AN INTRODUCTION TO GREEK TRAGEDY

This book provides a brief and accessible introduction to Greek tragedy for students and general readers alike. Whether readers are studying Greek culture, performing a Greek tragedy, or simply interested in reading a Greek play, this book will help them to understand and enjoy this challenging and rewarding genre. *An Introduction to Greek Tragedy* provides background information; helps readers appreciate, enjoy, and engage with the plays themselves; and gives them an idea of the important questions in current scholarship on tragedy. Ruth Scodel seeks to dispel misleading assumptions about tragedy, stressing how open the plays are to different interpretations and reactions. In addition to general background, the book includes chapters on specific plays, both the most familiar titles and some lesser-known plays – *Persians, Helen,* and *Orestes* – in order to convey the variety that the tragedies offer readers.

Ruth Scodel is currently D. R. Shackleton Bailey Collegiate Professor of Greek and Latin in the Department of Classical Studies at the University of Michigan. Her most recent books are *Epic Facework: Self-Presentation and Social Interaction in Homer* (2008) and *Whither Quo Vadis? Sienkiewicz's Novel in Film and Television* (2008). She is also the author of numerous articles on Greek literature.

AN INTRODUCTION TO
GREEK TRAGEDY

RUTH SCODEL

University of Michigan

CAMBRIDGE
UNIVERSITY PRESS

CAMBRIDGE UNIVERSITY PRESS
Cambridge, New York, Melbourne, Madrid, Cape Town, Singapore,
São Paulo, Delhi, Dubai, Tokyo, Mexico City

Cambridge University Press
32 Avenue of the Americas, New York, NY 10013-2473, USA

www.cambridge.org
Information on this title: www.cambridge.org/9780521705608

First published 2010

Printed in the United States of America

A catalog record for this publication is available from the British Library.

Library of Congress Cataloging in Publication data
Scodel, Ruth.
An introduction to Greek tragedy / Ruth Scodel.
p.   cm.
Includes bibliographical references and index.
ISBN 978-0-521-87974-3 (hardback) – ISBN 978-0-521-70560-8 (pbk.)
1. Greek drama (Tragedy) – History and criticism – Handbooks,
manuals, etc.   I. Title.
PA3131.S39 2010
882'.0109–dc22   2010025326

ISBN 978-0-521-87974-3 Hardback
ISBN 978-0-521-70560-8 Paperback

CONTENTS

Preface   *page* vii

1   Defining Tragedy   1

2   Approaches   15

3   Origins, Festival, and Competition   33

4   Historical and Intellectual Background   56

5   *Persians*   72

6   The *Oresteia*   85

7   *Antigone*   106

8   *Medea*   120

9   *Hippolytus*   133

10 *Oedipus the King*   147

11 *Helen*   162

12 *Orestes*   174

13 Tragic Moments   186

Glossary   197

Dates   199

Works Cited   201

Index   213

PREFACE

This book is intended for speakers of English who want or need to know about Greek tragedy. It tries to perform several jobs: to provide background information about Greek tragedy; to help its readers appreciate, enjoy, and understand the plays themselves; and to give readers an idea of what questions professional scholars have been asking about tragedy. It also seeks to dispel assumptions about tragedy that seem still to be standard in high schools. I deliberately chose to write chapters about some of the tragedies that are most familiar but also a few that are less well known – *Persians*, *Helen*, and *Orestes* – in order to provide a broader sense of what a tragedy can be.

I have tried to be honest. There are many scholarly debates about tragedy. Where I have strong views, I have put them forward – the opportunity to express them was my main inducement to write the book – but I hope I have not been unfair to those who disagree. At the end of each chapter is a brief section of "Sources and Suggestions." The "Suggestions" are suggestions for further reading. I added "Sources" because I have also used this space to locate what I have said in ongoing controversies where I thought it would help a reader to place my views on the large continuum.

Not everything I cite in order to be honest will be accessible to the Greekless reader, but I tried to distinguish such references from those that readers are likely to want to pursue. I have tried to refer to works in English that do not quote untranslated Greek, but I have occasionally broken this rule to clarify an influence or to show with whom I am debating. The list of "Works Cited" includes several collections of articles, and I have not listed the individual articles separately there, but I do cite them with author's name in "Sources and Suggestions," with information about the original publication if the article was originally published in a journal. Sometimes, the original publication did not translate Greek, but since many such articles are available online through libraries (for example, in JSTOR), I gave these references so that the reader, referring to a translation as needed, can read them even without access to the reprint.

I have also, occasionally, mentioned that the text is uncertain, though I have not discussed textual issues or pointed to every problem. This, again, is a form of honesty. A translator usually had to decide what the Greek should be and then translate it; sometimes the translator can add notes that explain where there have been difficult decisions. But often these decisions are invisible, and I want my readers to realize that we do not always know what the poets actually wrote. Throughout, I have assumed that my readers are intelligent people who want both information and ideas that will help provoke their own responses.

Translations are my own and have no claims to convey the glories of the Greek. I have not recommended translations, because different versions are good for different purposes, and because new ones appear so often that my advice would be quickly dated. I have generally used the Latin forms of Greek names, although this is not fashionable, because they look a little more familiar, and tragedy is hard enough.

There is an immense scholarly literature about tragedy. I have not come remotely close to reading as much as I should have, and I have read a great deal. In this book, along with the bias toward English, I have introduced a strong bias toward recent work, especially because the nonspecialist is likely to find it hard to distinguish what is still valid from what more recent research has shown to be false. Still, although some older work is truly outdated, much is not, and I hope my readers will not imagine that valuable contributions to the understanding of Greek tragedy only began in the 1970s.

DEFINING TRAGEDY

The very term "Greek tragedy" carries an immense weight of cultural and critical baggage. Even though the cultural prestige of the genre is often the inspiration for us to read, produce, or see these plays, this very prestige interferes with our ability to appreciate them. However, we cannot expect simply to shake off all the assumptions we have inherited about what a Greek tragedy is supposed to be. We would not want to, since we could not make sense of the texts at all without the scholarship of the past. Yet with that scholarship come inherited assumptions and expectations that distort. If we can at least identify some of these assumptions, even if we cannot see the plays in some pure, neutral way – for we will always see them or read them both through our beliefs about the ancient Greeks and about the genre, and through the concerns and presuppositions of our own place and time – we can at least see them more freshly.

There is one basic tension in any encounter with Greek tragedy that we should not even want to escape. These plays come from an ancient culture that is in some ways very distant from our own. Yet we expect them to move us and even to help us better understand our lives. If we rush too quickly to find universal meanings, we will probably ignore or misread whatever is profoundly different. But if we read them entirely as documents from a foreign culture – a polytheistic, slaveholding, misogynistic culture – they will lose their power. Again, tragedy has attracted all kinds of interpretive approaches, and part of its enduring place in the canon of both education and the theater is surely the result of its adaptability. Any given way of reading or seeing is both liberating, because it releases us from the limits of previous methods, and confining, because it prevents us from seeing facets with which it is not compatible. So when we study Greek tragedies, we do best if we constantly shift perspectives, universalizing and historicizing. This is simply an especially demanding case of what we always do when we read a story or see a play, as we both use our expectations to make sense of the experience and modify our expectations as the work unfolds (in the "hermeneutic spiral").

It is not hard to produce a neutral definition of what we mean by "Greek tragedy" by defining Greek tragedy historically and formally. Tragedy is a form of drama, invented in the territory of Athens in the sixth century BCE. Almost all our surviving plays and fragments of plays were composed for performance at Athenian festivals of Dionysus, mostly the City Dionysia. A few were first produced elsewhere: Aeschylus composed a tragedy called *Women of Etna* on a commission from King Hieron of Syracuse for a festival to inaugurate his new city, Etna, and Euripides composed tragedies for King Archelaus of Macedon. Euripides' extant *Andromache* was perhaps composed for the city of Argos. These, however, imitated the Athenian model. Although almost all our surviving plays are from the fifth century BCE (Euripides' *Rhesus* is probably from the fourth), new tragedies continued to be produced at Athens until the middle of the third century BCE, and in this same century, at Alexandria, tragedy was patronized by Ptolemy II Philadelphus. Seven Alexandrian tragic poets were called the "Pleiad" (after the constellation Pleiades – but not all the sources give the same seven names). Two hundred sixty-nine lines are preserved from a tragedy by Ezekiel called *Exagogê* ("Exodus"), whose main character is Moses. This was probably written in the first century BCE; no choral fragments have survived, so we do not know whether it had a chorus, or whether it was ever produced or intended for the stage. Although the standard edition of the fragments of Greek tragedy lists authors of the fourth century CE, the *Exagogê* is the last ancient Greek tragedy of which a substantial fragment is extant.

So a Greek tragedy is a drama that Greeks called "tragedy" – but this is a painfully superficial definition. They must have had reasons for calling some performances "tragedies" and presenting them at festivals under this name rather than another. Tragedies have obvious formal similarities with each other, and these allow for a different kind of definition. First, by content: a tragedy was a drama usually based on traditional legend, set in a past that was already remote for the ancient Athenian audience, although great events of history, even recent history, could also serve as the basis for tragedy. The lost *Capture of Miletus* and *Phoenician Women* of Phrynichus and the surviving *Persians* of Aeschylus treated events from the lifetimes of many members of their audiences with all the grandeur of heroic tradition, and in the fourth century the unknown author of the "Gyges" tragedy of which a substantial piece has been found on papyrus took a story from the historian Herodotus. Late in the fifth century, the tragedian Agathon presented a play whose plot and characters were completely invented. But the traditional stories, often told in the old epic poems, were the standard. The tragedians only rarely used a story directly from the *Iliad* or *Odyssey*, but they took many of their plots from the "Cyclic" epics, the (now lost) poems that told what happened before and after the two most canonical poems.

Tragedy was a specific kind of drama. It was performed by actors (at Athens, no more than three) and a chorus of twelve, later fifteen, who sang and danced, assisted by a player of the *aulos*, a reeded wind instrument. For the most part, actors used spoken verse, mainly the iambic trimeter, or recitative, while the chorus sang between scenes, but the chorus leader could speak on behalf of the group during actors' scenes, while the actors could sing, both in responsion with the chorus and in monody. The structure was regular but flexible. The drama began with a prologue, which could be a monologue or a dialogue, but which always provided basic information about the setting and the initial situation. The prologue speaker(s) could exit, or could hide from another actor, or could stay to meet the chorus. After the prologue, the chorus entered in the *parodos*, a song in the course of which the chorus identified itself, for each chorus had a distinct identity within the play. The drama would then proceed with an alternation of scenes and songs, ending with a few final lines from the chorus.

The songs between episodes followed the norms of Greek choral practice. There were various types of rhythm available, each with its own short units, *cola*. For each song, the poet recombined these cola and variants on them to create a unique *strophe*, and the song then used this pattern again in an *antistrophe*. A different combination could follow, the *epode*, or there could be another strophic pair. The chorus danced along with these songs. Song was not confined to these act-divisions. Actors and chorus could sing in response to each other, an actor could sing a solo, or one actor could sing while another answered in spoken verse. The longest song in surviving tragedy is the lament/magical rite performed by chorus, Electra, and Orestes at Agamemnon's tomb in Aeschylus's *Libation Bearers*, with eleven strophic pairs (306–475). Especially in late fifth-century tragedy, there were astrophic songs in which there is no repeated pattern, particularly actors' solos. Every song was different, but songs fit into traditional, recognizable types until the late fifth century, when new, highly virtuosic styles became influential. Song had two main functions in tragedy: it could serve to move the singer(s) slightly away from the immediate action, to a different plane on which the singers could try to make sense of the action, or it could express emotions too powerful for ordinary speech.

Actors and chorus (exclusively male) wore elaborate costumes and masks that covered the entire head, but the *aulos* player was not masked and was not part of the imitated action. Even the spoken verse used a "high" diction, avoiding vulgar language completely and restricting colloquialism, while allowing words from earlier poetry that were not employed in everyday speech. Although sometimes actors spoke in an otherwise empty performance space, so that they effectively spoke to the audience, and choruses often sang when no actors were present, tragedy never explicitly broke the barrier and addressed the audience or acknowledged that it was a performance, as contemporary Old Comedy frequently did. (Many scholars, however, see tragedy as highly metatheatrical in more various ways.)[1]

---

[1] So, for example, on Euripides' *Bacchae* alone: Segal 1997, 215–71; Foley 1985, 205–58; Goldhill 1986, 265–86.

Tragedy also had defining characteristics beyond its formal features. Its main characters were noble, although they might be disguised as beggars or enslaved. Choruses, who could participate in the action by, for example, revealing secrets, could not stop an act of violence, so they were often women, slaves, or old men. The fates of the characters were taken seriously. The plots may end happily or sadly, but the stakes are always high. For example, Euripides' *Ion* has a happy ending, but only after Ion's mother has tried to kill him, and he has come close to killing her.

The possibility of divine intervention in the action also defines the imagined world in which tragedy takes place; this world is controlled by the traditional gods of Greek mythology, either under the supreme direction of Zeus or as individuals who may even criticize each other, as the Heavenly Twins, Castor and Polydeuces, say at the end of Euripides' *Electra* that Apollo's oracle telling Orestes to kill his mother was not wise (1246). The audience expects that all oracles and prophecies will be fulfilled, and the poets use these predictions to manipulate audience expectations – but a world in which all prophecies come true is not exactly the world any person has ever lived in. A god may deliver the drama's prologue or appear at the end to tell the characters what they must do, or the characters may complain of the gods' indifference so that the audience is aware of their absence, but a tragedy in which the gods are not relevant is hard to imagine.

While there are many other important details about how tragedy was structured, styled, and performed, these are the essentials that made a tragedy recognizable and distinct from a comedy, an epic recitation, or any other kind of performance. Thirty-two tragedies survive in mostly complete form, while there are fragments of many others, quoted in later authors or found on papyri in Egypt, ranging from a mere title or citation of a rare word to entire scenes. Sometimes a play had more than one title in use, since the original title, usually the name of an important character or the chorus, might be shared with many other tragedies. So Sophocles' famous tragedy was probably originally *Oedipus*, but people began to call it *Oedipus the King* to distinguish it from *Oedipus at Colonus*. If such a later title was quite different from the original, we do not always know whether two titles known from the ancient world represent two different plays, so we do not know exactly how many different plays are represented.

One difficulty of great concern for scholars of tragedy is invisible to the spectator in the theater or reader of a translation: the texts stand at the ends of long chains of transmission by manual copying. Errors are unavoidable. Sometimes they are easy to fix, like an obvious typo in a modern book, but often they are not. In some cases, the copy itself may go back to a text based on a performance that made changes to the original. Most experts think that the end of Aeschylus's *Seven against Thebes* is a later addition and that at least parts of the final section of Euripides' *Phoenician Women* are also later interpolations. Most also think that parts of *Iphigenia at Aulis* are not by Euripides, and they agree that its final messenger speech is not authentic. On the other side, parts of Dionysus's final speech in *Bacchae* are obviously missing. In any case, the play we read or see represents an editor's judgment, and of course often a translator's too.

All the surviving Attic tragedies come to us under the names of Aeschylus, Sophocles, or Euripides, although most scholars believe that Aeschylus did not compose *Prometheus Bound* (it may be by his son, Euphorion, and have been produced under his name) and that the *Rhesus* we have is not the one Euripides wrote but was confused with it.[2] The *Iphigenia at Aulis*, although its core is Euripidean, is so difficult that the standard edition of Diggle uses marginal signs to indicate the probability that any particular passage is by Euripides.[3] From each of these, a selection of plays (probably made in the second century CE), seven of Aeschylus and Sophocles, ten of Euripides, was copied in the Byzantine period. For Euripides, by pure luck one section of an alphabetical edition also survived, so that we have nine more plays (one is a satyr play). We do not know the principles of the selection, but it is striking that Electra plays by all three are included, suggesting that the selector(s) wanted comparison to be possible, and the *Rhesus* was

---

[2] *Prometheus*: Griffith 1977; Euphorion as author, West 1990, 51–72. *Rhesus*: summary in Kovacs 2002, 349–52.

[3] Diggle 1994, vi.

included even though its authorship was already doubted in antiquity (Hypothesis b), probably because it could be compared to the version of the same story in Homer.

Tragedy, however, is hard for us to disentangle from "the tragic." Greek tragedy is the beginning of a long tradition, and naturally we look for commonalities within this tradition: Greek tragedy should have features in common with Seneca and then with Shakespeare. Of course, it does have commonalities with its descendents. Revenge tragedy, for example, is a special subgenre that is well worth looking at comparatively. The entire tragic tradition, from Greek tragedy onward, concerns itself with some core issues: the vulnerability of human life; the value of facing the limits of our control with courage; and the powerful, sometimes inescapable, effects of our decisions. However, if we place "the tragic" at the center of what we expect from Attic tragedy, we will seriously distort the corpus that we have. Greek tragedy, in fact, is the ancestor not only of later tragedy but of important strands in comedy. Euripides, especially, composed plays in which long-separated relatives were reunited, including the extant *Ion* and *Iphigenia among the Taurians*, and *Hypsipyle, Cresphontes,* and *Antiope,* of which substantial fragments survive in papyrus.

The continuing influence of Aristotle's *Poetics* is part of the problem. Aristotle was probably the greatest literary theorist in history, but even now many readers treat him not as an early theorist and interpreter of tragedy, and one with his own prejudices, but as an authority. The *Poetics* is often a filter through which we see tragedy – and, indeed, literature in general. This, too, is a problem. It is also peculiar, because most of us are not actually followers of Aristotle, and Aristotle's way of reading tragedy is profoundly Aristotelian. Aristotle has very little interest in some aspects of tragedy that were obviously important for ancient audiences and that could be important for us – spectacle, for example, and music. He cared more about plot than anything else, and in looking at the emotional side of tragedy, he was mostly concerned to defend it against Plato.

So Aristotle defines the tragic emotions as pity and fear, and suggests that it is the task of tragedy to "purge" these emotions – the famous "catharsis." (There has been an endless debate about whether the analogy in "purging" is medical or religious.)[4] Plato had argued that tragedy harmed its audience by encouraging self-indulgent emotionality (*Resp.* ii 376e–398b9; x 595–608b10), so Aristotle claimed that it actually did not make people more emotional but less: viewing tragedy relieved excessive pity and fear. There is, as far as I know, no empirical basis for this claim, although it surely rests on the experience of feeling, after seeing a play, that one has passed through an emotionally wrenching experience. Nobody really knows what the longer-term effects of tragedy are. Although the vast debate about the meaning of catharsis, and whether it is a ritual or a medical purification, is important for understanding Aristotle, it has little to contribute to the understanding of tragedy.

Because Aristotle has very precise views about the conditions under which people feel pity and fear, he then has to define the proper tragic plot:

> So the organization of the finest tragedy should be not simple but complex, and it should be imitative of things that cause fear and pity, since this is the special area of this kind of imitation. First, it is clear that virtuous men should not appear changing from good to bad fortune: for this is neither pitiful nor fearful, but disgusting. Nor, again, bad men from bad to good fortune, for this is the most untragic of all, for it is neither sympathetic nor pitiful nor fearful. Nor, further, should an intensely bad man fall from good to bad fortune. Such a plot would have the sympathetic, but neither pity nor fear; for pity is for someone who is unfortunate but does not deserve to be, fear for someone like us, so that this outcome will be neither pitiful nor fearful. Such a man is the one who is not exceptional in excellence and justice who changes to bad fortune not through badness and wickedness but through some mistake, one of those of great good fortune and reputation, such as Oedipus, Thyestes, and the famous men of such

---

4 Halliwell 1986, Appendix 3 (350–6), summarizes the various interpretations.

families. It is necessary, then, that the good plot should, therefore, be single, rather than double as some say, and should change not from bad to good, but, conversely, from good to bad, not through wickedness, but through some great mistake, and involve a person either such as has been described, or better rather than worse. (*Poetics* 13, 1452b30–1453a17)

These few sentences have probably done more harm to the appreciation of Greek tragedies than any others. The word *hamartia* has often been rendered as "tragic flaw." This has led to an endless hunt for the faults in the characters of tragic protagonists, whether their misfortunes are the result of these flaws or not. Yet even when the word is translated "mistake" or "error," so that Aristotle can be describing the results of ignorance, there is no reason that we should follow Aristotle's rules for deciding what makes a tragedy good.

To be sure, some excellent tragedies can be described this way, especially the *Oedipus Rex*. Oedipus's terrible misfortune is certainly the result of mistakes. Yet even for the *Oedipus Rex*, the Aristotelian formula easily leads readers to trivialize the tragedy by providing an easy moral. The heroine of Sophocles' *Antigone* certainly has a difficult personality, and if she were less fierce, she would probably not bury her brother and so bring about her death; but she is doing the right thing, not making a mistake. Creon in that play fits the Aristotelian scheme much better. He wants to be a good king, but is ruined by his stubbornness. Still, even though we may want to see them as equally important characters, we can only make the play follow Aristotle's precepts by distorting Antigone's role – and *Antigone* is one of the most influential and popular of tragedies.

Many other Greek tragedies do not fit this rule at all. In the next chapter, Aristotle himself says that the best action belongs to tragedies in which the murder of a relative is prevented by a last-minute recognition, even though the tragedies he mentions, such as the surviving *Iphigenia among the Taurians* and the *Cresphontes* (fragmentary, but with substantial remains), had happy endings (*Poetics* 14, 1454a5–9). Many tragedies show a change from bad to good fortune without such a close escape from interfamilial killing. Euripides' *Helen*, for example, begins with the heroine a lonely, threatened exile in Egypt, and ends as she returns to Greece with her husband. In Sophocles' *Electra*, the heroine helps her brother kill her detested mother and stepfather. Some have characters who fall into misfortune without any obvious "error." In Euripides' *Heracles*, the evil tyrant Lycus plans to kill Heracles' family while the hero is in Hades, performing the last of his labors. In the nick of time, Heracles returns and kills Lycus. Then the goddess Insanity, under direct orders from Hera, drives him mad, and he kills his wife and children. He is certainly mistaken in thinking the children belong to his enemy, Eurystheus, but the madness is sent by a goddess who hates Heracles for reasons having nothing to do with his character. On the other side, many characters in tragedy commit terrible crimes knowingly and yet receive pity from the audience, such as Euripides' Medea, Phaedra in his *Hippolytus*, Electra in his *Electra*, and Orestes in *Orestes*, because Euripides often directs the audience's attention less to whether the character deserves to suffer than to the forces that have pushed the character beyond limits.

Only a few sentences after the passage quoted, Aristotle lists Telephus as a typical tragic hero, but the story is that Telephus is wounded while defending his own territory against the Greeks who attack him by mistake. Only the inflictor of the wound, Achilles, could heal it. All three of the famous tragedians composed tragedies about Telephus (there are considerable fragments of the one by Euripides). Telephus makes no tragic error, but he suffers rather than the Greeks. The plays about him were about how he came to Agamemnon's palace in disguise and made the Greeks help him – in Euripides' play, he took Agamemnon's infant son, Orestes, hostage. Philoctetes, also the subject of tragedies by all three (only Sophocles' survives), accidentally trespassed in the sanctuary of a minor goddess, Chryse, and was bitten by a snake. This is a "mistake," but it has no moral significance, and it has nothing to do with Philoctetes' character. Because his wound would not heal and stank, or because he screamed in pain, the Greeks abandoned him on the island of Lemnos. Later the Greeks learned from a prophecy that they could not capture Troy without Philoctetes, and the tragedies depict their attempts to persuade, trick, or bully him into rejoining the

Trojan expedition. These plays, like those about Telephus, end with the hero leaving his lonely exile. To be sure, the surviving *Philoctetes* can inspire abundant pity and fear in the spectator. When Philoctetes, who has been deceived and betrayed again, chooses to die of starvation, since the bow that is his only way of obtaining food has been stolen, rather than go to Troy, his plight certainly evokes the tragic emotions – but his only "error" has been to be too noble to be suspicious enough of the son of his old friend Achilles.

Homer was the most important inspiration for tragedy (as Aristotle points out). Every fourth year at the Great Panathenaea, starting in the sixth century, Athens sponsored a major international competition for rhapsodes, performers of Homer, and the poems were central to traditional education. Tragedies only rarely took their plots directly from the *Iliad* or *Odyssey*, but the epics taught the tragedies how to create characters and how to attain emotional effects; the audiences at rhapsodic performances, like those at tragedies, cried. In the *Iliad*, Achilles, Patroclus, and Hector all fit the Aristotelian model better than most tragic protagonists. Achilles, although his anger is justified, is too obdurate, and sends his friend, Patroclus, into battle to save the Greeks because his pride will not let him go himself. As a result, Patroclus dies. The compassionate Patroclus becomes so excited by his success in battle that he forgets Achilles' warning to return as soon as he has fulfilled his mission of driving the Trojans away from the Greek ships, and he is killed. Hector, the conscientious defender of Troy, becomes overconfident when he has a winning streak in Achilles' absence, and Achilles kills him. The Ithacan books of the *Odyssey*, though, provided a model for a very different kind of story, in which a cunning hero overcomes his enemies with the help of the gods, and where the most powerful moment is Penelope's recognition of her long-absent husband. So there were many tragedies of intrigue and recognition, including the surviving Aeschylus's *Libation Bearers*, Euripides' *Iphigenia among the Taurians*. Many extant tragedies also present households where the husband/father is absent and his return is a focus of longing or anxiety: Aeschylus's *Agamemnon*, Sophocles' *Women of Trachis*, Euripides' *Andromache*.

In tragedies in which a focal character suffers misfortunes at least in part through his own mistakes, such as Euripides' *Bacchae* or Sophocles' *Antigone*, the drama often ends with a lament. So readers think of a "basic" pattern for tragedy: error, catastrophe, lament. Sophocles' *Oedipus at Colonus* ends with lamentation, although the hero, in old age and after much misery, has been called to a mysterious death that is in some way a compensation for his suffering. Sophocles' *Women of Trachis* ends as Heracles is carried out, still living, to his funeral pyre, but there is no lament. A tragedy can show a hero who suffers through error but not end with a lament, and it can end with a lament without having the "Aristotelian" plot. In Euripides' *Hecuba*, the heroine, who has already suffered the fall of her city and the deaths of her husband and many children, loses her daughter as a human sacrifice and learns that her last son has been murdered. All these misfortunes are completely external, although the most terrible misfortune Hecuba suffers is the loss of her own humanity as she murders her enemy's children in revenge. There is no single pattern for the tragic action.

The tragedians evidently did not have any moral objection to portraying suffering characters who have done nothing at all to cause their own suffering. Even tragedies that have "Aristotelian" plots often show the incidental sufferings of completely innocent victims. In *Antigone*, for example, while both Antigone and Creon could be thought to have brought about their own fates, Creon's wife, Eurydice, kills herself in anguish over the death of her son, Haemon, although she has contributed nothing at all to the catastrophe. Tragedians are interested in human choices and actions, so when characters suffer misfortunes for which they bear no responsibility, the tragedy is about how they respond. *Trojan Women* is an obvious example. The play shows different women reacting to the fall of Troy, but only one of them, Helen, bears any responsibility for the catastrophe (unless Hecuba is to blame for allowing Paris to be born and survive, as Helen argues she is). The catastrophe, though, has already taken place when the play begins; it is about survivors. If tragic plots are not usually about how completely innocent people fall into terrible misfortune, that is not because the tragedians and their original audiences found such stories morally offensive, but because they were more interested in how such people react to suffering – often by seeking terrible vengeance.

It may be most useful, if we want to define tragedy, to use Wittgenstein's concept of "family resemblance." Most tragedies used legendary material for their plots, but plays that experimented with historical or entirely invented plots could be recognized as tragedies because they shared many other features with the tragedies that had legendary plots. Other standard features could change too. We do not know whether the *Exagogê* had a chorus, for example, but it was a drama that used tragic language and took its plot from an ancient story with high cultural importance, so Greeks would have recognized it as tragedy. If we had more remains of tragedies from the fourth century and later, we would probably see even more variety. A tragedy, though, could not have satyrs in it, because even if it had all the other characteristics of tragedy, it would look like a satyr play. A tragedy could not violate the metrical rule in the iambic line that specialists call "Porson's Bridge" or use obscene language, because even it if had all the other characteristics of tragedy, it would sound like a comedy. Tragedy had boundaries defined by other genres.

SOURCES AND SUGGESTIONS

On the transmission of tragedy, a quick introduction is the essay by David Kovacs in Gregory 2005 (379–93). Fragments in this book are quoted from the standard Greek edition (*Fragmenta Tragicorum Graecorum, FTrG,* in the bibliography under Snell 1971). Readers who want to get an idea of what the lost tragedies were like should look at Sommerstein/Fitzpatrick/Talboy 2006 for Sophocles and the two volumes of Collard/Cropp/Lee 1995 and Collard/Cropp/Gibert 2004 or at Collard/Cropp 2008/2009 (the Loeb) for Euripides. For Aeschylus, there is no such guide, but the fragments are available in Sommerstein 2009. Gregory 2005 includes "Lost Tragedies: A Survey" by Martin Cropp (271–92).

Taplin, especially Taplin 1986, has consistently stressed the barrier between the audience and the world of the performance, but recent scholarship tends to embrace metatheatricality and to incline the other way (especially influential has been Henrichs 1994 – 5) – I think too far. For fourth-century tragedy, Green 1994 (49–62) is instructive (this is a book not about dramas themselves but about their social uses, using archaeological evidence). The *Exagogê* is translated in Holladay 1989 (529) and Jacobson 1983.

General books on tragedy for nonspecialists include Rabinowitz 2008, which emphasizes feminist and contemporary political issues. Zimmermann 1991 is old-fashioned but gives much information briefly. The most thorough introduction is Lesky 1983, although it is inevitably dated (this is a translation of a German edition of 1972). Taplin 1978 is about stagecraft but can serve as an introduction to the genre. Goldhill 1986 offers close, often deconstructionist, thematically organized studies that fight against any definitive interpretation. The various "Companions" – Easterling/Goldhill 1997, Bushnell 2005, and Gregory 2005 – all have valuable contributions on various topics. McDonald 2003 is largely plot summary but offers much information about modern productions and adaptations. Storey/Allan 2005 is an introduction to the Greek theater as a whole.

For Sophocles, there is a useful quick introduction in Garvie 2005; for Euripides, Morwood 2002 is a survey of the Euripidean corpus by an author who loves all of it.

2

APPROACHES

If Aristotle is not a reliable guide to the purpose of tragedy, what was it for? In Aristophanes' *Frogs*, the debating tragedians make the claim explicitly that they should improve their audiences (1009–10) and that the poets have taught valuable subjects (1030–6). Taken for granted, however, is pleasure. When Euripides complains that Aeschylus's tragedies would have four chains of songs in a row while the actors were silent, Dionysus comments that he *enjoyed* this style (914–17). The Athenian audience could be loud and rude if not pleased: they yelled, hissed, and banged on the wooden seats, and sometimes performances simply stopped in the face of a hostile audience.

In traditional Greek culture, poetry was central to education, and its value was taken for granted. However, the sophists, who offered an alternative form of teaching, displayed their intellectual superiority by criticizing the poets, and by the late fifth century, intellectuals no longer assumed that poetry was valuable and instead began to theorize about it and to construct reasons why it was useful. Since tragedy obviously affected its audience, some critics, like Aristophanes, demanded that it be edifying. Tragedy could inspire emulation of heroic greatness or teach people how to argue. Plato, who did not think it could be morally beneficial, did not allow it in his ideal city.

The Athenians, however, clearly thought it was useful to the city; they devoted considerable resources to it. Its social benefits are harder to identify than the pleasure it offered individuals, but we can make some guesses. First, while not everybody would have had exactly the same response to any play, there would have been moments of powerful shared feeling that briefly united a usually quarrelsome citizen body. This bonding had value in itself. Scholars and critics tend to look at tragedy intellectually, and that is only natural, since there is much more to say about the meaning of a drama than about the emotional effect – but that shared feeling of sadness at the hero's death or delight in a brilliant escape is one of the main reasons why going to a theater is not the same experience as watching a play on streaming video.

Then, tragedy was educational in a very direct way. It presented extracts from the entire range of Panhellenic myth, and taught its audience about the world. Anyone who regularly attended the festival would be familiar with stories attached to most *poleis* and to their famous sanctuaries and monuments. Some tragedies include immense displays of geographical information, such as Prometheus's prophecy of Io's wanderings in *Prometheus Bound*. This was valuable knowledge; it enabled the audience to locate themselves in a Greek and even wider world made meaningful and alive by story. Tragedy was not the only vehicle for conveying this knowledge, which epic and lyric poetry also provided, but as the fifth century progressed it became the dominant source of new poetry. Furthermore, tragedy often gave an Athenian slant to stories from other places. The contest in Homeric performance at the Panathenaia brought the shared cultural heritage of Greece to Athens; tragedy put that shared heritage through an Athenian filter. These versions served Athenian self-promotion throughout the Greek world and promoted Athenian pride. Third, tragedy provided Athenians with a shared mode of expression. The characters of Plato's dialogues casually quote tragedy along with Homer; bits of tragedy are part of the furniture of their minds.

We, today, can certainly get something else of great value from tragedy. Tragedy reminds us that the outcomes of human action are very hard to predict. Plots that follow Aristotle's rules of probability and necessity educate their audiences in the complex chains of cause and effect. In the *hamartia* plot, a mistake has devastating consequences. In the revenge plot, those who commit crimes find that their apparently helpful victims manage to take terrible revenge – but may lose their humanity in the process. In the recognition plot, lives devastated by loss are unexpectedly redeemed. Whether or not tragedy offers a *catharsis* of pity and fear, experiencing tragedy can enlarge our sympathies, and make us more grateful for our good luck and better prepared for it to change. Tragedies engage both our intellects and our emotions, not always on exactly the same track. The experience is complicated and messy, but most people intuitively see a value in it that Aristotle's analysis sometimes seems to echo but does not quite address.

We will be able to respond to more of what tragedy offers if we resist the inherited narrative about tragedy's rise and fall. We already see the germ of what could be called "The Story" in Aristophanes' *Frogs*. This play was produced in 405 BCE, shortly after the deaths of both Euripides and Sophocles. The god Dionysus, unhappy with the surviving tragedians, goes to the Underworld to bring Euripides back to life (66–72), but when he arrives there, he discovers Aeschylus and Euripides are fighting over the throne reserved for the greatest tragedian (757–65). (Sophocles has too much respect for Aeschylus to compete [788–90].) Dionysus oversees an extended debate. Euripides accuses Aeschylus of being too obscure and difficult (927, 1122), and of having too many songs and not enough plot (945–7). Aeschylus claims that Euripides causes moral decadence with his plots full of perverse sex (850, 1077–88) and that his style lacks tragic dignity (1013–17). Finally, Dionysus brings Aeschylus back to Athens. In "The Story," the history of tragedy is almost entirely about these three poets. Aeschylus is grand but primitive, Euripides clever but decadent, Sophocles perfect and serene.

Aristotle's *Poetics* helps establish "The Story" as the basic history of tragedy. Aristotle, writing in the second half of the fourth century BCE, mentions some famous tragedians of his own time – Astydamas (1453b34), Theodectes (1455a9, 1455b29), and Cleophon (1448a12, 1458a20) – but gives them far less attention than Sophocles and Euripides, and some of it very critical. It is clear that he regards Sophocles as the greatest tragedian, and puts *Oedipus the King* at the center of his canon (1452a22–33). Although he obviously admires some plays of Euripides and defends him against criticism (1453a23), he also sees him as the first author in the "new" and inferior style

(1456a2). "The Story" is profoundly Aristotelian: tragedy develops until it reaches its perfection, its *telos*, and from that point it must stay the same or decline. Finally, Nietzsche in *The Birth of Tragedy* gives a new twist to "The Story," making Euripides responsible for killing tragedy by introducing a Socratic rationalism that was foreign to the essence of tragedy. *Frogs*, the *Poetics*, and *The Birth of Tragedy* have all been immensely influential.

"The Story," however, distorts the history of tragedy. The three tragedians were evidently special, and canonical by the fourth century. But tragedy did not stop being composed, and we have no way of knowing that it was bad. "The Story" forces all three tragedians to play fixed roles in a scheme that seduces us into ignoring all their characteristics that do not fit. It is perhaps most unfair to Sophocles, who is defined as perfecting the form. His works thereby lose everything strange, experimental, and uneasy. The Aeschylus of "The Story" is artistically primitive and straightforwardly pious and patriotic. Euripides is identified entirely with his experiments and innovations, and the many ways in which he continued the tradition vanish.

Quite apart from the way "The Story" interferes with our ability to see the surviving tragedians clearly, such narrow and absolute canons restrict audiences' pleasure by denying the value of whatever does not fit. Even if I think that *Anna Karenina* is the best of all novels, I would sadly limit my enjoyment if I evaluated all other novels by how closely they resemble *Anna Karenina*. Ancient audiences, according to the "hypothesis" (a sort of preface) to Euripides' *Orestes*, loved this play, although "all the characters are bad, except Pylades" (contemporary audiences and readers mostly find Pylades quite bad too). Until recently, modern scholars had nothing good to say about it; but it has qualities that appeal to postmodernist sensibilities and has attracted considerable scholarly attention. Whether or not one happens to admire and enjoy *Orestes*, it is not useful to begin from premises that automatically marginalize part of a canon that is not very large in the first place.

Aristotle and those influenced by him (almost everybody who studies tragedy) place a very high value on dramatic unity. For Aristotle, tragedy needs to portray actions that happen "according to probability or necessity." So he objects to random events or coincidences. He also prefers dramas that may have complex plots with more than one reversal but that are still clearly a single action. *Oedipus the King* and *Iphigenia among the Taurians* are thus both excellent tragedies (even though the *Iphigenia* has a happy ending). However, many tragedies refuse to be tidily unified. Euripides' *Hippolytus* and Sophocles' *Antigone*, dramas that have always been among the most admired in the canon, shift the focus of the audience's attention and sympathy. The first part of *Hippolytus* is about Phaedra, the second is about Hippolytus. The first part of *Antigone* is about Antigone, the final third or so about Creon. The assumption that unity requires that a play have a single "tragic hero" – especially if the interpreter feels compelled to identify a single tragic mistake – has led to pointless controversies about whether *Antigone* is Antigone's tragedy or Creon's (the number of essays on this topic available for sale to aspiring plagiarists is frightening). Sophocles' *Women of Trachis* is about Deianeira, until it stops being about Deianeira and is about Heracles.

Euripides' *Andromache* begins with Andromache, the Trojan captive who is the concubine of Neoptolemus, and her son in terrible danger from Neoptolemus's wife, Hermione. She is rescued about two-thirds of the way through the play by the arrival of Neoptolemus's grandfather, Peleus. Now it is her persecutor, Hermione, who is threatened; but Hermione's former lover, Orestes, appears and they run away, and then a messenger comes to report to Peleus that Orestes has had Neoptolemus murdered at Delphi. The sequence of events and shifts of attention are dizzying. Evidently, Sophocles and Euripides did not share Aristotle's views of unity. Even Aeschylus can shift the focus in a single play. In *Eumenides*, the initial problem is the Furies' relentless pursuit of Orestes, who has killed his mother. The center of the drama lies in Orestes' trial at Athens, where he is prosecuted by the Furies and defended by Apollo, while Athena presides. Yet when Orestes is acquitted and goes home, the Furies threaten to turn their anger against Athens, and the last part of the play is a protracted struggle by Athena to convince them to give up their anger and accept honor as revered divinities in Athenian cult. Is this a single action? Maybe.

The point is not that we should not ask about the unity of tragedies. We expect stories to show some coherence, to be able to see why a play begins at one point and ends at another. But if we approach tragedy with rigid expectations, we will find that we are being disappointed over and over. Instead, since tragedies typically present segments of much larger cycles of story, it is often exceptionally revealing to consider how tragedies define what actually happens within the drama in relation to this wider story. The tragedian had to decide not only what he would include within the actual dramatic time, but what further information he would provide or imply that would locate the dramatic action in a wider story. The conclusions of Sophocles' plays are often ambiguous about the future, so that readers disagree about whether *Women of Trachis*, for example, implies that Heracles will be taken to Olympus as a god.[1] Aeschylus's *Agamemnon* begins the drama with the beacon that announces the fall of Troy, and the story of the family with Thyestes' adultery with the wife of his brother, Atreus, Agamemnon's father (1193). Sophocles' *Electra* begins the drama with Orestes' return to Argos, but the wider story goes back to the chariot race of Pelops, Atreus's father or grandfather. Euripides' *Orestes* takes place after Orestes' murder of his mother, but the family's story starts with Pelops' father, Tantalus (4–10).

The assumption that tragedy can be a form of ritual can be a further obstacle to fully appreciating it. Many scholars believe that tragedy was developed from ritual. Certainly ritual background is important for understanding the tragedies we have. Tragedy is deeply engaged with ritual (often perversely, so that murder is described as if it were sacrifice). Some tragedies, such as Sophocles' *Ajax* and *Oedipus at Colonus*, point strongly to their protagonists' future status as cult heroes. Tragedies include choral song and dance, which were ritual activities. Occasionally, tragic songs seem to merge into "real" ritual performance. When the Furies are persuaded by Athena to bless Athens in Aeschylus's *Eumenides* (916–1020), the original audience may have experienced the song as a "real" blessing. Such slippage between the

---

[1] No: Stinton 1986; yes: March 1987, Robert Fowler in Griffin 1999, 161–75.

chorus as character in a play and the chorus as Athenians singing for their own city should not be assumed everywhere, however. While the local identity of the chorus can be attenuated, so that the audience may well have heard the songs as directly addressed to themselves, songs were still inside the world of the play, and tragedies as a whole did not "do" anything.

Tragedy was performed as part of a religious festival, but attending a tragedy was not like going to church (Greek athletic contests were also religious in this sense). Tragedy, unlike satyr play, really does seem to have "nothing to do with Dionysus." We can see reasons why he should be the patron of drama – he is represented by a mask on many vase paintings of worshippers, for example, so that he is an obvious patron god for a masked performance – but they are not profound reasons. Very few tragedies were about Dionysiac myth. As drama became popular around the Greek world, it was most often introduced into festivals of Dionysus, but sometimes other gods were chosen. Apparently Greeks did not see an unbreakable connection between Dionysus and the theater, although when actors organized themselves into an international guild (sometime before 275 BCE), they called themselves "The Artists of Dionysus."

While a fine performance would surely please Dionysus, the patron god of tragedy, who would be likelier to be benign to the Athenians in return, tragic performance was not prayer and did not make crops grow or women bear children. Plato (*Laws* 800c–801a) expresses his disapproval that, immediately following sacrifices to the gods, choruses sang laments, and whoever most effectively made the city that had just sacrificed cry won a prize. It is indeed worth considering that Athens, imitated by other cities, year after year presented, in a sacred context, representations of the most ill-omened actions imaginable. A sanctuary was defiled if someone died in it, but pretend murder was fine. Nobody ever seems worried about bad supernatural effects from the many perverted rituals in tragedies. Plato was probably unhappy about the ritual aspect of tragedy because he was already unhappy about its psychological effects. The Athenians judged tragedies largely on whether they had enjoyed them. Rituals are not evaluated on these grounds.

This is particularly an issue in practical theater. Although recent scholarship that emphasizes the ritual affiliations of tragedy locates it in a very specific historical context, theatrical interpretation of tragedy as ritual typically universalizes. In modern performance, directors who are fascinated by tragedy as ritual typically have little interest in the language of the play, at least as articulate speech. Andrei Serban's famous *Fragments of Greek Tragedy* and his *Agamemnon* made language purely phonetic, using bits of Greek, Latin, and other languages. Tragedy, in this approach, becomes an originary theater, with style and movement borrowed from traditions all over the world.

Many audiences have found immense power in these productions and other experimental productions, which remind us that tragedy was a fully embodied art. They can capture aspects of tragedy we cannot experience in reading, no matter how diligently we remind ourselves that these are plays to be acted. Even if we do not fully agree with what directors do, it is immensely annoying when academics pedantically try to control the theatrical life of ancient drama (and what is a mistake from the scholar's point of view is often a fertile source of creative energy). Indeed, strong performances of Martha Graham's adaptations of tragedy as dance, *Clytemnestra* (1958) and *Cave of the Heart* (1946, from *Medea*), are deeply moving.

Ritualized performance can show aspects of a work that we otherwise miss. However, they are also incomplete. All the evidence tells us that the words were the single most important element in tragedy for ancient audiences. People from the fifth century on read plays, as well as watched them. Aristotle thought that it was just as good to read a play and to imagine it as actually to see it. This was surely not a normal view, but it was not ridiculous either. Athenian spectators memorized speeches and turned lines into catchphrases, and they memorized the songs for pleasure – that is, they picked out the parts that they liked and valued.

While modern performances often universalize tragedy by bringing performance practices from various cultures together, they also, perhaps paradoxically, often deliberately estrange the audience. For contemporary Westerners, the original performance practices of Greek tragedy are very foreign: the stylized speech, the mask, the presence of the chorus, the dance. Many productions use this strangeness to push the audience away from expectations of realism. So, for example, Peter Hall's famous version of Aeschylus's *Oresteia* with the National Theatre of Great Britain uses masks, an all-male cast, and a translation by Tony Harrison that emphasizes the foreignness of the text (especially in its consistent use of "he-god" and "she-god"). It is a fascinating and in many ways effective performance. However, the way the modern audience reacts to Greek theater conventions is determined by our own very different conventions, and tells us very little about how the Greek theater worked on its original audiences. We know that the original audiences were profoundly moved by tragic performances, and wept at them. They also quoted them and argued about them.

Euripides' *Bacchae* is probably the play that most invites us to assimilate it to ritual. Unlike most tragedies, it is about the theater-god Dionysus himself. It shows the terrible fate of King Pentheus, who opposes the rites of Dionysus and is torn apart by his own mother in the ecstatic madness sent by the god. Yet even this play is *about* ritual rather than *being* ritual, and it is a play about revenge, as well as religion. Also, the last part of *Bacchae*, in which Dionysus dresses Pentheus as a maenad – that is, as a woman – and sends him to spy on the women in the mountains, has seemed to many interpreters metatheatrical, about the theater itself. Theatrical self-consciousness and effective ritual do not sit easily together.

Tragedy for the Athenians was essentially what theater is for us in the West: make-believe. Everybody knew that a poet had made up the words and that the actors had memorized them, and sustaining the make-believe required that the barrier be maintained: the audience could not affect the play, and the play's only consequences in the real world came from the emotional and intellectual response of the audience. Athenian Comedy regularly violated dramatic illusion, but tragedy did not. Philosophers and psychologists still do not have an adequate understanding of the experience of involvement in fiction, of how we manage simultaneously to care deeply about the people on stage and to be fully aware that they are actors. Even though we usually sit in the dark and they sat in sunlight, our actors wear makeup

and theirs wore masks, and all the other differences between their theater and ours, the experience, mysterious as it is, seems to have been
similar – but their imaginations had to work harder.

Many interpreters, though, argue that the style of Greek tragedy
defines appropriate limits for its interpretation. Very influentially,
John Jones in the book *On Aristotle and Greek Tragedy* argued that
plot is the important thing in tragedy, while character is at best secondary, both because Aristotle says that it is and because the conventions of the Greek theater did not permit subtle psychology. It is hard
to know how subtle we should expect the psychology of tragic characters to be. A large theater (the theater of Dionysus at Athens had room
for about 15,000 spectators) encourages acting that is broad and grand
rather than subtle. An actor wearing a mask cannot show fleeting
facial expression. Still, he can far more convincingly be a woman than
he could be without one, and in a large theater in which the actor's
face would not be sharply visible anyway, the audience can imagine
the expressions. Because so many tragedies presented variations on
stories of which many versions were already familiar, and because so
many more placed their characters in similar situations, at least some
members of the audience would have a ready mechanism by which to
make fine judgments: each Electra was different from every other.

This kind of definition of characters, though, is not quite the same
thing as providing them with complex inner lives. Greek tragedies are
comparatively short, and they are highly rhetorical; when characters
debate (especially in Euripides), they tend to make clever arguments
that reveal not how they, as individuals, think, but rather what someone
might argue in this particular situation. When Antigone argues (*Ant.*
904–20) that she would not have defied the city to bury a husband or
children, but acted as she did because it was the body of a brother in
need of burial, it is hard to decide whether her speech demonstrates
that she is emotionally cold toward Haemon, who loves her and wants
to marry her, or whether she is desperate to find an argument that the
chorus will understand, or whether the argument has nothing to do
with her as an individual but is simply something Sophocles thought
someone in her situation could say.

On the other hand, when the messenger in *Antigone* describes how Creon, coming to release Antigone, finds Haemon holding her corpse (she has hanged herself), Haemon first lunges at his father with his sword and misses, and then turns his sword on himself. The narrator calls Haemon "angry at himself," but we do not know whether he is angry because he has attempted parricide or because he has failed (1221–37). Whether or not tragedy has subtle psychology, it often makes some motives explicit while leaving others obscure, and so invites the audience to see the characters as having inner selves about which we can only guess – like real people. The tragedians also were adept at depicting the flaws in how people judge each other's thinking and make decisions. There are passages where we are almost forced to say that a character is rationalizing.

Freudian interpretations assume that characters have not only hidden motives but unconscious ones, or that tragedy in general operated by addressing the unconscious fears and desires of its audience. Perhaps because tragedy was so important for Freud himself, many critics have applied psychoanalytic theory to tragedy. Freud, in 2009, is no longer very visible in the curricula of psychology departments, but he continues to be a powerful force in the study of literature, especially through the influence of the French psychoanalyst, Jacques Lacan. Certain plays almost irresistibly invite modern Westerners, for whom some Freudian ways of thought have become part of everyday popular psychology, to see their characters as victims of Freudian neuroses. In Euripides' *Hippolytus*, Hippolytus's aversion to sex is easy to see as sexual disgust connected with his illegitimacy and uneasy relationship with his father. In Euripides' *Bacchae*, Pentheus believes that the women who are worshipping Dionysus in the wilderness are having illicit sex (225), and he passes quickly from revulsion to a desire to spy on them (812). Those who have grown up with Freud almost automatically interpret his anger and disgust as a sign of repressed desire.[2]

---

[2] Segal 1986, "Pentheus and Hippolytus on the Couch and on the Grid: Psychoanalytic and Structuralist Readings of Greek Tragedy," 268–93. Originally published in *The Classical World* 74: 129–48.

It would be wise to be cautious, however. Many tragedies do not offer much basis for Freudian understanding, even as they invite it. *Oedipus the King* is the great example. Oedipus does not live the "family romance" with the father he kills or the mother he marries, for he has never known them.[3] The play may exploit the Oedipus complex in its audience, if there really is such a thing, but its protagonist does not experience it. Some scholars argue that Antigone in Sophocles' play feels incestuous desire for the brother she buries, Polynices. Since the Labdacid family alternates between incest and kin-murder, it seems to be a natural way to interpret her statement "I shall lie beside him, dear one with dear one" (73).[4] Still, there is no hint in the play that Antigone even knows Polynices (it is not clear how long he was in exile) or has any personal relationship with him – he simply belongs to the category "brother."

The Freudian understanding of *Bacchae* is a solution to a problem that is pervasive in tragedy and in Homer too. Pentheus is obviously in some way enchanted by Dionysus when he decides to spy on the women, just as the women themselves have been driven into the mountains by the god. In many instances in Homer and elsewhere, it is clear that the gods influence people in ways that fit their characters: Athena gives Odysseus good ideas because he has good ideas on his own. Modern audiences typically see this "double motivation" whenever the gods affect characters' minds, because the plots are more meaningful that way. Phaedra, in *Hippolytus*, falls in love with Hippolytus because Aphrodite wants revenge on him for refusing to honor her, as Aphrodite explains in the prologue. Phaedra herself, though, compares her own passion to the erotic misfortunes of her mother and sister (337–43), and the modern spectator can easily make this family pattern into a predisposition that belongs to Phaedra herself. In Euripides' *Heracles*, Hera forces the goddess Madness to attack the hero and make him kill his children. Again, interpreters often see Heracles' madness as a "natural" effect of the extreme violence that he has directed against his enemies.[5]

---

3 Vernant in Vernant/Vidal Naquet 1981, 63–81.
4 Griffith 2005.
5 Foley 1985, 147–204.

If characters have repressed desires, the gods are no longer essential to understanding events. That does not mean that such interpretations are wrong. Still, we need to be aware that there is always a temptation to make an ancient drama easier for ourselves.

In Aristophanes' *Frogs* (959–63), Euripides accuses Aeschylus of making his audience incapable of critical reflection, of stunning them with big and exotic sights and sounds, while he composed his tragedies about everyday life, so that if he made a mistake, the audience could have recognized it and shown that he had done something wrong. Both Aeschylus and Euripides here are caricatures, but the opposition captures a tension in the experience of serious drama. The audience may be completely carried away or critically judging every aspect of a play and its performance; or some spectators may be utterly absorbed and lost in the make-believe while others are bored and irritated; or, hardest to understand, individuals may simultaneously be deeply moved by the sufferings of a dramatic Hecuba and be consciously impressed that the actor has devised a gesture that conveys her anguish effectively. The experience can involve a variety of apparently contradictory reactions: strong emotion and intellectual evaluation, sympathy and revulsion for the same character.

Since the same stories were used many times by different tragedians and had already been used many times by earlier epic and lyric poets, everyone knew that any particular tragedy could not be literally true. The audience, or at least most of its members, believed that the characters of the tragic legends had once lived and that these stories had taken place, but they also recognized that the poets were inventing details and imagining motives. Indeed, the tragedians competed with earlier poetry, with earlier tragedians, and with their own contemporaries to create versions of the old stories that were more exciting, more plausible, more relevant, or more profound. Sophocles and Euripides composed versions of *Electra* within a few years of each other, probably in direct response to a revival of Aeschylus's *Libation Bearers*. They were obviously competing with each other, although scholars debate who was earlier, and both were competing against Aeschylus.

Tragedies contradict each other. The Antigone of *Antigone* says that she has personally washed, adorned for burial, and poured libations for her father, mother, and brother (900–2). In *Oedipus at Colonus*, she is forbidden even to see his grave (1756–63). The two plays are by the same author, but Antigone was composed almost forty years earlier. Odysseus is an admirable character in *Ajax*, despicable in *Philoctetes*, both by Sophocles. There is no fixed consistency of character from play to play. Although Odysseus is always clever and persuasive, he can be compassionate or ruthless. Menelaus sometimes conforms to the Athenian stereotype of the arrogant, bullying Spartan – but not always.

A few tragedies used material from recent history, and the audience of *Persians* knew very well that Aeschylus did not know how the Persian court had reacted to the Athenians' defeat of the Persians at the battle of Salamis. Indeed, tragedians could invent entire plots that fit within the basic edifice of legend. Aeschylus in *Eumenides* probably invented the story that Orestes came to Athens and was tried for the murder of his mother by the Areopagus. Euripides invented the story that he went to the land of the Taurians to bring back a statue of Artemis and there rescued his sister, Iphigenia, who had been brought there by the goddess when the Greeks thought her father, Agamemnon, had sacrificed her.

In the late fifth century, the tragedian Agathon made up a tragic plot from scratch, not even using the names of legendary characters. This did not, as far we know, create any great scandal, but he did not start a fashion. The tragedians mostly continued to create variants on the familiar plots. These had various advantages. As Aristotle points out in the *Poetics*, they had a built-in verisimilitude, since people believed that they happened. Since tragic plots are often about exceptional and extreme actions, especially murders of close relatives, this a priori credibility was helpful. It also made exposition easier. Tragedies never take the audience's knowledge of the stories for granted to the extent of not providing essential information. It is possible to follow a performance of tragedy without knowing the story at all. Sometimes, though, it is not easy. Relevant information may be presented rapidly and allusively. In Sophocles' *Electra*, for example, the story of the chariot race of Pelops is told in a lyric as the origin of the troubles of the family. Someone who did not know the story would probably not understand the song. To be sure, not understanding this song would not severely limit the spectator's comprehension of the whole play, but something would be lost. Most important, tragedians set their own versions against those with which at least some members of the audience would be familiar. Euripides' Electra in *Electra*, for example, is married and living in the country – unlike the unmarried Electra in the palace of other versions. Euripides' Helen in *Helen* has spent the entire Trojan War in Egypt. Euripides did not invent this variant, which he took from the lyric poet Stesichorus, but it was very different from the usual story.

The traditional plots did not remove suspense from among the emotions a tragedy could arouse. It has been demonstrated experimentally, in any case, that people can feel suspense when they hear a story whose outcome they already know, and we are all familiar with the intense suspense we can experience when watching films in which we may not know the story already, but the genre is enough to tell us that the hero cannot be killed. In tragedy, certain outcomes were fixed. Agamemnon would be killed by Aegisthus or Clytemnestra or both together, and his son, Orestes, would kill them in return. The Trojans lost the Trojan War. Oedipus's sons, Eteocles and Polynices, killed each other. Much, however, was open to variation, and tragedies sometimes pushed the inherited stories to the limit. At the end of Sophocles' *Philoctetes*, the deified Heracles appears and tells Philoctetes and Neoptolemus that they are to sail not to Philoctetes' home in Greece but to Troy. Philoctetes has adamantly refused to go to Troy as the story demands, but once Heracles instructs him, mythological order is instantly restored. At the end of Euripides' *Orestes*, Orestes, with his sister, Electra, and his friend, Pylades, beside him, along with his cousin, Hermione, whom he has taken hostage, is about to burn down the palace. Apollo appears and suddenly restores everyone to the proper future, which requires that Orestes marry Hermione.

While familiarity with Greek mythology adds to the pleasure of tragedy, it does not seem to be required. Tragedy has been open to a variety of purposes and interpretations in the long history of its reception; it is there to be used by directors, actors, readers, and even scholars. For the last three decades of the twentieth century, it has been a very lively field of study. Because, in tragedy, opposites often seem to turn into each other, and the boundaries of basic cultural divisions such as male/female and city/wild are overturned, structuralism had much to contribute to it. René Girard's *Violence and the Sacred* argues that sacrifice served to deflect social tension onto the victim, but that when this mechanism failed, social order collapsed, violence erupted, and a scapegoat was the only way to restore order; this book had considerable influence on the study of tragedy in the 1980s.[6] Because it is so engaged with problems of language and communication, it invited deconstruction. Because it was a public form in which the cultural anxieties of Athenian society were on display, New Historicism could study it as a manifestation of cultural issues and tensions. Because it so often concerns marriage and women, feminism engaged intensively with it. There has been a long tradition of careful study of the formal qualities of tragedy and their relation to interpretation, and the development of narratology gave these new energy. Because tragedy addresses universal human problems, philosophers can examine its ethical assumptions. Once interest in tragedy as theater revived, the study of how it has been and continues to be produced and adapted in the theater gradually developed into a field of its own. No approach is inappropriate as long as it does not exclude the possibility that the plays can continue to be powerful and meaningful.

Tragedy, then, is a dramatic form full of suspense and surprise, of violence and unexpected happiness. Even at its most horrific, it can provide a pleasure that is peculiar to itself, and maybe, if we allow it, it can also teach us something.

SOURCES AND SUGGESTIONS

This chapter owes a debt to Heath 1987, especially on the question of unity, though I think that he goes too far in denying tragedy's intellectual

---

[6] Girard 1977; his influence is manifest in Foley 1985 and Goff 1990.

side. Earlier debates about unity were prompted by the work of Tycho von Wilamowitz-Moellendorff, who argued that Sophocles aimed only at a powerful effect scene by scene, not at unity. Others extended similar arguments to other tragedians; for an appraisal, see Lloyd-Jones 1972 (untranslated German, especially in footnotes, but a reader without German can follow the main points). The main proponents of a ritual approach are Sourvinou-Inwood 2003 and Seaford 1994; for a quick introduction, see, in Bushnell 2005, Sourvinou-Inwood, "Tragedy and Ritual" (7–24) and Seaford, "Tragedy and Dionysus" (25–38).

Characterization in Greek tragedy was an area of intense debate following a paper by Gould 1978 (itself a response to Easterling 1973); there are discussions by both Easterling ("Constructing Character in Greek Tragedy," 83–99) and Goldhill ("Character and Action, Representation and Reading: Greek Tragedy and its Critics," 100–27), in Pelling 1990. Although it is a scholarly monograph with untranslated Greek, the introduction of Gibert 1995 (13–54) is an accessible discussion of the characterization problem.

For structuralism, see Vernant/Vidal-Naquet 1981. Segal 1981 is a structuralist study of Sophocles. Deconstruction is a powerful influence in Goldhill 1986 (though not the only one). The founding work for New Historicism in the study of tragedy is Winkler/Zeitlin 1990; Goff 1995 is a deliberate demonstration of the method; Hall 1989, however, is an important and influential example. (These works did not define themselves as New Historicism, a term that gained currency in the study of early modern literature, but they reflect the same intellectual trends and it is convenient to refer to them this way.) New Historicism, which looks at underlying ideology, has also revived historicist reading more broadly, as in the papers in Pelling 1997. Feminism has appeared in a variety of forms. Zeitlin's argument in "Playing the Other" that the women of tragedy are either instruments in stories about men or ways for men to think about themselves first appeared in 1985. Rabinowitz 1993, Wohl 1998, and Ormand 1999 are all, in different ways, intensely theorized studies of tragic women; McClure 1999 and Foley 2001 are sophisticated but easier reading. Goldhill's survey, "Modern critical approaches to Greek tragedy," in Easterling/Goldhill 1997 (324–47) is helpful. Dunn 1996 looks at one formal element, closure, and how Euripides fights stable interpretation; de Jong 1997 offers a meticulous narratological study of messenger speeches, which are not as neutral as they appear to be. Nussbaum 1986 is an especially important philosophical study of tragedy; for Sophocles, Blundell 1989 looks at the central ethical problem of retaliation.

Taplin 1977 began the revival of interest in staging that produced many specialized works. Goldhill 2007 is a prescriptive discussion of modern staging.

3

ORIGINS, FESTIVAL, AND COMPETITION

A. ORIGINS

Almost everything about the origins of tragedy is disputed, because the evidence is scanty, and scholars disagree profoundly about how reliable most of it is. Unfortunately, the very real questions about how tragedy began have become entangled with two issues of great importance for its interpretation: how religious tragedy was and how democratic it was. Scholars tend to assume that if tragedy began as a ritual dance, it must be interpreted as a religious event; if it began under the democracy, it is likely to be engaged with specifically democratic values. Neither of these assumptions is necessarily true. Tragedy could have continued to serve the same religious, social, and political functions through time, or it could have changed as circumstances changed. However, because scholars assume that we would know something crucial about tragedy if we knew its origin, they become too invested in different possible accounts. Furthermore, we tend to forget that three innovations must have taken place for tragedy as we know it to exist. First, somebody created a new kind of performance by combining a speaker with a chorus and putting both speaker and chorus in disguise as characters in a story from legend or history. Second, this performance was made part of the City Dionysia at Athens. Third, regulations defined how it was to be managed and paid for. It is theoretically possible that all these were simultaneous, but it is not likely.

We can start with what we hear about Thespis. According to the Marmor Parium, a famous Greek inscription of 264–263 BCE giving the dates of important events both mythological and historical, Thespis first acted and produced a play "in the city" (the stone is not entirely legible and this is a guess), with a billy goat as the prize, between the capture of Sardis (540 BCE) and the reign of Darius (520 BCE). (The word *tragoidos*, "performer in tragedy," means "one who sings in connection with a billy goat.") The Byzantine encyclopedia *Suda* says that he came from the Attic village of Icaria, and was, as a maker of tragedy, depending on which authority one followed, the sixteenth in line from Epigenes of Sicyon, or second, or the first. He first used white lead on his face, then a herbal preparation, and finally used masks of fine linen, first producing in the sixty-first Olympiad (535–532 BCE). There are various problems with these testimonies. The dating by Olympiads belongs to an artificial scheme that dated the first productions or victories of the great pre-Aeschylean names (Phrynichus, Choerilus, and Thespis) at tidy three-Olympiad (twelve-year) intervals before the competition of Choerilus, Pratinus, and Aeschylus between 499 and 496 BCE.[1]

Various other testimonies about Thespis show that throughout antiquity he was the main candidate for the inventor of tragedy, although his claims were not undisputed. Sicyon's claim is especially interesting because the fifth-century historian, Herodotus (5.67.5), says that the Sicyonians honored the hero, Adrastus, with "tragic choruses" until their tyrant, Cleisthenes, transferred the choruses to Dionysus. This Cleisthenes was the grandfather of the Cleisthenes who established the Athenian democracy, and ruled early in the sixth century. We have no way of knowing, however, whether the "tragic choruses" that Herodotus mentions at Sicyon were called that in the early sixth century, or whether Herodotus calls them "tragic" because the Sicyonian choruses of his own time resembled tragedy as he knew it. The Peloponnesians disputed Attica's claim to have invented tragedy, and ancient scholarship ascribes the invention of tragedy not only to Epigenes of Sicyon but to Arion of Methymna, whom Herodotus regards as the inventor of the literary dithyramb (1.23). Earlier choral

---

[1] West 1989.

song-and-dance forms were precursors of tragedy, and those connected with goat sacrifices were probably called "tragic."

However, our most important source for the history of tragedy is Aristotle's *Poetics* (1449a) – and he never mentions Thespis there. Whether we actually know anything about how tragedy began depends to a large extent on whether we believe that Aristotle knew anything. This is what he says about it:

> Starting from an origin in improvisation – both tragedy and comedy, the first from those who led off the dithyramb, the other from the phallic songs that are still today customary practice in many cities – gradually it became great, as they added each element of it that became visible. And tragedy, after undergoing many changes, stopped, once it had its own nature. And Aeschylus first brought the number of actors from one to two and diminished the choral role and had speech take the main part. Sophocles introduced three actors and painted scenery. And about its size: from small plots and ridiculous diction it became serious late by changing from the satyric.

This passage is extraordinarily difficult. The classical Athenian dithyramb ("circular chorus"), which was performed at the same City Dionysia as tragedy, was a song for a chorus of fifty; some dithyrambs represented characters and had a "dramatic" quality (Bacchylides 18, in which a soloist and chorus respond to each other), but many scholars think these show the influence of tragedy rather than the opposite. When Aristotle refers to "those who led off the dithyramb," he could be thinking of dithyrambs like the one mentioned in Archilochus fr. 120W, where he says "I know how to start off the beautiful song of Lord Dionysus, the dithyramb, when I am thunderstruck in my mind with wine." In such a performance, the main singer probably sang verses, perhaps improvised, and the others responded with a refrain. Any improvisatory performance, however, could only be a distant precursor of tragedy.

Did tragedy arise from satyr play or from a shared proto-drama, which then divided into satyr play and tragedy? This is tricky. There are many vase paintings from the sixth century on which satyrs, with or without nymphs, form a chorus. There are also paintings of choruses of men in various costumes – horse riders, dolphin riders, and birds. The dramatic satyr, however, does not appear until the very end of the century. The *Suda* says that Pratinus of Phlious first wrote satyr plays; he competed against Aeschylus and Choerilus in the seventieth Olympiad (499–496 BCE). The evidence, weak as it is, all suggests that satyr play was later than tragedy or roughly contemporary with it. To moderns, the name *tragoidos/tragoidia* has suggested a connection between tragedy and satyrs – but the satyrs of the archaic and classical period are horse men, not goat men. One ancient theory connects satyr play with the proverb "nothing to do with Dionysus" (used to mock irrelevance), saying that originally dithyramb was Dionysiac in its theme but then began treating all of mythology, and that satyr play was introduced so that Dionysus would not be forgotten at his own festival.

A famous Athenian inscription nicknamed the *Fasti* lists annual winners in the "revel"/circular chorus, comedy, and tragedy from 472 to 328 BCE (but not much is legible). Originally, it went back to about 501 BCE, and that is probably when the official record of the contests started. There was little solid evidence from any earlier time, although Aristotle certainly had an abundance of archaic and early classical poetry that we do not.

In the classical period, there are four distinct forms: circular chorus, satyr play, tragedy, and comedy. They may not have evolved in as tidy a progression as we would like. For examples, the animal choruses are obviously reminiscent of the choruses of fifth-century comedy, but they do not have the padded costume of classical comedy (which is similar but not identical to the costume found on Corinthian and Attic "komast" vases). There is no reason to assume that every form of choral dance in the sixth century had a fifth-century descendent or had only one. The forms surely evolved in relation to each other. As the forms became institutionalized, they needed to be defined for competition, and features excluded by one genre could then help define another.

The date of the institution of the festival itself is disputed. It honored Dionysus of Eleutherae, a village on the border of Attica and Boeotia that joined with Athens in order to avoid domination by Thebes and was incorporated into Attica. The image of Dionysus in the temple in the theater's sacred precinct was believed to have come from Eleutherae. Eleutherae was not one of the Attic demes established by the reforms of Cleisthenes in 308–307 BCE, so some scholars believe that the festival must be later than that date, while others think that Eleutherae could have entered into an alliance with Attica and sent the ancient statue as a sign without being annexed.[2]

It is, in the end, hard to know whether tragedy had very much to do with Dionysus. Still, the chorus sang and danced in a space in which there was an altar. Spaces created for dancing do not require altars – there is no mention of one, for example, in Homer's description of the dance floor on the Shield of Achilles in the *Iliad* (19.590–606). The altar may have been an accident in relation to tragedy, for the dithyramb was a circular chorus of fifty that used the altar as its center – but nonetheless it was always present and visible, a reminder of relations between humans and gods.

Tragedy was a deliberate invention, a brilliant idea. The archaic Greeks had a well-established tradition of choral songs about the heroes of the past. Some of these songs, as we know from the fragments of Stesichorus, included direct speech by the characters, along with narrative. Greeks also had performances of Homer by professionals, the rhapsodes, who probably did their best to impersonate the characters as they delivered the extensive speeches that constitute much of the epics. Finally, there were choruses that were disguised, as animals or (probably) as satyrs. Somebody, presumably Thespis, decided to combine spoken verse with choral song. Instead of using a narrator who would switch into speaking as a character, he decided to make the performer represent the character(s) without narrative. (The Greek word for "actor" is *hypocrites*, which means "answerer" or "interpreter," but the word cannot tell us anything about tragedy's origins, since we

---

[2] Anderson 2003, 179–84; Connor 1989, 7–32; Buck 1979, 99, 113.

do not know when it came into use.) He used masking to make this impersonation complete. Although it is only a guess, there is no reason to think that the inventor of the actor did not also decide to make this a dignified rather than a raucous performance, and so also decided that the chorus, though in costume, would be human. The traditions of choral song that tragedy adapted were ritual, but the spoken sections were not.

Greek literature associated particular literary forms with particular dialects. Epic poets, for example, used a special form of the language that nobody spoke. The dialect of the spoken parts of tragedy was a poeticized form of the everyday Greek of Athens. The sung portions, however, changed the Attic long *ê* to the long *â* characteristic of the Doric family of Greek dialects, marking them unmistakably but very superficially as part of the tradition of Greek choral poetry, which was predominantly Doric. This distinction between the spoken and sung parts shows how self-conscious the creation of tragedy must have been.

Although we do not have any plays that only use one actor, Aeschylus's *Suppliants* has only one scene in which the actors speak to each other. (This made scholars assume that it was Aeschylus's earliest play, until a papyrus revealed that Aeschylus had been victorious over Sophocles with its tetralogy.) As tragedy developed, the actors began to interact more with each other, and the role of the chorus became smaller. At the beginning, the actor's speech was powerful in part because of how it changed the chorus, which did not sing a single song as in other performances, but changed its rhythms and melodies repeatedly. Tragedy was thus a dazzlingly innovative kind of show. It combined the best features of rhapsodic performance of epic and choral lyric, offering singing, dancing, costumes, a refreshingly vivid way of presenting traditional legends that invited intense emotional reactions, and a new story every time. It is not surprising that the Athenians made it an official part of a major civic festival.

They are unlikely, however, to have instituted a major competition in a newly invented and untested genre. Thespis is a shadowy figure, maybe even a legend. (The name means "divinely inspired" and is an epithet of epic singers in Homer; either it was a name assumed professionally, or the father of Thespis planned for him to be a poet.) He is, however, consistently associated with the country, particularly the village of Icaria or Icarion, and the testimonies that say tragedy began at a rural festival and then was brought to the city have a certain inherent plausibility.

Choerilus is almost as dim a figure as Thespis, though he is certainly historical; his one surviving title is *Alope*. She belongs to the mythology of Eleusis, a village in Attica: her father, Cercyon, killed her after she had a baby whose father was the god Poseidon. Pratinus of Philous, a small city-state in the Peloponnese, was recorded as the inventor of satyr play, and one substantial fragment of a song (probably not from a drama) complains about excessive domination of the *aulos* over singers. His tragic titles are *Dymaenae* or *Karyatides* (these were types of women's chorus in Sparta), *Perseus*, and *Tantalus*. Since all his fragments were preserved in treatises about music, they are all about music. For practical purposes, the first tragedian we know anything about is Phrynichus.

Phrynichus is now remembered mostly because he composed two tragedies on the theme of recent history. The *Capture of Miletus* recalled the fall of Miletus to the Persians in 494 BCE, during the Ionian Revolt, which the Athenians had supported. Herodotus (6.21) says that he was fined for reminding the Athenians of their misfortunes. *The Phoenician Women* was about the Persian Wars and was set in Persia. His other plays, though, were mythological: *Women of Pleuron* (the story of Meleager), *Egyptians* and *Danaids* (like Aeschylus's *Suppliants*, about the descendents of Io), *Tantalus*, *Antaeus* (a giant defeated in wrestling by Heracles), and *Alcestis*. Aristophanes was an admirer of Phrynichus, and this is interesting in itself, because Aristophanes was a very young man in 427 BCE and cannot have seen the first productions of plays by Phrynichus. Elements of his choreography were remembered, so that Aristophanes says "do the Phrynichian kick, so that the spectators will cry 'Oh!' when they see the high leg" (*Wasps* 1525–7), and some of his songs were evidently still sung late in the century.

B. THE FESTIVALS

Whatever tragedy's ritual origins, in classical Athenian practice, tragedy was completely embedded in the festival of the City Dionysia. The festival took place in late March or April, after the beginning of the sailing season, and it was an occasion on which the Athenians displayed the splendors of their city to the Greek world at large. Before the festival proper, the poet, actors, and chorus made a public presentation, wearing garlands but unmasked, at an event called the *Proagon*, introducing the performances to come. After 444 BCE, this event was held in the Odeon near the theater; we do not know where it took place before the Odeon was built, if indeed it took place at all. Before or at the start of the festival, the statue was taken to a small shrine at the Academy, outside the walls on the way to Eleutherae. It was then formally brought to the theater in a torchlight procession. It would have been brought into the theater itself for the performances.

There was a formal sacrificial procession, probably on the morning of the first day of the festival. It included a bull for sacrifice and various other animals, and the men who were paying for the dramatic and dithyrambic performances paraded in elaborate, magnificent robes. (The meat from such public sacrifices was distributed among citizens, so that festivals were also feasts.) As was usual in a procession honoring Dionysus, there were large models of an erect phallus carried on poles, the *phalloi*. Then there were the performances: three sets of three tragedies and a satyr play; five comedies; and ten circular choruses performed by adult men and ten by boys. The simplest arrangement would be five days, with either tragedies or circular choruses first and a comedy later. The arrangement is not certain, but tragedy was clearly first.

Before the performances began, there were a number of patriotic ceremonies. During the period of the Athenian empire, from which all our tragedies except *Rhesus* come, the tribute of the allies was displayed in the theater. The sons of men who had died fighting for Athens were brought up at the city's expense, and, before the tragedies, a herald stationed those who had reached young manhood in armor before the crowd and delivered a proclamation wishing them good fortune and inviting them to take seats at the front. The city could also announce other important public matters, including proclamations of honors for service to the city. Other proclamations were made, too, without public authority: men announced honors they had received from their districts, or from other cities, and sometimes the manumissions of slaves. Since the theater audience was the single largest gathering in the Athenian year, it is not surprising that people tried to use the occasion for any declaration for which they wanted the widest possible publicity. The ten generals poured libations at the altar in the theater itself.

It is hard to evaluate how all this pageantry influenced the effects of the tragedies themselves on their audiences. There may have been, as Simon Goldhill has suggested, a tension between the patriotic values of the presentation of the war orphans and the proclamations of honors and the questioning of these values that is so common in tragedy.[3] Yet it is clear that the performances were as much a display of Athens' greatness as were the other ceremonies.

This question leads to another: when did tragedy become part of the program at the City Dionysia? Until recently, scholars, relying partly on the evidence of the Marmor Parium, thought that tragedy was introduced into the festival in the sixth century, during the rule of Peisistratus. If that were so, tragedy was considerably older than the patriotic rituals, and, even more important, tragedy was not a product of the democracy. But, just as many recent scholars doubt that Aristotle had real knowledge about tragedy before the fifth century, some have suggested that all the sources that present information about tragedy before the inscriptional record began in 502–501 BCE are retailing guesses. So some think that tragedy began when it was recorded, under the democracy. The lost section of the inscription known as the *Fasti* did not go back before c. 502 BCE, but its partially preserved heading said that it recorded victories from the beginning.

Whenever it was instituted, the tragic contest was far less "democratic" than the contest of dithyrambs. In the dithyrambic

[3] Goldhill in Winkler/Zeitlin 1990, 97–129.

contest, each of the ten "tribes" into which the constitution of Cleisthenes had divided the Athenian citizen body had choruses of men and boys, each of fifty, all members of the tribe, with a *chorêgos*, who paid the expenses, also from the tribe. The inscriptions recording victors, remarkably, did not include the poet's name, although in the early fifth century, some very famous poets participated. When the dithyrambic contest was instituted, the system of ten tribes was less than ten years old, and the arrangement was obviously intended to make citizens identify with the tribes.

The tragic contest could not have been more different. It had far fewer participants, and the contestants were poets and *chorêgoi* who represented only themselves. The record of victories gave the names of the poets and *chorêgoi* along with the titles of the plays. There is no obvious ritual or political basis for having exactly three competitors; it appears to have been a practical decision about how many performances would be ideal, how many competitors were needed for an exciting contest, how many good poets would be available, and how many *chorêgoi* would be available year after year. The combination of dithyramb and tragedy in the festival mirrors in microcosm the tensions within the democratic system, which needed simultaneously to proclaim its egalitarianism, to attract and reward excellence, and to exploit the rich without alienating them. There is also a balance between local and Panhellenic interest. The dithyrambic poets were not always Athenians, but the prize went to an Athenian. The tragic prize, however, sometimes went to Pratinus of Phlious, Aristarchus of Tegea, or Ion of Chios.

In 442 BCE, tragedy was added to the program at the Lenaia, a winter festival of Dionysus. Two tragedies each by two poets were performed (at least in the fifth century), and there were no satyr plays. It appears that although comic poets made little distinction between competition at the Lenaia and at the Dionysia, for tragedians the Dionysia had more prestige. For one thing, the Lenaian audience was almost exclusively Athenian. No representatives of the allies were present, and the sailing season had not started yet. Plato's *Symposium* takes place at a party celebrating Agathon's victory at the Lenaia of 416 BCE.

Then there were rural festivals. The demes – the smallest units of government in Attica, originally villages and neighborhoods – held performances of tragedy at their celebrations of the Rural Dionysia or at other festivals. Most of the evidence comes from the fourth century BCE. These sometimes encored plays that had been well received at the major festivals. Even though the theater of Dionysus was large, it could not begin to accommodate the potential audience, so there would be many who would be eager to see a play that was being talked about, and doubtless many who would be eager to see it again. In Plato's *Republic* (475d), Glaukon refers to people who "run around to the Dionysias, skipping neither those in the cities nor those in the villages, as if they had rented their ears for listening to every chorus." But they may also have premiered the tragedies of poets who had not yet been granted a chorus in the city. Athenian tragedy also interested Greeks outside Athens, and, beginning in the late fifth century, performances outside Athens took place not only when a wealthy king chose to patronize a poet, but in various cities.

After Aeschylus's death, the Athenians passed a decree that anyone planning to produce his plays should receive a chorus, and there was a production of *Libation Bearers* sometime in the late 420s. Starting in 386 BCE, "old plays" were produced at the Dionysia. Euripides was evidently the most popular. There is also evidence for performance of Sophocles in this period, but Aeschylus seems to have been more revered than produced.

C. FINANCES AND CONTEST

Like other state-sponsored performances, tragedies were produced in competition with each other. The system required rigorous rules. A tragedian first had to apply to the magistrate in charge of the festival, the archon. We do not know exactly how he chose, but a passage of Plato (*Laws* 7.817d) suggests that the poets read samples. The tragedians did not need to be Athenians, and we know of several successful tragedians who were not. The archon also had the job of appointing the *chorêgoi*.

Chorêgus means literally "chorus leader," but in Athens it refers to the men who were responsible for paying for the chorus – their training and their costumes, probably the clarinet player who accompanied them, and the extras tragedies required. The archon had to find *chorêgoi* as soon as he entered office, because they were supposed to be those most financially able to handle the expense, and the individuals selected could object and propose someone else. Extended legal wrangling could result. A lot of money was required for a good show: we hear of twenty-five or thirty minae (dithyramb, with fifty singers, cost even more, although each was probably paid considerably less than the twelve, later fifteen singers of the tragic chorus).

The financing of tragedy is truly extraordinary. The actors, two in the early period, later three, were paid by the city, and the city paid the poets, although we do not know how much. The *chorêgos*-system was the democracy's way of adapting traditional aristocratic competition for its own purpose. By spending generously, a rich man could buy goodwill and prestige. The famous politician, Themistocles, was *chorêgos* for Phrynichus in 476 BCE for his *Phoenician Women*, a play about the defeat of the Persians (to which Themistocles had made a great contribution). He must have volunteered. Pericles as a young man was *chorêgus* for the production that included Aeschylus's *Persians* in 472 BCE, and whether or not he had specific political goals connected with the plays being shown, he surely wanted to promote himself. We do not hear of famous men as *chorêgoi* for tragedy later.

The city paid for the actors, and the competition required that each poet be allotted the same resources. In our earliest plays of Aeschylus, there are two, in the *Oresteia* and later, three. The actors therefore played multiple roles, and the restriction also meant that only three speaking characters could be on stage at the same time. Extras were a way of working with those limits. An actor who had a speaking part in one scene could exit and change mask and costume. He could then reenter in a different role, and his earlier character could still be present, played by an extra in the mask and costume, as long as the character had no lines. Extras were also needed as "spear carriers" – not infrequently, a king in tragedy will speak to an attendant whose presence has not been noted so far. The high-status characters were always followed by attendants. So extras must have been a financial issue sometimes.

Sometimes these doublings of roles seem to be significant. In Sophocles' *Women of Trachis*, for example, the same actor played Deianeira, the wife of Heracles who kills him with a poison that she thinks is a love-potion, and Heracles himself. We do not know, however, to what extent audiences really noticed that the actor inside the costume and mask was the same person. A strong and beautiful voice was important for an actor, but the sources do not say to what extent the actors tried to sound different in different roles.

The tragedians produced and directed their own plays, although the chorus had a trainer as well, at least later on. In the early days of tragedy, they were probably actors too. Starting in 449 BCE, there was a competition for tragic actors, and acting was evidently professionalized. Only the first actor, the protagonist, competed for the prize, although in developed tragedy, the second and third parts could be extremely demanding. We hear about special relationships between tragedians and individual actors, so it appears that before the introduction of the actor's prize, the tragedians hired their protagonists, although later the archon distributed the actors by lot. The protagonists then apparently hired their own second and third actors. In the fourth century, each tragedian at the Dionysia received each of the three actors for one tragedy, but in the fifth century, the same actor seems to have performed an entire tetralogy.

The system for judging the competition at the Dionysia was complex. Judges were nominated by the ten tribes into which the citizen body was divided. The names were vetted, and then lots with these names were sealed in jars, one for each tribe. The jars were opened only in the theater, just before the performances began. The most recent and plausible reconstruction of the voting procedures is this. After the performances, the judges cast ballots into an urn, voting only for the winner. The first five ballots were drawn and publicly read; if any of the productions had three or more votes, it won. If none did, another two ballots were drawn and read. If any production had four or more votes, it won. If none did, another ballot would be drawn until a winner emerged. If the second place was a tie, second place may have gone to the production that received this number of ballots first, or they may have voted again. This system also ensured that often (roughly eighteen percent of the time), the winner was not the production that had received the most votes.[4]

The element of chance allowed the god to intervene, but leaving decisions to the gods was not an Athenian habit. In trials, Athena had a tie-splitting vote, but it always favored the defendant. Public officials were chosen by lot to make sure they represented ordinary citizens, not to call for divine intervention. This system has an interesting side effect. If tragedians had resented losing too much, or if younger poets had felt they had no chance against established favorites, the festival would have failed, for the supply of potential tragic poets was not unlimited. Both Aeschylus and Euripides died outside Athens, and the ancient biographical traditions have them leave in resentment at losing a contest or being treated unfairly (in neither case is there any reason to think they planned more than a visit elsewhere). The element of chance was small enough that the victory itself was not diminished, but large enough to mitigate the effects of making valuable people angry. There was a first-time victor every three or four years.

D. THE THEATER AND ITS CONVENTIONS

According to the usual unreliable sources, the theater of Dionysus was built on the southeast slope of the Acropolis after the seating used previously in the *agora* collapsed sometime between 500 and 496 BCE. This is of course possible, but it is also likely that the city would have wanted a venue that would allow large audiences to enjoy the spectacles into which it was putting immense resources.

The performance space in an ancient Greek theater is called the *orchestra*, a place for dancing, and the essentials for tragedy were a space for the chorus to sing and dance, a space for the actors, a place

4 Marshall and van Willigenburg 2004.

where actors could go to change masks and costumes, side entrances and exits, and seating for the spectators. (This last space is not controversial – there were wooden benches on the slope of the Acropolis.) There is endless discussion about the shape of the theater. The theater of Dionysus has been rebuilt repeatedly, and only a few stones set in an arc remain from the fifth century, their significance endlessly debated. Archaeologists and theater historians cannot agree on whether the auditorium as a whole was a trapezoid or circular, and whether the acting and dancing space was circular or rectangular.[5] Argument tends to proceed by analogy, but there is no agreement about the best analogy. For example, a rectangular theater in the Attic deme of Thorikos has been excavated whose fifth-century form is not obscured by later remodeling. It could hold more than two thousand spectators. However, it seems clearly to have been a multipurpose space, used for meetings and rituals, as well as performances of various kinds, and the theater seems to have adapted to existing buildings on the site. Every theater presents such issues: the exact shape would depend on what the building was for, what the strengths and weaknesses of the site were, and what existing structures needed to be accommodated. Fourth-century theaters often have a circular *orchestra*. Since dithyrambic performances were among the most important functions of the Theater of Dionysus, a circular *orchestra* seems somewhat more likely. But the most important thing to realize about the theater is that we really do not know.

Another issue is the stage. It is clear that physical interaction between actors and chorus was possible, so most scholars believe that in the classical period, there was a low stage. Behind the stage stood a tent in the early period, but by the *Oresteia* of Aeschylus in 458 BCE, there was a building (the Greek word for the stage building literally means "tent"). In Aeschylus's *Persians*, the setting is an open-air meeting place, and the palace is at a sufficient distance for the Queen to make her first entrance on a chariot, while in *Agamemnon*, the house is so important that it is effectively a character. The building quickly became integral to tragedy. The Watchman in *Agamemnon* opens the play lying on the

5 Circular: Wiles 1997, 53; rectangular: Rehm 1994, 33.

house's roof, and going through the door is a fateful action. Relatively long passages, called *parodoi*, led off on each side; the chorus entered along these, and it is because they were long that often the chorus or a character onstage announces a new entry before the entering character engages with those already present.

The theater quickly developed particular devices with their own conventions. Since the setting must be outdoors, there was a wheeled platform called the *ekkyklêma* that could be pushed out through the central door. By convention, actors and props on the *ekkyklêma* were still indoors, but they were visible to the audience. The *ekkyklêma* is used in *Eumenides* to show the interior of Apollo's temple at Delphi with the ghastly Furies besieging Orestes, and in Sophocles' *Ajax* for the inside of Ajax's tent, where he sits amid the cattle he has slaughtered. (What you see when you look inside a building in tragedy is unlikely to be pretty.) The other celebrated device was the *mêchanê*, the "machine," a crane that allowed gods to appear in the air, or Bellerophon to fly on Pegasus. A *deus ex machina* is a god who flies into the play to provide a final resolution. Gods could also appear on the *theologeion*, a raised platform above the roof.

There were limits on what could be shown. First, violence normally took place only offstage. In Aeschylus's *Agamemnon*, the murder takes place inside the stage building, and the audience hears Agamemnon's cries. Second, changes of scene were rare; in our surviving tragedies, *Eumenides* moves from Delphi to Athens, and Sophocles' *Ajax* moves its scene from the space directly in front of Ajax's tent to a lonely spot by the sea. Both times, the chorus leaves the *orchestra* and reenters. This is unusual, however. Usually events outside the defined setting and violent actions must be reported. In Euripides' *Heracles*, the chorus and audience hear the cries of Amphitryon as the mad Heracles attacks his family, and then a messenger comes from inside the house to narrate in detail what has happened. In most tragedies, a messenger enters to describe offstage events to the chorus and characters, like the messenger in Euripides' *Medea* who reports to Medea how her poison has killed Jason's bride and King Creon, or the messenger who tells the chorus about the suicide of Jocasta and the self-blinding of Oedipus in *Oedipus the King*.

The time that passes during a choral song is fluid. Sometimes it must be days. For example, in *Agamemnon*, the chorus has no sooner doubted that a signal relayed by beacon fires really proves the fall of Troy than Clytemnestra sees the herald coming (493–4). Still, tragic performance feels continuous, and several tragedies, such as Sophocles' *Ajax* and Euripides' *Medea*, emphasize that they take place in a single day.

E. BIOGRAPHIES AND DATES

Aeschylus, Sophocles, and Euripides do not dominate the genre only through an accident of survival. They all had long and prolific careers. The most famous tragedians of the high classical period after the Big Three were Ion of Chios and Agathon. Ion apparently wrote thirty or forty plays (some satyr plays), but only twelve survived for later Greek scholarship. Agathon first produced at the Lenaia of 416 BCE, had gone to the court of King Archelaus in Macedon by 405 BCE, and died there. The Three among them composed a substantial percentage of all the tragedies produced in the fifth century.

Furthermore, they were in a peculiarly favorable position for becoming almost instantly canonical. Aeschylus began producing plays early in the fifth century. Sophocles and Euripides both died in 406 BCE, just before the fall of Athens at the end of the Peloponnesian War. The Three were active at precisely the period of Athens' greatest power, and perfectly suited to represent Athenian prestige. In addition, they were all Athenian citizens.

We are generally safe from the temptation to make facile connections between the tragedians' life and their plays because we know very little about their lives. Of Aeschylus, we know that he came from Eleusis and fought against the Persians at the battles of Marathon and Salamis, and that his brother Cynegeirus was killed at Marathon. He wrote a play to celebrate the foundation of the city of Etna by Hieron, the tyrant of Syracuse in Sicily, and probably traveled to Sicily to produce the play. Late in life, he went to Sicily again, and died at Gela.

Both his son, Euphorion, and his nephew, Philocles, were successful tragedians.

Aeschylus often, but not always, composed his plays as tetralogies, in which each play presented one episode in a larger story. The *Oresteia* consists of the tragedies from such a tetralogy. The satyr play, *Proteus*, was about Menelaus's adventures in Egypt on the way back from Troy; it is lost. (Scholars often ignore the satyr plays and refer to these connected tragedies as "trilogies.") Of Aeschylus's other surviving plays, *Persians* was not part of a connected group, but both *Suppliants* and *Seven against Thebes* were. Later tragedians seem to have linked their plays for the Dionysia only occasionally. Euripides in 415 BCE produced *Alexandros, Palamedes*, and the surviving *Trojan Women* together, and a few titles of what seem to be trilogies survive from minor tragedians. The turn away from the tetralogy was probably mainly a poetic decision. Both the *Oresteia* and the Oedipus trilogy to which *Seven against Thebes* belonged showed the workings through time of a family curse and the interaction between free will and an inherited fate. While the later tragedians sometimes hint that a family curse is at work, they do not emphasize the theme.

We know a little more about Sophocles' life for two main reasons: he held important public offices, and his acquaintance, Ion of Chios, wrote a book about famous people he knew, from which a long fragment survives about Sophocles at a party on the island of Chios during his generalship. Sophocles, from the village of Colonus a little outside the walls of Athens, was born in the mid 490s BCE. He had his first production and victory in 468 BCE competing against Aeschylus, and continued to have an exceptionally successful career (he never placed third in the contest). He served as the chair of the board of Treasurers of the Greeks in 443–442 BCE – the treasurers were responsible for receiving the tribute from Athens' allies, paying the tithe to Athena (one-sixtieth of the total), and disbursing the funds when they were authorized by the assembly. It was a highly responsible job, and his subsequent election as general must mean that the Athenians thought he was both honest and a competent administrator.

At the party Ion describes, which probably took place when Sophocles was collecting reinforcements for the Athenian blockade of Samos, Sophocles managed to trick a good-looking young slave into getting close enough that Sophocles was able to kiss him. Sophocles commented that he was a better "strategist" than Pericles thought. At the same party, Sophocles quoted a line of the tragedian, Phrynichus, to praise the young man's beauty, and when a "teacher of letters" objects to Phrynichus's description of a beautiful boy's cheeks as "red," because a painter would not use red for them, Sophocles cited Homer, Pindar, and Simonides to prove that poets and painters do not follow the same rules. Everyone laughed, but Sophocles was clearly annoyed by the contemporary (sophistic) practice of demonstrating one's own cleverness by finding mistakes in famous poets. Ion says that he was fun over wine and witty, but in politics, no more astute or active than any typical upper-class Athenian. As for the slave and the kiss, there is abundant evidence that Sophocles was powerfully attracted to both men and women. His son, Iophon, was a successful tragedian who sometimes competed against his father; the son of his illegitimate son Ariston, Sophocles II, was also a tragedian.

Late in life, he served as one of the special commissioners to propose constitutional changes after the Sicilian disaster. This was a fiasco; the commissioners opened the way for an oligarchic coup. The episode, however, does not seem to have harmed his immense popularity. Sophocles was a symbol of all that was best about Athens in his own lifetime.

Euripides was born around 480 BCE. He apparently never held public office, and the biographical tradition makes him the opposite of Sophocles in every way: socially dysfunctional, preferring solitude, sexually interested only in women, and betrayed by his wife. The Euripides of ancient biography is a caricature, although there evidently was some scandal about his wife. The biographical tradition makes him humorless, although his tragedies contain some deliberately very funny incidents, such as the sequence in *Ion* when Xanthus emerges from the temple of Apollo after being told that the first person he meets will be his son: he tries to embrace Ion, who evidently thinks that Xanthus is making a sexual advance. However, he seems not to have liked composing satyr plays. One of his extant plays, the *Alcestis*, was fourth in its tetralogy. If we did not know it replaced a satyr play, we would simply think it was an unusually short tragedy, but because we know, some features, like the cartoonish character Death, seem to push the limits of the tragic register downward. He may have substituted such lighter tragedies in other productions too. Also, several satyr plays of Euripides were lost early, suggesting that he made no attempt at preserving them.

The dates of first production are important because we tend to think of the Three as a sequence, Aeschylus – Sophocles – Euripides. But Euripides' first production in 455 BCE was only a few years after Aeschylus's last in 458 BCE, and the influence of Aeschylus on Euripides is more visible and more powerful than any influence of Sophocles – and so is his resistance to it. When Euripides was young, Aeschylus was the acknowledged master, while Sophocles was a rising star. Both Sophocles and Euripides developed primarily in response to Aeschylus, and only secondarily to each other.

F. THE AUDIENCE

Scholars have discussed the audience of Athenian drama extensively, especially whether women attended. These debates have focused entirely on the City Dionysia, on the assumption that plays were composed entirely for that single performance. The City Dionysia was clearly the most important venue. But the tragedies that we have all survive as written texts, which means that somebody (probably, first of all, the poets and their families) kept copies of them after that initial performance. Written copies could serve as prompts for reperformances at local festivals or as aids for individual memorization (for which comedy provides abundant evidence). If a play was a failure, it probably was never reperformed, and not many people would want to learn one of its songs or a speech as a party piece (although there may

have been popular songs that survived from otherwise forgotten tragedies, just as many standards today originated in obscure musicals). As
for reading, Aristophanes' *Frogs* provides the first evidence for individual reading of a tragedy (52–3, Euripides' *Andromeda*), but we can
safely assume that there were readers earlier, often probably in groups
of friends rather than solitary consumers.

Still, the Dionysia was crucial. The city gave out a contract to a private individual or group to maintain the theater, and the lessee then
took money for seats, probably in cash. It cost two obols to attend,
which was not a trivial amount of money for the poorer Athenians
(three obols a day was the wage of a laborer on the Acropolis).
According to our sources, the city introduced payment for seats in
order to control entrance to the theater, because with free seating,
people had camped out and fought over seats. Under Pericles, around
the middle of the fifth century, the city set out to make the experience
equally available to all citizens by subsidizing attendance with pay-
ments from the Theoric Fund. Any properly registered citizen who
was not abroad could collect an amount that would pay for the theater
and other costs of the festival. The dithyrambic contests involved five
hundred men and five hundred boys, and their friends and relatives
must have wanted to attend at least on the days when the circular
choruses performed. Many poorer Athenians probably had other pri-
orities than the theater, and the city does not seem to have imposed
any limits on how the recipients actually spent the theoric subsidy;
but if ordinary citizens had not valued the theater, they would not
have continued to spend civic money on it. Even the liturgies, after all,
had public opportunity costs – the city could have had those *chorêgoi*
spend their money in other ways. So while there were probably more
elite and wealthy people in the theater than in the general population,
the theater was not exclusive.

Comedy and other sources prove that at least foreign residents (met-
ics) attended both the Dionysia and the Lenaia, while many foreigners came to the Dionysia. Comedy also shows that boys were present.
In Theophrastus's *Characters*, written in the late fourth century, the
"Man without a sense of propriety" (9.5) buys theater seats for foreign

guests but the next day brings his sons and their pedagogue (a slave) instead.

The most energetic debate has concerned the presence of women in the theater. Comedy often addresses the audience, and the word used is "men" (as in the assembly). The "notional" audience consists of men. Comic evidence suggests that men would often go without their wives; for example, in Aristophanes' *Women at the Thesmophoria*, a speaker complains that men come home from the "bleachers" after seeing Euripides, look their wives over, and start searching for an adulterer in the house (390–7). However, other comic passages give the strong impression that women were present, and Plato famously says that "educated women," young men, and most people generally would select tragedy as their favorite performance (*Laws* 658c–d) – although he may be thinking of performances at smaller festivals. Since women did not receive the subsidy, among citizen women, attendance would depend on their families' willingness and ability to pay. Among non-citizen women, the expensive courtesans (*hetaerae*) surely attended, both to be seen and to be able to talk intelligently to clients.

Although the theater had a capacity of 15,000 or more spectators, this was not even close to the citizen body at the height of Athenian power, especially since foreigners, resident aliens, children, and probably women were there. It was, however, a significant segment of it – anywhere from a fifth of voters to half. Tragedy was a popular entertainment. While the cleverest intellectuals in Athens and the Greek world evidently engaged with it, it appealed to a very broad audience, both at first performance and later. While tragedies can be very subtle, to be successful they needed to be able to make a large crowd feel as if everybody was sharing the same feeling – even when individual responses, if closely analyzed, would have differed.

SOURCES AND SUGGESTIONS

For a presentation of the traditional view of the origins and early form of tragedy that relies on Aristotle, see Lesky 1983 (1–36). For a discussion that is very strongly opposed, see Scott Scullion, "Tragedy and Religion: the Problem of Origins" (23–37), in Gregory 2005 (a more accessible version of Scullion 2002). Csapo/Miller 2007 is a collection of essays that brings comparative evidence to bear on the development of drama from ritual. The best discussion of the poetic background of tragedy is Herington 1985. My view of origins is much influenced by Herington and Scullion, though I am a little less skeptical of the evidence than Scullion.

The standard work on the festival is Pickard-Cambridge 1988 (for scholars only, with untranslated Greek). Evidence about the theater, production, and audience is collected in translation in Slater/Csapo 1995. On women in the audience, Goldhill in Easterling/Goldhill 1997 (54–68); Henderson 1991. On the choregic system, Wilson 2000 is extremely informative. Green/Handley 1995 presents vase paintings based on dramatic scenes.

4

HISTORICAL AND
INTELLECTUAL
BACKGROUND

Whether or not tragedy first became an established part of the festival under the democracy, the Three and their rivals knew it as an institution of the democracy, and it was the cultural product by which imperial Athens most proudly presented itself to the Greek world and to itself. It was profoundly a product of the Greek *polis*, the city-state. A *polis* was a town and its countryside that formed a political unit, and whatever the form of government, a *polis* was formed of citizens who had membership in it, and it had its own laws. Tragedies usually assume the *polis* as setting, even though the *polis* did not exist in the legendary past. Often the concerns of the *polis* are a significant background: in *Libation Bearers*, for example, Orestes' assassination of Aegisthus and Clytemnestra frees the *polis* from illegitimate and tyrannical rule (973). Not infrequently, its institutions and practices are imported into the heroic world: in Aeschylus's *Suppliants*, the king of Argos insists on consulting the people before he agrees to protect the Danaids, because this could lead to war and the whole *polis* must take responsibility for the decision (398–401).

The crucial events that define the world of Attic tragedy are the revolution of 508–507 BCE that established the constitution of Cleisthenes; the battle of Marathon in 490 BCE; the Greek-Persian War of 480–479 BCE and the subsequent formation of the Delian League; the reforms of Ephialtes c. 463 BCE; the gradual transformation of the Delian League into an Athenian Empire; the ascendancy of Pericles from 461–427 BCE; the Peloponnesian War, with the Archidamian War from 431–421 BCE, the disastrous attempt to conquer Sicily from 415–413 BCE, and the Decelean War from 413–404 BCE. Some tragedies directly reflect contemporary events, such as the reforms of Ephialtes in Aeschylus's *Eumenides*. Scholars disagree about other possible allusions – whether, for example, the character and fate of Sophocles' *Ajax* respond to the career of Cimon. There is no question, however, that tragedies were profoundly engaged in the broader ideological tensions of democracy and imperialism.

The constitution that emerged from the conflicts of 508–507 BCE involved a considerable reorganization of Athenian political and social life. Henceforth, the Athenian population was divided into ten "tribes," each with a tribal hero selected from a long list of possibilities by the Delphic oracle. (Most of these heroes were eventually the subjects of tragedies, but not all.) Each tribe was divided into thirds representing one of the main regions of Attica, and the thirds were made up of demes, villages, or neighborhoods. This structure made it difficult for big landowners to use their local power. The Assembly was supreme, and the Council of Five Hundred that conducted most business was selected by lot. Each year, the assembly had the power to "ostracize" one person, which required him to leave Attica for ten years; this was a further attempt to prevent anyone from having too much power. Such was the constitution under which the Athenians defeated the Persians when they landed at Marathon on a punitive expedition, because the Athenians had supported the Greeks cities of Ionia in their revolt against Persian rule. Persia then attempted a full conquest of Greece, invading in 480 BCE. The Persians occupied Athens; but the Greek alliance, in which the Athenians, who had retreated to the island of Salamis, were the most important contingent, defeated the Persians at sea. This victory is the subject of Aeschylus's *Persians*. The following year, the Greeks, led by Sparta, also defeated the Persian army on land, at Plataia in Boeotia.

In the following year, as Greeks continued operations against Persia, it soon became clear that Sparta did not want to lead the Greeks in ongoing warfare, but Athens did, and Athens became the leader of the Delian League, a permanent alliance against Persia. Initially, this was an alliance of near equals, with many city-states providing ships, but more and more either preferred simply to provide money, or were forced to substitute tribute for ships after a failed attempt to secede. Athens had by far the biggest and best-trained navy, and Athens controlled the money – under Pericles, spending it on the grand temples whose remains are the most famous tourist attractions of today's Athens.

Starting in the late 460s, the reforms of Ephialtes and further developments under the leadership of Pericles created the "radical" democracy. The jurisdiction of the Areopagus, the old, aristocratic body, was greatly reduced. The power of the popular courts, with their large juries, increased, and since political power struggles often played out in the courts, this development had serious political consequences, making ordinary people the arbiters of struggles among the rich. Property qualifications for most offices were removed, and most offices were filled by lot. Pay for public service was introduced – for holding various offices, serving on juries, even at some periods for attending the assembly. This made popular sovereignty *de facto* instead of *de jure*. Peasants in the countryside are not likely to have made the serious effort to attend routine assembly meetings – the Pnyx, the assembly place, had a capacity of about 6000 – but participation in political life was genuinely open to everybody.

Everybody, that is, who was an adult male citizen. Athens was full of slaves; historians debate whether the economy was dependent on slaves, but they were certainly important. Women were, except in religion, officially invisible. They were an essential part of the *polis*, but ideally never as agents for themselves, only through and for their fathers, brothers, husbands, or sons. Tragedy, however, is consistently concerned with people other than adult male citizens. Choruses, who are so important in guiding the audience's responses, are most often not male citizens but young girls or women, or slaves. This is almost inevitable, because the chorus cannot intervene to prevent violence, so choruses are composed of the powerless. Choruses of men are often elderly, wise, but frail, as in *Agamemnon* or *Oedipus at Colonus*; or they are composed of subordinates, like Neoptolemus's followers in Sophocles' *Philoctetes*. Even beyond the chorus, tragedy consistently places women in situations where men are unavailable or unwilling to act for them. Tragedies present transgressive women, like Clytemnestra in *Agamemnon*; victimized women, like Andromache in *Andromache*; and women who act against female norms because their nobility trumps their gender, like the Electra of Sophocles' *Electra*.

In Aristophanes' *Frogs*, Euripides boasts that in his plays, everyone talked: "the woman and the slave no less, and the master and the young girl and the old woman," and he says that this was "democratic" (949–52). Dionysus warns him against this theme – apparently Euripides was not regarded as a supporter of the democracy – but it is interesting that Athenian democracy, which from a modern perspective excluded so many, could see itself as inclusive (and the pamphlet by the author nicknamed the "Old Oligarch" indeed complains that slaves and resident aliens could not be told from free men on the street (10–11) and show no respect. Distinctions between slave and free were certainly obvious on the tragic stage. One democratic principle, that anyone may have wise advice to offer, is extended in tragedy beyond the limits of Athenian practice. It is a general rule of tragedy that characters who reject advice because a social inferior offers it are making a mistake. Creon in *Antigone* will not listen to his son. Sympathetic characters pay respectful attention to the words of social inferiors, although their advice is not always good (Phaedra in *Hippolytus* should not have listened to the Nurse, and Creusa in *Ion* should not have followed the Pedagogue's suggestions).

The protagonists of tragedy are always of noble birth, but women enslaved in war are significant characters in tragedy and protagonists in Euripides. The Peloponnesian War between Athens and its allies and Sparta and its allies began in 431 BCE. It led to large-scale enslavements of Greek women by other Greeks (when a war was really nasty, the victors would kill the men in a captured city and enslave women and children). The fall of Plataia in 427 BCE was the first occasion of this kind in the war, when the Spartans killed and enslaved the Plataians, but the Athenians did the same to Scione in 423 BCE. It is no coincidence that Euripides in the mid-420s began composing plays about the fates of Trojan women after the city's fall. But he also wrote overtly patriotic, almost propagandistic plays that used favorite Athenian stories in which the Athenians came to the rescue of the oppressed, such as *Children of Heracles* and *Suppliant Women*. In *Suppliant Women*, Thebes has refused burial to the bodies of the *Seven against Thebes*, and their mothers have come to Eleusis to ask for help from King Theseus of Athens. This story had been dramatized by Aeschylus in his *Eleusinians*, where diplomacy was successful, but in Euripides' play, Athens must fight Thebes. In 424 BCE, after the battle of Delium, the Thebans had refused the Athenians the customary truce for burial of the dead for seventeen days. The issue was far more complicated than in the play, since the Athenians were using a temple as a fort, but Euripides did not hesitate to exploit anti-Theban feeling.

Suppliants also presents a Theseus who is not a monarch, but the founder of the democracy. He announces that he will ask the people to approve his actions to recover the bodies of the Seven, and says that they will, if he asks – but that they will be more supportive for having discussed the issue (349–53). In a vigorous debate with the herald of Thebes, he praises democracy and criticizes monarchy (399–456). Tragedy was always concerned with political leadership. The earliest surviving tragedies, Aeschylus's *Persians*, *Suppliants*, and *Seven against Thebes*, all explore the themes of wise and foolish rule, effective and ineffective leadership. The period when Pericles' unique position made Athens "in name a democracy, but in practice the rule of the best man" in Thucydides' famous formulation, made this theme even more powerful. *Suppliants*, produced a few years after Pericles' death, seems to model Theseus on Pericles. Sophocles' *Oedipus the King* is certainly not "about" Pericles, but the Oedipus of the first part of the play, who asks for advice but then has already taken the action others suggest, would not be quite the same character if there had been no Pericles. And during the Decelean War, tragedy reflects deep dissatisfaction with the leading politicians in Athens. Both Sophocles' *Philoctetes* and Euripides' *Orestes*, *Phoenician Women*, and *Iphigenia at Aulis* take place in worlds where political operators and cynical self-interest dominate.

Both Sophocles and Euripides died before Athens' fall, and the collapse of Athenian power is not reflected in tragedy. Sophocles' *Oedipus at Colonus*, produced only after his death and after Athens' defeat, presents the idealized Athens of Euripides' suppliant plays, generous and powerful.

The interactions between particular events and contemporary institutions and tragedy were complex and often indirect. Some interpreters see many allusions to particular individuals, but almost every such allusion proposed is challenged elsewhere.[1] Tragic convention allowed the tragic world to be more or less like the contemporary world familiar to its audience.[2] It could present legitimate kings, but it could also transfer democracy to the heroic past, along with the alphabet and coinage, or imagine practices that might have been customary in the distant past. This blurring is sometimes just convenient, but sometimes it makes it difficult to be sure how the original audience would have understood the norms of the heroic past.

The politics of tragedy are not consistent from drama to drama, or even within particular tragedies. The production of tragedy was both a presentation of the democratic city to itself and to the Greek world, and an occasion for the richest Athenians to display their prominence. Tragedies show a complex interweaving of old aristocratic values with assertions of democratic ideas. Furthermore, Athenian democratic ideology tried to appropriate aristocratic language for itself and to treat all Athenians (mythologically all descended from the ancient king Erechtheus) as "well born." The genre was often profoundly ambiguous in its allegiances.[3]

A. THE INTELLECTUAL WORLD

Tragedy was responsive not only to political events but to the fervent intellectual controversies of its time. In the fifth century, traditional cultural certainties were being challenged from many directions in what is sometimes called the Greek Enlightenment. Science was defining its

[1] Vickers 2008 is an example of allegorical political interpretation.
[2] Easterling 1985.
[3] Griffith 1995.

boundaries; it is in this period that for the first time a polemical medical treatise, *On the Sacred Disease*, claims that all natural phenomena have natural causes.

Tragedies refer directly to theories of the philosopher Anaxagoras, a friend of Pericles. In Aeschylus's *Eumenides*, Apollo follows Anaxagoras when he says that children are the product only of male seed, and that mothers only nurture (this utterly wrong speculation was to have a long history), while Euripides' *Orestes* alludes to his famous suggestion that the heavenly bodies were metallic rocks heated by friction as they moved through the sky. Euripides was also evidently interested in the scientific theories of Diogenes of Apollonia, who identified human intelligence with air. Such theories aroused great anxiety among the traditionally minded, because they took power over the world away from the traditional gods, but they did not necessarily lead to atheism. Indeed, Euripides created characters who combine such scientific thought with deep piety, such as the Egyptian priestess Theonoe in *Helen*.

Tragedians were interested in contemporary science, but even more important for tragedy were the developments in anthropology, rhetoric, and ethics associated with the sophists. Until the fifth century, those who could afford to send their sons to school for a formal education expected them to learn the basic skills of literacy and arithmetic, gymnastics, and music. Boys memorized poetry and performed songs to the lyre. The sophists offered a more advanced education for young men who were finished with school: they promised to teach everything needed to be successful in private affairs and in politics. The sophists claimed to teach *aretê*, all-round excellence (often translated "virtue").

This offer to teach *aretê* was in itself a challenge to traditional aristocratic ideas. Greek elites believed that the capacity for *aretê* was inherited. Teaching was important because it helped realize a potential that is in a person's nature from birth (*physis*). If *aretê* could be taught in exchange for money, anybody could theoretically learn it, although sophistic training was expensive and so not a practical threat to the rich.

Characters in Sophocles, especially, use the traditional language of inherited excellence. In *Ajax*, for example, the hero is certain that his son, if the boy is truly his, will not be frightened by the blood that covers his father, and says that he should be trained in the "raw folkways" of his father and so "make his nature similar" (545–9). Ajax's assumption that his son will share his own toughness and fearlessness is especially salient because the passage echoes *Iliad* 6.466–70, where Hector's young son is frightened by his father's helmet. In *Philoctetes*, much of the conflict in the play is about whether Neoptolemus will remain true to the *physis* he has inherited from his father, Achilles, or will be corrupted by the bad teaching of Odysseus.

The curriculum promoted critical thinking over a wide range of topics and skills in debate; people said that they taught their students "to make the worse argument the better" – that is, to be convincing when advocating any position, including a bad one. Euripides in particular shows the influence of this new rhetorical training. He gives clever and sometimes perverse arguments to many characters: the Nurse in *Hippolytus*, for example, uses examples from mythology to try to convince Phaedra that she should act on her sexual desire for her stepson and that resisting sexual desire is fighting against the gods (433–91). Sophocles, too, occasionally inserted provocative arguments: Oedipus in *Oedipus at Colonus* argues that he would have been justified in killing his father even if he had known who he was (547–8). Euripides regularly stages formal debates; Sophocles also does this once, in the *Electra*. Sometimes these seem barely relevant to the main action, like the debate about whether archery in warfare is cowardly or intelligent in *Heracles* (157–64, 187–203).

One particular tool of the new speech training was argument from probability. Whenever facts were lacking (or if the facts pointed the wrong way), a speaker in court could evoke what was likely. There are two outstanding examples in extant tragedy of this kind of argument. Creon in *Oedipus the King* argues that he would not have tried to overthrow Oedipus, because as the ruler's brother-in-law, he has all the advantages of being close to power but avoids the dangers and responsibility (584–602). Hippolytus in Euripides' *Hippolytus* must argue from probability that he would not have tried to rape his father's wife (1009–20). Both are indeed innocent, but neither persuades the interlocutor inside the drama.

The engagement of tragedy with rhetoric, though, went far beyond its use of a favorite device. Tragedy was probably deeply concerned with persuasion from its beginning, since verbal persuasion was central to Greek public culture (even before democracy), and attempts to persuade are inherently dramatic. The second half of Aeschylus's *Eumenides* is a celebration of the possibility of good persuasion, as Athena refuses to give up until she has convinced the Furies to abandon their anger and come to live as revered Athenian divinities. Sophocles' *Antigone* and *Electra* both include sharp exchanges in which sisters try, and fail, to persuade each other to choose a different response to the painful situation in which they are placed.

The slogan attached to sophistic speaking, however, was that it could "make the worse argument the better." Learning to argue by defending opposite sides of the same issue is routine for us but was new for the Greeks, and the practice made skill in speech available even when the speaker was completely insincere. Greek literature of the late fifth century, and the courtroom speeches of the fourth, reveal a widespread anxiety about the "clever speaker." This danger of being too easily persuaded, of falling victim to clever speaking, was an obsession of Euripides. He wrote at least four plays with plots of the "Potiphar's wife" type, in which a woman who has been sexually rejected persuades her husband that the man she now hates has assaulted her (*Sthenoboea, Phoenix,* and two versions of *Hippolytus*). In *Medea,* he shows how Creon is destroyed because he is fooled by the pathetic self-presentation of Medea. The character of Odysseus, a superb orator in earlier Greek poetry, becomes the tragic figure who most embodies fears about sophistic speeches and demagoguery. In *Hecuba,* he persuades the Greek army to offer the Trojan captive Polyxena as a human sacrifice to Achilles' ghost (131–40). In *Iphigenia at Aulis,* his ability to sway the army constrains Agamemnon, even though Agamemnon is the commander. This cunning, manipulative Odysseus is also a character in Sophocles' *Philoctetes.* Yet Euripides can present good rhetoric, too, when Theseus in *Heracles* persuades Heracles not to commit suicide, for example (1313–39). Theseus, strikingly, uses the same argument – that the gods act badly, too – in a good cause that the Nurse in Hippolytus uses in a bad one (*Heracles* 1314–21, *Hipp.* 451–8), although Heracles explicitly rejects that part of the argument, denying that the gods have committed incest or imprisoned each other (1341–6). Yet Heracles has killed his wife and children in a fit of madness sent by Hera; whether or not the gods have committed the precise crimes he mentions, the plot of the play depends on the familiar all-too-human gods of mythology. Euripides often creates such tensions between the inherited mythology and new ideas.

Sophistic speculation abandoned the traditional notion that a Golden Age long ago had been the best period of human existence. For the sophists, human life had undergone a protracted progress. They guessed that the earliest human beings had lived in caves without technological skills, and had gradually developed agriculture, seafaring, medicine, political institutions. (This line of thought is associated with the sophist Protagoras.) Sophistic anthropology finds repeated echoes in tragedy, where it can be combined with mythology. So, in *Prometheus Bound*, Prometheus becomes the donor to humanity not only of fire but of the ability to use the stars to follow the seasons, of arithmetic, writing, and the domestication of animals (442–71). He also, at some length, details the practices for divining the will of the gods that he has taught humanity (484–500), set between medicine and metallurgy (we need to be careful not to assume that "advanced" Greek thought was like modern thought). The catalogue of Prometheus's gifts evidently adapts a list of human inventions. In Sophocles' *Antigone*, the famous "Ode on Man" describes a Protagorean humanity that has taught itself language, domesticated animals, created tools for hunting, learned agriculture and seafaring – but, the chorus insists, the well-being of the city demands that he revere the *nomoi* of the land and the justice grounded in oaths of the gods (332–75). In Sophocles' *Philoctetes*, the life of the hero, abandoned alone on an island, is modeled on that of primitive humanity in sophistic thought.[4] In Euripides' *Suppliants*, Theseus introduces his scolding of Adrastus for his foolish attack on

[4] Rose 1976.

Thebes with a lecture on how a god brought humanity from its early animalistic existence with intelligence, language, agriculture, sailing, and divination (201–15). Adrastus ignored the warnings of prophets. The course of the play both makes Theseus admirable and undercuts his optimism about the human condition.

During this period, the Greeks came to learn a great deal more about other cultures, while the Persian Wars gave them a much sharper sense of their shared identity. Hecataeus of Miletus early in the century, followed by Herodotus (who gave public readings of his work in Athens in the 440s), practiced ethnography – accounts of the customs of other peoples. Ethnographic knowledge could reinforce self-complacency by defining others as different and exotic, but it could also stimulate self-criticism. Tragedy sometimes reflects the general fascination with foreign ways, as when Oedipus in *Oedipus at Colonus* compares his children to Egyptians, because in Egypt men stay at home and women go out to work, and his daughters care for him while his sons do not (337–41).

Intellectuals, inspired by this awareness about the variety of human cultures, developed the opposition between *physis*, "nature" (the same word as aristocratic inherited "nature"), and *nomos*, "law" or "custom." *Physis* was universal, always and everywhere the same, while *nomos* obviously varied greatly from place to place. In Euripides' *Helen*, Helen and Menelaus are able to fool the Egyptian Theoclymenus into providing a ship so that she can observe a Greek *nomos* she has invented about the ritual for those who have died at sea (1241–76). The heroine of *Iphigenia in Tauris* speculates that the local custom of sacrificing strangers to Artemis does not actually reflect what the goddess wants, but is an expression of the bloodthirstiness of the people (389–90). Particular thinkers or speakers could treat *nomos* as "mere" custom whose only authority was public opinion, or praise it, despite its local variations, as the foundation of civilization, or try to reconcile it with nature, postulating universal *nomoi* or speaking of *nomoi* from the gods. Fifth-century thinkers did all three. The sophist Protagoras wrote a constitution for the Athenian-led colony at Thurii in Southern Italy. Xenophon's *Memorabilia* (4.4.19–25) shows the sophist Hippias discussing "unwritten laws" with Socrates. Socrates defines these as norms that are either universal among human beings or that enforce themselves if they are violated. Socrates suggests that the gods are responsible for these *nomoi*. However, the most culturally visible promulgators of the nature/culture antithesis were those who used it to deny the genuine authority of traditional rules and restraints. Plato depicts characters like Callicles in the *Gorgias* and Thrasymachus in the *Republic* as defending a life of pure self-interest. Meanwhile, Socrates, who spent his life forcing prominent Athenians to admit that they could not define terms such as "courage" and "piety," gave a further tool to those inclined to ignore traditional morality. If people could not agree precisely on what "piety" was, it was easy to decide that it was whatever was convenient.

In tragedy, speakers (especially in Euripides) use the nature/culture opposition as a rhetorical tool. It leads to a cultural relativism that enables characters to defend practices abhorrent to Greeks but perhaps allowed elsewhere. In a fragment of Euripides' *Auge*, the heroine, having given birth in a temple (strictly forbidden), says "Nature wanted it, and does not care about *nomoi* at all" (265a). A much-quoted line in Euripides' *Aeolus* defended incest on relativist grounds based on the *physis–nomos* contrast: "What is shameful, if it doesn't seem that way to those who practice it?" (fr. 19). At least sometimes, such speakers of paradox were sympathetic characters. The *physis–nomos* contrast also offered a position from which Greek norms could be criticized. A fragment of Euripides' *Antigone* says "The illegitimate man is blamed because of the name, but his nature is equal" (fr. 168).

Euripides could treat cultural difference with dramatic complexity and irony. In *Andromache*, Hermione takes Andromache's (forced) sexual relationship with the son of her husband's killer as a typical instance of non-Greek behavior, and claims that "barbarians" regularly practice incest and murder their relatives, with no *nomos* holding them back (173–6). Andromache insists "shameful behavior is shameful there and here" (244). By denying that cultural difference is significant, she overturns Greek assumptions that Greek women are more self-restrained than barbarians.

Sophistic and scientific thought was most anxiety-provoking when it justified unethical behavior or disturbed traditional religion. Speakers in tragedy do not just defend particular forbidden actions; sometimes they endorse a sort of antimorality. Eteocles in *Phoenician Women* first mentions that people do not agree in their use of moral terms, and then announces that he regards *Tyrannis*, supreme power, as the greatest of gods, and will do anything to keep it (499–525). He uses the difficulty of agreement about moral terms to excuse his greed for power. Odysseus in *Philoctetes* says that he can be whatever kind of person an occasion requires. His nature is to win, and he can be just and noble if there is a contest for that (1049–53).

In sophistic and other intellectual circles, myths were rationalized or allegorized. It is hard to know how ordinary people felt about such criticism. The *Histories* of Herodotus, who was unquestionably pious, open with versions of myth from which the supernatural parts have vanished. Rationalizing particular myths is not a problem, because the existence and power of the gods do not depend on the truth of particular legends. If every miracle in Greek myth was explained away, however, the gods themselves could be explained out of existence. In Euripides' *Electra*, the chorus sings about how the sun and stars had reversed their path in horror at Thyestes' seduction of his brother's wife and theft of the golden lamb that was the proof of sovereignty. Then, however, they announce that they do not believe this story – the sun would not react to mortal affairs – but that such tales are useful for making people care about the gods. Clytemnestra did not have them in mind when she killed her husband (726–46). This must have been truly disturbing, since it comes close to implying that such fables are needed to make people believe in and care about the gods. Near the end of the same play, Castor, appearing with his brother Polydeuces (they are the Heavenly Twins), tells Orestes and Electra that "Phoebus, though wise, did not give you wise oracles" when he told Orestes to kill his mother (1246). Still, Castor then announces what "Fate and Zeus" have ordained, and it is hard to disentangle the oracle from these powers, which he does not criticize.

In Euripides' *Bacchae*, the prophet Tiresias tries to convince King Pentheus of Thebes that Dionysus is really a god. He argues, though, in the terms of contemporary speculation:

> Demeter the goddess is Earth – call her whichever your like. This goddess nourishes mortals on dry food. The one who came next, the offspring of Semele, discovered the corresponding liquid drink of the grape-cluster and introduced it to mortals ... This one, a god is poured as libation to the gods, so that people have the goods they have through him. (275–85)

Dionysus-as-wine itself echoes a theory of the sophist Prodicus, that religion began when human beings came to see the essentials of life as divine. The theory would seem atheistic, but Tiresias uses it to encourage the worship of Dionysus.

Tragedy had always addressed the problems of Greek religious belief. The Zeus of Aeschylus's *Agamemnon* is the ultimate arbiter and the only explanation for events, but his justice is incomprehensible – he uses Agamemnon to punish Troy and punishes Agamemnon for destroying Troy. Sophocles' gods are often inscrutable and often cruel: Apollo in *Oedipus the King*, Athena in *Ajax*, Zeus in *Women of Trachis*. Euripides, though, was different. The other tragedians allowed their characters to question the justice of the gods, but they did not usually present new and unsettling ideas in the clearest way possible, even framing innovative views or critiques so that they could not passed unnoticed. When the servant in *Hippolytus* tells Aphrodite that she should pretend not to have heard Hippolytus's disrespectful speech, an expression of the arrogance of youth, because gods should be wiser than mortals (117–20), it is impossible to miss the message that Aphrodite does not listen.

Sophistic or philosophical ideas may be even more overtly marked. Hecuba in *Trojan Women* prays to Zeus:

> Support of the earth and having your seat upon the earth, whoever you truly are, most difficult to know about through

> thought, Zeus, whether necessity of nature or mind of mor-
> tals, I pray to you. For traveling along a silent path you con-
> duct all mortal affairs according to justice. (884–8)

Menelaus immediately comments that this is an original prayer, in case anyone had failed to notice that it combined the traditional structure and addressee of Greek prayer with philosophical speculation. Zeus here is evidently identified with the air. In the sixth century BCE, the presocratic Anaximander had talked about the physical processes governing the universe in terms of justice, but here, although Zeus is no longer an anthropomorphic being, he is the guardian of human rules of justice, as he is in traditional Greek moral thought.[5] Yet Hecuba's prayer will not be answered.

Euripides did not just critique traditional religion, but tried to use the new thought to make sense of it in new ways. This involvement of tragedy in the fifth century need not make it irrelevant today. The political and intellectual crises of fifth-century Athens were not exactly the same as ours, but they were also not so different that we cannot recognize some of their worries. The twenty-first century has its own conflicts between tradition and modernity, religious belief and scientific inquiry, global power and its limits, conflicts that can make a tragedy, even if we study it within its historical context, meaningful for the present in spite of its foreignness.

SOURCES AND SUGGESTIONS

On the sophistic movement, see Guthrie 1977 and Kerford 1981.

Recent scholarship has strongly emphasized tragedy as a specifically democratic and deeply political practice. Vernant in Vernant/Vidal-Naquet 1981 stressed that tragedy belonged to the particular "moment" at which democratic ideology was in conflict with inherited aristocratic view of the world. Meier 1993 (in German 1998) examines Aeschylus and early Sophocles politically. Goldhill's "The Great Dionysia and

---

[5] Buxton 1982.

Civic Ideology" in Winkler/Zeitlin 1990 (97–129), which argues that tragedy questions the values of its festival context, has been influential. On the other side, Griffin 1998 (accessible except for some footnotes). On the politics of tragedy, Pelling 2000 (164–88). On rhetoric, Buxton 1982, Halliwell's "Between Public and Private: Tragedy and Athenian Experience of Rhetoric," in Pelling 1997 (121–41).

I have stressed Euripides' difference from the other tragedians because leading scholars have recently tended to stress his similarity to them – for example, Mary Lefkowitz, "'Impiety' and 'Atheism' in Euripides' Dramas," in Mossman 2003 (102–21), and Kovacs 1987 (71–7) (there is no untranslated Greek in this section). There is a quick survey of Euripides' use of sophistic ideas in Conacher 1998.

5

PERSIANS

A. SYMPATHY FOR THE PERSIANS

Aeschylus's *Persians*, the oldest surviving tragedy, is also among the most obviously political. Produced in 472 BCE, it dramatizes the response at the Persian court to the Greeks' defeat of the Persian fleet at the battle of Salamis only eight years earlier. Not only was the war recent, it was not over. Following the failure of the Persian invasion in 480 and 479 BCE, the Greeks had launched counterattacks to free the Greek city-states that had been under Persian rule when the war began. Athens was the leader of a permanent alliance against Persia, the Delian League. The League was itself to become an oppressive empire, and it is possible to see the play as a prescient warning to the Athenians against becoming like their enemies.

Persians was not the first tragedy on this theme. Phrynichus's *Phoenician Women* was probably produced in 476 BCE with Themistocles, the Athenian most responsible for the victory, as *chorêgos*. The play opened as a eunuch put cushions on seats for the councillors and reported the defeat of Xerxes. While Aeschylus's tragedy also puts Persian luxury on display, it does not have any eunuchs; castrating boys was an "Eastern" practice, and this opening negatively defined the Persians very emphatically from the beginning. Aeschylus's opening line closely echoes the opening line of Phrynichus's play, seemingly inviting the audience to compare the two treatments.

Persians is one of the many dramas descended from the *Odyssey* and other stories about the returns of heroes from Troy, in which the characters who are present are waiting for the return of someone absent (these are often called *nostos* plays, from the Greek for "return home"). *Persians* has the simplest of all actions. The elderly courtiers, who form the chorus, and the Queen apprehensively wait for news of the military expedition of King Xerxes. When a messenger tells them of the calamitous loss of the fleet, they perform a ritual to summon the ghost of Xerxes' father, King Darius, who severely criticizes his son's rashness and predicts the further defeat of the Persians at Plataia. The Queen leaves, hoping to meet her son on his way home and provide him with new clothes, but he enters wearing the robes he has torn in his distress at the outcome of the battle, and the play ends as he laments with the chorus.

For a long time, it was relatively neglected. In the academy, starting in the 1980s, it began to receive fresh attention, as developments elsewhere in literary studies more generally made it more interesting. For example, the spreading influence of Edward Saïd's *Orientalism* (1978) and the postcolonial theory it inspired drew scholars to look again at this early Greek text in which the West imagined the East. The New Historicism prompted scholars to think about tragedies in relation to central problems of Greek culture and identity, and this drama, set among the Greeks' enemies, was an obvious choice. In the theater, similarly, the play became an anti-imperialist piece: the Gulf War of 1991 inspired the production of an adaptation of *Persians* directed by Peter Sellars, while the United States' invasion of Iraq not surprisingly led to a widely noticed production in 2003.

All this interest, however, has not led to any agreement about the play. It is open to very different interpretations about the most fundamental questions, because readers disagree about how the play directs the sympathies of the audience. Aeschylus chose to write a tragedy about how the Greeks, and Athens in particular, had defeated a foreign aggressor, and to set the tragedy in the aggressor's home. He could easily have composed a play that was unabashedly triumphalist, making the Persians despicable villains, full of greed and arrogance, so that the audience would simply enjoy seeing their enemies' misery. He certainly idealizes the Greek resistance to Persia. Because his Greeks are viewed only from a distance, by their enemies, he can tell a story that omits all inter-Greek squabbling, rivalry, and disunity. On the other side, he could have made the Persians exactly like Greeks so that his audience would identify with them and feel the pain of their defeat. He did not do either of these things. The play's Persians are sometimes very much like Greeks, but they have distinctively Persian qualities too – some authentically Persian, some a product of Greek imagination.

For example, the Queen first enters in a chariot (150–8). She is elaborately dressed and probably surrounded by attendants. The elders prostrate themselves, and call her the spouse of a god (Darius), and, unless an ancient supernatural force has turned against the army, the mother of a god (Xerxes). Chariot entries were probably not uncommon in early tragedy, since before the stage building was available, the action did not take place directly in front of a palace, and royal characters were unlikely to walk. The chorus's greeting, though, is profoundly un-Greek and in a way that could invite Greeks to smug superiority: they did not treat mortals as if they were divine. Yet after the messenger speech, the Queen announces that she wants to make offerings to the gods and brings gifts for Earth and the dead, in the hope that the future may be better (522–6). When she reenters, she is carrying the offerings, and is on foot, in simple clothing, and alone. Her reaction to the disaster is indistinguishable from that of a pious Greek, and it is hard to imagine that any audience would feel no sympathy for her.

The very beginning of the play displays this complexity. *Persians* has no prologue. The chorus of Persian elders, chanting in a marching rhythm, enters a space marked by a tomb (of King Darius) and seats. They identify themselves as the guardians of the "rich and golden palace," appointed by "the lord himself, Xerxes, the King, born of Darius" (3–6). This alone is enough to make a Greek audience aware that these men are more subordinate than they ought to be. In Greek epic poetry, the poet constantly mentions the gold and splendor of his heroes, because these identify them as belonging to a more glamorous time; but in tragedy, too much talk of wealth and luxury is a signal of a dangerous complacency, a failure to recognize the importance of knowing one's limits. Yet this negative beginning is immediately modified, for the elders announce that they are worried and anxious (8–11). They are not overconfident at all. They then list names of leaders from different parts of the empire – to a Greek ear, foreign-sounding names – and the heroic catalogue emphasizes the immense power of the Persian force (14–58). As they end their first section, however, they describe the army as the "flower" of Persia (59) and speak of the longing of the land for them (61–2), and of their parents and wives who tremble as time passes (63–4).

As they go from chant to full song, they celebrate the army, and assert that it is irresistible – but then consider that "no mortal can flee the cunning deceit of a god" (94–5). This is the pattern. At one moment, they are unmistakably the enemy. They seek to enslave Greece, and their power is overwhelming. In the next, though, they are vulnerable mortals whose moral reflections are typical of a tragic chorus. The elders believe that a fate from the gods ordained that the Persians fight wars with cavalry and destroy cities, but that the Persians learned to behold the sea and to rely on cables (the cables that held together Xerxes' famous bridge over the Hellespont, 101–14). This worry that Persia has exceeded the limits of its fated success is again typical of the thought of Greek tragedy, so that for the original audience, it made the Persians sound familiar, as they say what was appropriate for the situation.

Throughout the play, the Persians appear as different and obviously inferior to Greeks. They are luxurious and effeminate, while the messenger's speech especially stresses the discipline, self-control, and unity of the Greeks. Yet the chorus, Queen, and ghost of Darius, though they look at the disaster slightly differently, all use the terms of Greek morality. Greeks were accustomed to warning about excess, and they had to know that they were not immune to the delusions that had led the Persians to catastrophe. Queen and chorus follow a different strand in Greek morality from Darius: they stress the danger inherent in great wealth (163–4) and the hostility of a malign divine force (515–16). Darius says:

> … being mortal, one should not think arrogantly. For *hybris*,
> flowering, ripened into an ear of disaster, from which it reaps
> a harvest full of lamentation. (820–2)

Hybris is behavior that ignores one's limits and the respect due to other people and to gods. Notably in *Agamemnon*, Aeschylus distinguishes the worry that the gods resent too much good fortune and tend to overturn it from the idea that too much prosperity can lead people to *hybris*, and that it is only the hybristic deed that causes ruin. Whether these are so distinct here is not so clear.

Darius, when he attributes *hybris* to the Persian army, is commenting on their failure to respect altars and temples during their invasion (808–14). The imagery of *Hybris* as a cereal whose crop is *Atê*, Disaster, was familiar particularly from the Athenian poet Solon (fr. 13 West). Precisely because such moralizing was so common among Greeks, Darius's reference to *hybris* must have bridged the distance between Greeks and Persians; Greeks, too, had been known to fail to respect shrines during warfare. Only Darius speaks of *hybris*, and he predicts that this *hybris* will cause the mass deaths of Persians at the battle of Plataia (816–30). The entire army is implicated in it, though Xerxes is mainly responsible. Elsewhere in the play, Plataia (where Sparta took the leadership) is almost ignored.

The play returns several times to Xerxes' bridge over the Hellespont (67–72; 114–15; 130–2; 722–4), and finally Darius's ghost makes the moral explicit:

> He expected to hold fast with bonds the sacred Hellespont in
> its flow, the Bosporus, stream of god ... a mortal, he thought
> he could have power over all the gods – no wise plan – and
> over Poseidon. (745–50)

These repeated references to the bridge exemplify the ambivalence of the play. Xerxes' bridge over the Hellespont was a perfect symbol for Greeks of Persian excess and immoderation, of the failure to recognize mortal limits (of *hybris*). But in Aeschylus's own *Agamemnon* of 458 BCE, the Greek conqueror of Troy enters his house on a walkway covered in tapestries, and the dialogue makes it clear that he is behaving in accordance with the stereotype of an Eastern potentate (*Ag.* 935–6). Oriental kings were especially likely to forget their mortal vulnerability, and habitually were treated with adulation not proper for mortals, but losing respect for limits was a danger to anyone who was too successful.

Indeed, the play characterizes Xerxes as a reckless young man (although he was over forty when he invaded Greece), and the Queen explains his folly as his response to being rebuked by "bad men" for not increasing the wealth of Persia as his father had (753–8). It was a Greek expectation that a young man would be likely to listen to such bad advice, so this, too, universalizes the play. The play idealizes Darius, even though he, too, attacked Athens and was defeated at Marathon, and Xerxes hoped that his expedition would exact vengeance for his father's defeat (243–4, 473–7). The play insistently blames Xerxes, and thereby almost removes blame from the other Persians except his evil advisors.

In the choral ode that follows the messenger speech, the name "Xerxes" in one strophe hammers out his responsibility in three successive sentences ("Xerxes led, *popoi*, Xerxes destroyed, *totoi*, Xerxes foolishly placed everything on ships on the sea," 550–3), while the answering antistrophe repeats "ships led, *popoi* ..." The ships mark the proper boundaries of Persian power; they were defeated at sea because they should never have tried to expand their empire over the sea. The lesson is potentially universal.

The tragedy is certainly open to interpretations and productions that emphasize that imperialist ambition is dangerous for any powerful state and that it can lead to terrible suffering both abroad and at home. Still, Aeschylus produced *Persians*, after its success in Athens, in Sicily for Hieron of Syracuse, who had defeated Etruscans and Carthaginians at the Battle of Cymae in 474 BCE. Hieron was as ruthless a ruler as the play's Xerxes, and his secret police was famous. The Syracusans did not enjoy the freedoms the play celebrates: free speech and accountable rulers. Yet Hieron evidently thought that he could use the tragedy propagandistically, encouraging the Sicilians to see themselves in the play's Greeks. This was surely a thoroughly triumphalist performance.

B. FREEDOM AND ATHENS

The great contrast between Greeks and Persians in the play is the contrast between slavery and freedom. The Persians seek to place a "yoke of slavery" on Greece (50). The Queen assumes that the Athenians must have a "master" over their army, and is puzzled that they can resist foreign invasion if they are "neither slaves nor subjects of any man" (241–3). The Greek audience, in contrast, assumes that the Greeks resist precisely *because* they are not slaves; they fight to defend their freedom. At the moment battle is joined at Salamis, the messenger reports

> And a great shout was heard all at once, "Sons of the Greeks, come, free your fatherland, free your children, wives, the seats of your ancestral gods, the graves of your forefathers. Now is a struggle for everything! (401–5)

It is completely unclear who speaks these lines: a Greek leader, all the Greeks together, or a god. That seems to be the point. The Greek devotion to freedom is uncanny and absolute, and it stands in sharp contrast to Persian slavishness.

Early in the play, the Queen narrates her dream (181–99). Two beautiful women, one in Persian dress, one in "Doric" (the short and simple form of Greek dress), appeared and began to quarrel. Xerxes came and restrained them, and yoked them both in a chariot. The Persian woman submitted, but the Greek fought, smashed the yoke, and overthrew Xerxes. King Darius appeared and showed pity for his son, but Xerxes tore his robes in anguish.

The dream is fascinating because not every detail of its interpretation is obvious. The dream is prophetic, but in a way that reflects the Queen's own imagination: that Xerxes tears his robes in shame before his father reflects her understanding that he attacked Greece in order to escape rebukes that he was inferior to his father (753–8). It has a genuinely dreamy effect, for the Queen does not indicate surprise that Xerxes yokes women to his chariot. The clothing of the dream women identifies them as Greece and Persia, and they are sisters. One has been allotted Greece, the other the non-Greek land – so not just Persia, but the lands of the Persian Empire. That they are fighting when Xerxes intervenes, though, is striking. The play certainly mentions Darius's attack in 490 BCE, but the play generally treats Xerxes' invasion as a war of choice. The dream transforms the attempt of Xerxes, already Great King, to add Greece to his empire into an attempt at simultaneously mastering Persia and Greece. In the dream, hostility between Greece and Persia is natural and inherent, but the audience cannot know whether this is part of the divine message of the dream, or represents the Queen's view of the world, in which Persian imperialism is benign and ends unnecessary conflict.

In any case, the Persian woman stands "like a tower" and bears the reins, but Greece rebels and overthrows Xerxes. This calamitous event points to the Queen's obvious worry about the future of the entire empire (213–14), when she concludes her speech by reassuring herself that Xerxes will still be King. Later the chorus laments that Asia, too, will refuse to be ruled by Persia (584–94). So while the Greeks' refusal to submit is inherent in the Greek character, the play does not imply that Greeks alone desire it. The Greeks see themselves as potentially exemplary, demonstrating that with courage and self-control it is possible to defeat even the might of Persia.

What exactly is the "freedom" that is so profoundly rooted in the Greek character? "Freedom" for Greeks had the same ambiguities it has today, although its meaning was sharper because the presence of slaves was a constant reminder of what extreme nonfreedom is. Slaves lack both the ability to do what they want and the right to social respect, and Greek freedom includes both of these. A nation can be called "free" because it is independent, or because it has democratic institutions. The play sets Greek freedom primarily against Persian monarchy. The Queen, reassuring herself, says that Xerxes is not *hypeuthunos polei*, "answerable to a city" (214). The Athenians were especially proud that every magistrate, at the end of his term, had to submit his accounts for auditing, *euthynai*. This accountability was especially central to democratic ideology, but any city-state with a constitutional government could see itself as free in contrast to the arbitrary rule of a monarch. The chorus, in its fear of rebellion, emphasizes first that the inhabitants of Asia will not pay tribute or prostrate themselves, and then that they will say what they think: "the people have been released to speak freely" (592–3). Again, the Athenians were deeply proud of their ability to say whatever they thought, both in everyday life and in the assembly. Many other Greeks, however, would also have believed that they had freedom of speech.

So the play creates an idea of freedom whose primary characteristic is the rule of law and established institutions that guarantee individuals respect and the absence of arbitrary impositions. From a modern point of view, Greek women were not very "free," but the exhortation to free them was completely clear to a Greek ear, for the victors could literally enslave them and deprive them of the respect to which they were entitled. In at least one Greek view of freedom, a woman was free when she married a man her male relatives had chosen, but not when she was raped by a stranger, because the arranged marriage provided her with honor and with legal protections.

It is a striking feature of the play that not a single individual on the Greek side is mentioned by name, while the Persian leaders are named in the first song, the messenger gives a list of the dead and their fates (302–30), and the final lament is an additional catalogue of the great Persian dead (958–1002). Persian "slavery" is not incompatible with personal glory. The suppression of individual contributions on the Greek side has at least two effects. First, just as the catalogues of Persian heroes implicitly place all the blame for the defeat on Xerxes and malignant gods, the silence about Greek heroes gives credit for the victory to the ordinary rowers in the fleet. Greek success is a success of everyone. The night before the battle, the Greeks prepare "not in a disorderly way, but with a mind obedient to those in charge" (374) – but the obedience matters, while who is giving the orders does not. Even though the play emphasizes the Athenians as the crucial opponents (if Athens were defeated, all Greece would be, 233–4), it regularly refers to "Greece" and "Greeks." It avoids distinctions. Similarly, the messenger devotes a section of his narrative to the episode on the tiny island of Psyttaleia, where Greek infantry massacres a force of elite Persians (441–64), mentioning both an initial attack with stones and arrows and a final assault by the heavy infantry, so that the rowers, the light infantry, and the heavy infantry all have their contribution recognized (459–64).

The messenger narrates the famous trick by which the Persian fleet was lured into doing battle in the narrow strait of Salamis, where their greater numbers would give less advantage and the maneuverability of Greek warships would be most valuable. In the account of Herodotus, Themistocles sent his slave, Sicinnus, with a false warning that the Greeks were going to try to flee in different directions (8.75). In the version of the messenger, a "spirit of vengeance" or "hostile divinity" came from somewhere (354), for a "Greek man" from the Athenian army came with the false message (355), and Xerxes did not understand "the Greek's deceit or the gods' resentment" (361–2). Many in the Athenian audience certainly believed that gods had assisted them. By not naming any individuals, the Greek victory is collective, while the accomplishments of particular individuals are not denied but become manifestations of supernatural forces.

C. *PERSIANS* AS DRAMA

Persians has a simple plot, but it shows how fully Aeschylus thought as a dramatist. Since the messenger speech comes early in the play, the spectator could have wondered what else could happen; either Xerxes would return, and the rest of the play would actually focus on him, or some other action would intervene as a delay. The drama carefully balances anticipation and surprise. For example, the Queen at her first exit tells the chorus, as loyal advisors, to contribute loyal advice, and to send Xerxes to the palace, if he arrives before she returns (529–31). Xerxes does not arrive, and the chorus does not deliberate but sings a lament. The Queen leaves to bring offerings, but only at the end of her speech after her reentry does she direct the chorus to invoke the ghost of Darius (620–1). The raising of the ghost and the Darius scene turn out to be the delaying action.

Throughout, word and spectacle are completely interdependent. For example, the play repeatedly uses images of yoking as a metaphor for exerting power. People yoke animals to pull vehicles or plows, but in the play Xerxes seeks to yoke Greece and yokes the Hellespont with his bridge. Aeschylus, however, does not just have the characters talk about yokes. He has the Queen make her first entrance in a chariot, probably pulled by two horses, so that when she narrates her dream of Xerxes' attempt at harnessing a chariot drawn by women, the visual analogue of the "normal" chariot is there for the audience to see. When the Queen enters again, on foot, the metaphorical force of her earlier entry is revealed. The bow also moves from language to visual sign. The Queen learns that the Athenians are close-fighters, not archers (239), and Xerxes at the end shows the chorus his empty quiver (1020–2).

Similarly, the women in the dream can be distinguished only by their clothing. The drama is obsessed with clothing. In the dream, Xerxes tears his clothing, apparently in shame, and the messenger then narrates how he tore his clothing when he saw the massacre of his best men on the island (468). Darius's ghost tells the Queen to go home and fetch clothes for her son, who in his grief is still wearing the rags remaining from the clothing he tore. The Queen duly exits, hoping to meet her son with the change of clothing (845–51), but when he enters, he is still in rags. Of course, it is not exactly likely that he would still be wearing these rags, but Darius makes it clear that he is doing so deliberately, "under the pain of his misfortunes" (835). As Xerxes was excessive in his arrogance before the calamity, he is excessive in his response to it, continuing to wear rags instead of responsibly trying to decide what would be best for his people. Similarly, Priam in *Iliad* 24 does not eat or sleep in his grief for Hector, until Achilles convinces him to eat (*Iliad* 24.635–42; he also rolls in manure). Such grief may arouse pity, but it needs to be controlled.

Just as the Queen is unable to bring her son fresh clothing, she does not have the chance to follow the rest of Darius's advice:

> Calm him in a kindly way with words. For I know that you
> are the only one he will endure listening to. (838–9)

Darius's advice is, theatrically, a series of misdirections to the audience. It also carries much of the moral of the drama. Darius, who sees his son's behavior as *hybris*, tells the chorus to persuade Xerxes, with "well-framed rebukes," to avoid further overproud offenses against the gods (830–1). He also advises the elders, for themselves, to try to enjoy life despite their misfortunes (840–2). None of this takes place.

The final scene is a striking theatrical surprise that also suggests that Persia will not change for the better. Xerxes enters with recitative anapests, and the chorus answers in the same way, before they spend the rest of the play in responsive lament. They sing exclusively when they should also be talking analytically. This is the final episode of Persian failure. Wisdom is available in Persia: Darius is truly wise, the Queen is wiser than the elders, and the elders are wiser than Xerxes. The Queen, however, does not meet her son in time, and the elders do not do what Darius told them. The torn clothes represent Xerxes' inability to learn anything from his terrible mistakes, except that Greeks are valiant (1025).

If the audience had not heard Darius's recommendations, the rags and the laments would easily seem purely a stage effect. The tragic genre itself sometimes seems to like to wallow in misery, and a lament is entirely appropriate after the Persian calamity. Yet it was already proverbial in Homer that lamentation does not accomplish anything (Iliad 24.524). Especially because Darius has reminded the spectator that Xerxes needs to hear voices of reason, the sung lament in the absence of any spoken dialogue is both pathetic and self-indulgent. The chorus should pull Xerxes back to the present and the need to plan for the future, but the elders succumb to the pleasures of grief instead. Whatever else it may be, Persians is a cautionary tale about how not to respond to national disaster. This warning was not one the Athenians typically needed in their political life; the Corinthians in Thucydides say that they "give the least ground when they are defeated" and that if they fail to get something they want, they turn their hopes to something else and get that instead (1.70). So the original audience, confident in their own strength when they met with reversals, may have responded to the play's conclusion with self-satisfaction, for it made their enemies seem weak and likely to be easy to fight. A modern audience, though, is likely to feel both pity and frustration.

SOURCES AND SUGGESTIONS

Hall 1996 provides the Greek text and a translation with an introduction and commentary (this is an entry in the Aris & Phillips commentary series), while Rosenbloom 2006, in the Duckworth "Companions to Greek and Roman Tragedy" series, provides a perfect complement. Rosenbloom stresses the universality of the play and its application to Athenian ambitions, while Hall emphasizes how it portrays the Persians as effeminate and Other. Harrison 2000 argues aggressively that is celebratory, but also argues against scholars who have seen it as taking a partisan position within Athenian politics.

6

THE *ORESTEIA*

A. READING *AGAMEMNON*

The story of Agamemnon's murder and the revenge taken by his son, Orestes, was familiar to Greek audiences. In the *Odyssey*, different characters tell parts of the story for their own purposes. Agamemnon was the leader of the Greek army at Troy. Aegisthus seduced Clytemnestra while Agamemnon was at Troy, and killed Agamemnon at a banquet when he returned. Eight years later, Agamemnon's son killed Aegisthus (*Od.* 3.307–10). Zeus tells how he warned Aegisthus, to show the mortals unjustly blame their troubles on the gods (1.32–43); Athena tells Telemachus about the glory Orestes has won, to inspire him to action (1.298–300); Agamemnon's ghost describes how he was killed, to warn Odysseus against trusting his wife (11.405–56). Because Orestes is a positive example, the epic never explicitly says that Orestes killed his mother, as well as Aegisthus, though it is clear that he did. Also, although other evidence makes it clear that the story of Iphigenia's sacrifice was old, Homer never mentions it. The lyric poet, Stesichorus, composed a long poem (two papyrus scrolls) about Orestes that included his rescue from his father's murderers by his nurse, Clytemnestra's dream of a snake, the Furies' pursuit of Orestes after the matricide, and the support of Apollo for Orestes.

Aeschylus's version of this story, the trilogy *Agamemnon, Libation Bearers*, and *Eumenides* (collectively, the *Oresteia*) is the only one of his trilogies to survive complete – and even this complete tragic trilogy has lost its satyr play, *Proteus*, about Menelaus's adventures in Egypt.

85

The trilogy, especially *Agamemnon*, has been immensely influential in the history of theater, and is regularly performed. It is dramatically brilliant, with an extraordinary texture. The action moves relentlessly but slowly toward the single goal of Agamemnon's return and murder, and the audience is held in painful suspense as the moment of inevitable violence is delayed. When Agamemnon finally enters, in a chariot with the captive Cassandra (a surprise) at his side, the grand entrance becomes an exit over red tapestries that look as if the house is bleeding: with *Agamemnon*, the possibilities of visual meaning were fully exploited, perhaps for the first time.

The songs are very difficult. The chorus of elders does not know what is going to happen. They know enough to be deeply anxious, and they reflect on the past and on possible futures in songs that twist back on themselves. When the chorus celebrates the fall of Troy, the song reflects on why Troy fell, which, in a tragic chorus, means not what its political or military weaknesses were, but what offenses turned the gods against Troy. Inevitably, the wrongdoing of the Trojans is eerily reminiscent of the wrongdoing of the Greeks. So every song has multiple referents, and there is almost more meaning than the words can support.

The play also tricks the audience. In its long entry song, the chorus ponders the implications of the omens and events beginning with the departure of the army for Troy, and particularly worries about the sacrifice of Iphigenia. Only in Cassandra's lyric exchange with the chorus does the audience learn that the earlier terrible history of the family is also relevant: Thyestes committed adultery with Atreus's wife, and Atreus killed Thyestes' children and served their bodies to him at a feast. This new context becomes immediately relevant after the murder, when Clytemnestra argues that she was not the real killer of Agamemnon: the ancient spirit of vengeance, an *alastor*, took her shape (1497–504). The chorus rejects her claim to bear no responsibility, but agrees that an *alastor* could have been involved. The framework for making sense of the action has shifted. The trilogy is about claims and counterclaims to justice, and it does not give the spectator any simple position from which to decide who is right.

In *Agamemnon*, the songs of the chorus especially pull the audience to recognize that Agamemnon is doomed by his own actions, but at the same time to want him to escape and to feel little sympathy for his killers. In *Libation Bearers*, the audience must sympathize with Orestes, while realizing that, in killing his mother, he becomes like his mother. *Eumenides* apparently resolves these conflicts. Orestes is purified by Apollo but still pursued by the goddesses who avenge crimes against relatives, the Furies (in Greek, *Erinyes*), and he is tried in Athens and acquitted through Athena's tie-breaking vote. The liveliest disagreement about the trilogy concerns the *Eumenides*: does the final play, with its establishment of a homicide court and its endorsement of patriarchy (for the struggle has come to be about the relative value of mothers and husbands) really settle anything?

The first requirement for thinking about the trilogy is understanding at a basic level what the choral songs say and how they relate to the action (not a simple task). The prologue speaker of *Agamemnon* is a Watchman who is on the roof of the building, complaining about the wretched task that requires him to stay awake all night, and also lamenting that the house is not well managed "as it used to be" (19). Seeing the beacon for which he has been waiting, he rejoices and calls to Agamemnon's wife – but there is something he does not want to talk about, that the house itself could best say, if it could speak (37–8). So the prologue establishes that Clytemnestra is in charge, but that her own household mistrusts her.

The following entry song of the chorus begins at line 40 and continues to 257. The chorus begins by announcing that it is the tenth year since Menelaus, the plaintiff at law against Priam, and his brother Agamemnon departed for Troy (40–1). They were like vultures whose young have been taken from the nest (49–54), and who cry for help to a god, who send an avenging spirit, an Erinys (55–9). Even so, Zeus, the protector of guest friends, sent the sons of Atreus against Alexander (60–1), who will not be able to appease the gods' anger with offerings (69–71). In the rest of the song, the chorus members explain who they are, old men (70–82), and ask Clytemnestra why she has ordered sacrifices throughout the city (83–104).

The moral situation here is almost straightforward. Alexander, in eloping with Helen, the wife of his host, Menelaus, violated the laws that Zeus protects, and the Greek expedition against Troy is the just response. Yet even here, the situation is more complicated than it sounds at first. Helen is called a "woman of many men," which may hint that she was not worth fighting for, especially because the song goes to some detail of the struggle the war entails for both Greeks and Trojans. It is a little disturbing that the Atridae are first victims who call on the gods and then the god's agents, so that they become Erinyes.

Because the sacrifices indicate news, the elders go back to the moment that connects past and future, the omen that appeared as the army prepared to depart: two eagles attacked and ate a pregnant hare. Evidently, the eagles are the sons of Atreus, Agamemnon and Menelaus, who have turned from vultures who lost their young into eagles who consume the young of others. The prophet of the army interpreted the omen to mean that Troy would, in time, fall. But he was concerned that divine anger might cast a shadow over the army, for Artemis, pitying the hare and its young, resents the sacrificing "winged hounds of her father." The omen turns out to be both good and bad, for Artemis may cause winds that will prevent the army from sailing in order to cause "another sacrifice, lawless and without a feast, an innate builder of quarrels, not man-fearing. For a fearful, later-arising crafty, housekeeper awaits, remembering Anger that avenges a child" (150–5). The strophe, antistrophe, and epode of this section all end with a refrain, "Say 'woe, woe,' but let the good prevail."

Parts of this are completely clear for the reader, who knows the story and has time to unravel the compressed and evocative language. The "other sacrifice" is that of Agamemnon's daughter, Iphigenia, and Clytemnestra will remember her death and takes vengeance for it. Still, the passage is profoundly perplexing, because it is unclear exactly why Artemis is angry. In earlier epic, she was angry at Agamemnon because he had boasted that he was a better hunter than she was, but the chorus's song excludes this story. It makes no sense for her to be angry at the eagles and demand a sacrifice from Agamemnon; the eagle symbolizes him, but he did not send it. It is also perplexing that, in her anger at the killing of the innocent young of the hare, she should demand the death of Agamemnon's equally innocent daughter. And it is hard to understand how the supreme god, Zeus, can support the expedition and send his eagles to predict its success, while his daughter, Artemis, creates this dreadful obstacle to it. So it is not entirely surprising that the chorus turns away from telling the story, completely changes the rhythm of its song, and sings a hymn to Zeus.

Zeus, this hymn declares, is the one who

> ...set mortals on the path to understanding, who made "learning by suffering" to be an authoritative rule. A pain that reminds of sufferings drips before the heart instead of sleep. Even to those who do not want it, *sophrosyne* comes. (176–81)

There was a proverb in Homer: "the fool learns when he suffers." It is all too easy to assimilate learning through suffering to a Christian model, but it probably means not that suffering is actually beneficial, but that actions have unavoidable consequences, and people who make mistakes will recognize them when the consequences arrive. The pain is probably the chorus's own anxiety as they consider the likely results of the events they have been singing about. *Sophrosyne* here may not be the knowledge of limit, but their enforcement. Turning to Zeus has not alleviated their fear, but has made it even worse.

"And then," they sing, resuming the story – how, when the fleet could not sail, the men were hungry and the cables rotting, Agamemnon finally decided to sacrifice his daughter. But once he had "entered the yoke-strap of Necessity" (218), his mind turned so that he would do anything. They describe the preparations for the sacrifice in all their horror, only at the actual moment of killing saying that they did not see and do not know. "Justice weighs out learning to those who have suffered" (250) – but there is no point worrying about the future.

The elders' thoughts repeatedly follow similar paths. They are supporters of Agamemnon, who is their legitimate ruler, and they want him to succeed at Troy and return to rule. They also believe that the war had a just cause and that Zeus favors it. Yet they have doubts whether the cause, though just in itself, was great enough to compensate for the vast suffering it caused for both Greeks and Trojans. The anger of Artemis, mysterious as it was, made that calculus real. Artemis insists that if Agamemnon is to destroy Troy in revenge for the theft of his brother's wife, he must sacrifice his own daughter just as he causes the deaths of innumerable Greeks and Trojans. Once Agamemnon decides to kill his daughter, he is no longer fully sane, and he has entered the cycle of action and counteraction. It is at least possible that the destruction of Troy is so excessive a vengeance that it will in itself call forth a countervengeance, but it is almost certain that the sacrifice of Iphigenia will be paid for later. So the thinking of the elders brings them to a conclusion that they do not quite have the courage to accept. This is the pattern their next two songs also follow. The end of their song shows that Clytemnestra has entered and hears them, as they wish that future events "go well, as this nearest sole-guarding defense of the Argive land wishes" (225–7). In the world of this play, where what is said tends to appear, to wish that things turn out as the Queen wants is not wise. The elders, however, are intimidated by the Queen, even as they underestimate her because she is a woman. Because they cannot confront their fear for Agamemnon, they cannot acknowledge how dangerous she is.

The characters of Agamemnon are not rounded people, but they are vividly defined. The song gives a few lines to Agamemnon's anguished speech as he considers what to do, but this song, and the play as a whole, are not very concerned with individual motivation. He calls Iphigenia "splendor of the house" (207), but the play never shows or tells whether he loved his daughter, whether he welcomed an opportunity to attack Troy, whether he had been a good husband. At the end of the first choral song, Clytemnestra enters, and she is the dominant character in the play. The legend did not require that Clytemnestra be what she is in this drama; in the *Odyssey*, Aegisthus is the murderer and her seducer. Clytemnestra of *Agamemnon* is a nightmare of the Greek male imagination: a woman who has all the capabilities of a heroic male and who ignores the customary limits on female action. The Watchman at the very beginning speaks of her "man-planning" heart (11), but she is actually more intelligent than any of the men around her, and more in control of language. For Clytemnestra, too, an analysis of complex motives is out of place. She is, in the first choral song, called "Anger that takes vengeance for a child" (155). In Agamemnon's absence, she has taken a lover who has his own desire for vengeance and his own claim to the throne, but who is a weakling and allows her to handle all the dirty work. When Agamemnon enters with a concubine, the captive Cassandra, she kills her, too, with explicit relish (1447). So it is not the case that her motives could not be of interest, but nowhere does the play say anything about how her relationship with Aegisthus began; for instance (at *Libation Bearers* 920), she implies that she was lonely without Agamemnon, which seems unlikely. Instead, it powerfully sets out the different aspects of the situation. She has a strong claim to justice because of the sacrifice. But she is a fearfully transgressive woman who obviously enjoys her (culturally inappropriate) power.

Gender, then, is central from the moment she enters. In the scene that follows the first song, Clytemnestra explains to the chorus about the system of beacons that has transmitted the news from Troy, and powerfully imagines the scene of Troy's fall. She expresses concern that the Greeks may fail to respect the sanctuaries of the gods as they sack the city, and the gods may not grant them a safe return home (338–50). The audience cannot know whether her prayer is sincere, because she wants the satisfaction of murdering Agamemnon herself, or whether by mentioning the chance that the Greeks are offending the gods she hopes magically to bring it about that they will. Some of Clytemnestra's power comes from her opacity.

In the following choral song, the chorus begins by praising Zeus who has thrown a net over Troy (355–66). Paris exemplifies the man who has ignored Justice and fallen prey to the dangers of excessive wealth (385–403). The thought of Paris leads to thoughts of Helen and how she left the house (404–8), and to the misery of Menelaus when she was gone (412–29). This is the pivot of the song, because the unhappiness of Menelaus evokes the much greater unhappiness caused by the war. The relatives of men who have died for Helen mutter resentfully against Menelaus and Agamemnon (428–55), and the chorus comes to see that Agamemnon is threatened by divine vengeance (456–74). So the elders start to doubt whether the beacons really mean that Troy has failed (475–87) – but the herald enters to report that Troy has indeed fallen (503–37), though a terrible storm came up as the Greeks sailed home, and Menelaus disappeared (620–33). (This information prepares for the satyr play.)

The chorus repeatedly tries to blame all that has happened on the two women, Helen and Clytemnestra (who are sisters), and repeatedly it becomes clear that the women are able to destroy men because men allow it. So in their next song, they sing about Helen the destroyer. They tell a fable about a man who kept a lion cub as a pet (717–19). Young and helpless, it was delightful (720–6), but when it grew up, it became a lion and ravaged the house (727–36). So Helen at first came to Troy "a spirit of windless calm, a gentle ornament of wealth, a soft arrow of eyes, a heart-biting flower of desire" (740–3) – Aeschylus had an extraordinary gift for poetry of erotic dreaminess. But then she became an Erinys (744–9). (But the fable of the lion cub turns out to be applicable to almost all the characters of the trilogy.) It is easy to blame Helen, but the elders go on to consider profounder causes – whether it is excessive prosperity in itself that leads to misery (750–6). They do not think so; it is the impious action that leads to more impious actions (758–60). Once the general moral reflections move beyond the figure who first prompted them, they always apply far more widely.

Hybris generates further *hybris* and Ruin (764–6). "Justice shines in smoky houses" but turns away from the rich who have dirt on their hands – and she directs everything to its end (774–82). At that moment, Agamemnon enters, in a chariot, with his concubine Cassandra and, probably, slaves carrying booty, so that the audience cannot be unaware who is rich but not clean. The elders struggle to address him properly (782–98) – to show their loyalty without denying that they disapproved of the war and the sacrifice (799–804), and to warn him that something is wrong (805–9). But neither the elders nor Agamemnon imagine that Agamemnon's enemies could act so quickly.

Clytemnestra has slaves bring out precious dyed cloth so that he can walk over it into his house (908–13), and Agamemnon and

Clytemnestra argue over the propriety of this behavior (918–43). It is a scene of exquisite tension, even though it does not exactly accomplish anything. Whether or not Agamemnon walks on the tapestries, she will kill him when he enters the house. The Persian king never touched the soil, so walking on them makes Agamemnon an arrogant Eastern potentate; they are precious, and it is an act of deliberate waste that invites resentment from both mortals and gods. Clytemnestra persuades Agamemnon to behave in a way that will make him look bad, and also exerts her own power: she controls his entrance.

Once Agamemnon enters the house, the audience is waiting for the murder, as the chorus sings of its anxieties (975–1034). But after the song, Clytemnestra comes out again, to order Cassandra to come inside (1035). Cassandra not only does not obey, but does not speak, and Clytemnestra gives up and goes back inside (1068). Cassandra, the enslaved Trojan, can resist Clytemnestra's power. Only after Clytemnestra goes inside does Cassandra begin to sing, and her song laments the fall of Troy and her own imminent death, predicts Agamemnon's murder, and proclaims that the Erinyes have long inhabited the house (1072–172). Then, in spoken verse, she explains her prophecies to the chorus. She sees the ghosts of the children of Thyestes (1217–22). Only now does Aegisthus (Thyestes' son) really enter the play, as a "lion without valor" (1224) who plans vengeance on Atreus's son. Cassandra enters the house only after she predicts also that she, too, will be avenged, when a son returns from exile to kill his mother (1279–84). Once she goes inside, cries from within announce the murders (1343, 1345).

So the story begins with Atreus and Thyestes, but this new information does not cancel the effect of all the earlier reflections on the war and the sacrifice of Iphigenia. It complicates the question. Neither the abduction of Helen nor Artemis's anger stands in any direct causal connection with the crimes of Atreus and Thyestes, yet Agamemnon's willingness to kill his child is a repetition of his father's killing of his brother's children. The chorus has used reproductive imagery for *hybris*, saying that crime "begets" crime like itself, so that the similarity between father and son is more than an accidental repetition;

but there is no "curse" that would make Agamemnon any less responsible for his own actions. Clytemnestra and chorus debate what has
happened in song (1372–567), and they reach a surprising conclusion.
When the chorus insists, "While Zeus remains on his throne, it remains
that the doer suffers: that is the established order" (1564), and fears
that the family is doomed, Clytemnestra agrees (1567–8). She offers
an agreement to the spirit of the family: she will give up most of the
wealth of the house if the spirit will go elsewhere (1567–76). This is
not a feasible bargain, if the choral songs have been right. She cannot
commit the murders she wanted and make the cycle stop. And that it
is not feasible is immediately demonstrated by the entry of Aegisthus,
who has no interest in surrendering the wealth of the house. At the end
of the play, Aegisthus's threats to the chorus make it clear that the new
régime is a tyranny.

The central problem, then, is not resolved within the play and seems
incapable of resolution. "Justice" in the world of this play means vengeance, but every avenger commits a further injustice and brings on
new vengeance. Once the cycle begins, it cannot be stopped.

B. RECURRENT IMAGES: THE ERINYES

The power of the play, though, lies in its language and its dramatic technique, which cannot be separated from each other. If *Persians* already
demonstrates that Aeschylus had mastered the resources specific to
drama, the *Oresteia* shows a perfected dramatic technique whose influence has been profound. The stage building had not existed for long
when Aeschylus produced it in 458 BCE, but the building is completely
integral to the dramatic design – the preceding summary is enough to
show how important the house is. The trilogy develops even further
Aeschylus's favorite technique of recurrent imagery in the poetic language that sometimes becomes literally visible in the stage action.

The Erinyes are the most obvious such metaphor-become-real. In
Hesiod's *Theogony*, the Erinyes are born from the blood of Ouranos
when he is castrated by his son, Cronos (186), the first violence committed by a son against a father. Associated with blood and sometimes

identified with curses, they have an inherent fluidity that Aeschylus exploits, since they can fulfill their task of punishing murderers, oath breakers, and offenders and hospitality and the rights of parents either through human action or their own. That is, they can often be understood as a divine analogue to human revenge, but they can also simply enforce curses: in the *Iliad*, Phoenix's father calls on the Erinyes to curse his son with childlessness (9.454), and an Erinys hears the prayer of Meleager's mother for his death (9.570–1). Sometimes they enforce divine law more broadly, as when they silence the prophetic horses of Achilles (*Iliad* 19.418), either because horses are not supposed to talk or because their prophecy is telling Achilles more than he is supposed to learn. In all these functions, they are invisible, travelling in a supernatural darkness. But they can also serve as an external manifestation of what moderns call "conscience" (for which Greek does not have a word until the late fifth century). Someone whose violence has caused deep ritual pollution or who has broken the most sacred rules of the culture could sense their presence.

The preceding section has traced their most important appearances in *Agamemnon*. Agamemnon and Menelaus, sent by Zeus to avenge the theft of Helen, are their own Erinyes. Helen herself turns from an embodiment of breathless, supreme erotic desire into an Erinys when she brings destruction on Troy. The chorus, reflecting on the anger of the people who have lost relatives at Troy, consider that the Erinyes wear away those who are lucky without justice, and still pursue them in death (463–7). Clytemnestra refers to a "paean of the Erinyes" that is appropriate for news of military defeat, but not for the mixed report of the victory and the storm (645). The chorus's heart sings a "lament of the Erinyes" as the elders express their worry after Agamemnon enters the house (990–3). Then, however, the clairvoyant, Cassandra, actually sees the Erinyes:

> A chorus never leaves this house that sings in unison but not with beauty. It does not speak propitiously. Indeed, having drunk mortal blood, so that it is bolder, it stays in the house, a band of revelers hard to get to leave, of Erinyes who are born in the family. (1186–90)

In myth, the Erinyes are born of blood, but they are also vampires who drink the blood of those they torment. The Erinyes are both a chorus and a *kômos* – a group of partygoers who would ordinarily go from party to party. Yet after the killing, both Aegisthus and Clytemnestra speak confidently of the Erinyes: Clytemnestra has sacrificed her husband to them (1433), while Aegisthus now believes in divine justice, seeing Agamemnon "in the woven robes of the Erinyes" (1580).

In *Libation Bearers*, Apollo threatens Orestes with the Erinyes if he does not avenge his father (283). The chorus insists that it is the rule that spilled blood demands blood, and that the Erinys of the dead cries out for further ruin (400–4). Orestes imagines how the Erinys will drink Aegisthus' blood (577–8) as a third drink. The chorus again sings of the Erinys just before Orestes knocks on the door of his ancestral house:

> The famous, deep-planning Erinys, in time brings a child to the
> house for paying the contamination of old blood. (648–50)

These lines exemplify Aeschylean density. The trilogy has repeatedly emphasized that one crime, one act of violence, produces another as parents produce children, and "of old blood" could modify "child," as well as "contamination." Clytemnestra's name means "famous for her plans," and the epithets of the Erinys here point to her, especially because the avenger is literally her child. "Paying" is ambiguous. Clytemnestra and Aegisthus will "pay" for the crime, but the child who enters the house, Orestes, will in turn pay for his. Throughout the two plays, characters fall into the delusion that *this* Erinys will be the last. At the end of the play, Orestes begins to feel an intense fear that he realizes is the harbinger of madness (1021–6). At 1048, as the chorus assure him that he has freed Argos from a pair of serpents, he sees Gorgon-like beings who are covered with snakes, and he recognizes the "angry hounds of my mother" (1054). (In Clytemnestra's dream, he himself was a snake, 526–33.)

Finally, in the last play, the audience actually sees the Erinyes. First, the priestess at Delphi comes out of the temple unable to describe clearly what she has seen. They are not women, or like Gorgons, but they are something like Harpies, but they have no wings (46–59); they are completely beyond her experience. At last, after Apollo sends Orestes to Athens, the *ekkyklēma* reveals the Erinyes themselves – and they are asleep, as Clytemnestra's ghost tries to rouse them, complaining that they are not repaying her for the offerings she made them (106–10). These Erinyes can still terrify when they rouse themselves and sing against Orestes. They make terrible threats against Athens when they lose their case. Surprisingly, however, making them visible turns out to represent a kind of progress. They are now plainly distinct from the human agents who have acted with or for them, and it has become possible to debate with them and in the end to persuade them. Finally, they are incorporated into Athenian cult. Aeschylus probably invented the idea that the *Semnai Theai* ("Revered Goddesses") who were worshipped in Athens in connection with the court of the Areopagus had once been Erinyes. At the end of *Eumenides*, the Erinyes again become invisible, but now in a relationship with the city that has enlisted their help in support of its institutions. The change of their name to *Eumenides*, "Kind Goddesses," is not preserved, but Athena must have announced it in her final speech.

C. RECURRENT IMAGERY AND DRAMATIC TECHNIQUE

One strength of the trilogy is that the three plays have utterly different kinds of plot. *Agamemnon* is built around waiting for his arrival, his murder, and its aftermath. *Libation Bearers*, in contrast, is at one level a thriller. The audience is on Orestes' side, so that the dynamics are the opposite of those in the first play. Sympathy goes to the attacker, not the victims, the deceivers and not the deceived. Its first stage is the recognition of Electra and Orestes and the song at Agamemnon's tomb in which they call on the power of the dead man and the gods. The play is ruthless in its forward movement. When Electra asks the chorus what to do with her mother's offerings (87–95) and sees the signs of Orestes' presence (168–211), she becomes the focus of audience attention and sympathy – but once the intrigue is underway, she disappears and is never mentioned again. The second segment is the intrigue by which Orestes and Pylades gain entry into the house, and the chorus has the Nurse fetch Aegisthus without his bodyguard. The play uses some of the same techniques as Agamemnon to surprise the audience, but with very different effect: when Orestes plans the murders, he assumes that Aegisthus will be home, and the audience expects Aegisthus to die first. Then Clytemnestra comes to the door instead (668). Clytemnestra is hospitable, and seems genuinely grieved at Orestes' death, so that the spectator expects her to be killed before Aegisthus, and is likely to be confused about how to react. But then the Nurse appears, claiming that Clytemnestra's grief is faked (737–41). The chorus then turns her into an assistant in the plot by having her fetch Aegisthus alone, without a bodyguard, and it turns out that he is killed first, so that there is no anticlimax. The celebration of the liberation of Argos ends quickly with Orestes' vision of the Erinyes and departure for Delphi. Although the songs carry forward the main themes of *Agamemnon*, it is possible to watch the play mainly for its exciting action. The third play has at its center the courtroom drama. A trial in itself indicates that the story is about to end; the series of violent events has ended, and now the problem is what judgment will be made about it. The settings, Delphi and Athens, are new, and the house no longer serves as a center of attention and a reminder of the past. In the last part of the play, the anger of the Erinyes at Athens creates a completely new issue. In this play, the deceptive speech that dominated the first two becomes an honest attempt at persuasion.

Within this difference, however, the repeated themes are expressed in images that constantly repeat with variation. The Erinyes are only one of the terms to pass from metaphor to literally visual. Only one killing in Agamemnon is actually a sacrifice, but all are linked by sacrificial language. Cassandra smells blood in the house, and the chorus reassures her that she smells only the sacrifices that give thanks for Agamemnon's return (1309–10). Clytemnestra calls her third stroke an offering to Zeus below the earth (1385–7), parodying the custom of pouring three libations at the banquet, and she takes an oath that she has no fear "By Justice achieved for my child, by Ruin and the Erinys, to whom I ritually slaughtered this man ..." (1432–3). *Libation Bearers* almost entirely avoids sacrificial language, but it returns in *Eumenides*, where Orestes is a victim the Erinyes plan to consume alive, without slaughter at the altar (304–5).

Clytemnestra kills Agamemnon by throwing "an evil wealth of cloth" around him as he bathes, "like a fish net" (1382–3), so that he is entangled and cannot defend himself. As she describes the killing, she stands over the body on the *ekkyklēma*, so that the audience sees it: as a net, it recalls the net Zeus threw over Troy (357–8) and the hunting net that in this very speech was her metaphor for the hypo-critical words she used to trap Agamemnon (1375–6). Cassandra sees a "net of Hades," but then redefines the snare as Clytemnestra her-self (1115–16). Aegisthus calls the cloth "woven robes of the Erinyes"; weaving was the woman's task, and the image unites Clytemnestra and the Erinyes as female killers. But the killing cloth also recalls the tap-estries on which Agamemnon walked into the house, and perhaps the saffron robes that fell around the body of Iphigenia as she was lifted over the altar (239). These red tapestries, spread from the door of the house to Agamemnon's chariot, look like a river of blood flowing out of the house, and so make visible the repeated references to shed blood, while the moment at which Agamemnon walks on them make real the metaphor of trampling on sacred things. Language is a net, cloth is a net, Zeus's justice is a net. When Orestes presents the cloth again, along with the bodies of Aegisthus and his mother (1098o–4), he speaks of it as a binding and as fetters, and images of binding also reappear in dif-ferent forms. Later, in *Eumenides*, Orestes is a fawn who has escaped the hunters, leaping over the nets (111–13), and the Erinyes sing a "binding song" to enchant him (332, 345). In a trilogy whose central theme is a nightmarish repetition of evil in new forms, language also repeats, but constantly takes new associations.

Certain stage effects also repeat themselves in new form. When, in *Agamemnon*, Clytemnestra addresses Cassandra and Cassandra does not reply, a spectator familiar with the rules of the theater will assume that Cassandra is being played by an extra, not an actor, and so will not speak unless she exits and reenters. So it is a shock when she suddenly breaks into song at 1072 and calls on Apollo with a lament (the chorus finds this ritually inappropriate). The same trick returns in *Libation Bearers*, but with a twist. Pylades has been a silent character since the play started, and he is the kind of character we would expect to remain silent, a sidekick. Orestes and Pylades are inside the house when Aegisthus goes in, and he screams as he dies at 870. A slave runs out to call for help, and as Clytemnestra enters he tells her "the dead are killing the living" (886). The slave exits, and a moment later Orestes enters. When she begs Orestes by her breast to spare her, he turns to Pylades if he should – and Pylades answers:

> Where then in future will be the oracles of Apollo declared
> at Delphi, and trusty oath-keeping? Consider all men your
> enemies rather than the gods. (900–3)

The actor has entered the stage building and changed costume and mask to turn around and enter behind Orestes. Speaking when so unexpectedly, and referring directly to the oracle, he acquires almost the god's own authority.

D. *EUMENIDES*: THE TRIAL

The first two plays of the trilogy present what seems to be an impossible problem. Every act of revenge demands a further revenge. Orestes pushes the difficulty to its limit. As the trilogy defines the play's world, there is no person on whom the task of revenge could fall. Yet he has committed the most appalling of murders. So the third play of the trilogy replaces human avengers with the Erinyes themselves, and lifts most of the action to the divine level. (In a real Athenian court, the Erinyes would not have standing to prosecute, since they are not related to Clytemnestra.) In Greek poetry, interactions of gods among themselves are often comic, and there may be some humor in the abuse exchanged between Apollo and the Erinyes.

The third play is unlike the preceding two in another way also. *Agamemnon* and *Libation Bearers* do not present psychologically complex characters, but the network of images and moral reflection in which those characters act is extremely complex. Their dilemmas are real dilemmas. Orestes, especially, is threatened by Apollo with dire penalties if he does not avenge his father, but he is tormented by the Erinyes when he does. The trial scene pays homage to this complexity in one way, for the jury's vote is evenly divided, and Orestes is acquitted by Athena's vote. But the arguments in the Athenian court do not match the richness with which the problems have been examined in the two preceding plays (and they may even be intended to be comic).

In *Agamemnon* and *Libation Bearers*, the overlapping images bring out the similarities in different actions. This play is largely devoted to legal argument, which concerns itself with fine distinctions. When Apollo order the Erinyes to leave his temple, though, and asks why they did not pursue Clytemnestra, they answer that she did not murder a relative (212). Apollo responds that this argument is disrespectful to the marriage of Zeus and Hera and to Aphrodite, but a debate about the importance of marriage as an institution is not in the spirit of *Agamemnon* or *Libation Bearers*. In the earlier plays, it was not clear that they observed such restrictions, especially because the evil seemed to belong to the house, as well as to the family. Clytemnestra's ghost wakes the Erinyes, while in *Libation Bearers*, Orestes, Electra, and the chorus seek to win help from the angry shade of Agamemnon, and the slave's way of reporting Aegisthus's death, "the dead are killing the living," implies that Agamemnon is there. In the earlier plays, vengeance from human agents, from the gods generally, from the dead, and from the Erinyes are not sharply distinguished. The technique of making images visible means that there is no precise boundary between metaphorical and literal. Once the Erinyes appear as a chorus with an individual personality, these distinctions are unavoidable.

The trial itself is very odd. When Athena solemnly founds the Areopagus as a homicide court, she acknowledges her dilemma. She cannot simply ignore the demands of the Erinyes, who have the power to harm her city, but she must respect Orestes as a suppliant, while the decision is too hard for any one mortal to decide (470–81). For the first time, a character confronts such a dilemma and finds a way to escape it. Athena's arrangement echoes a basic premise of democratic ideology: where no one individual can judge, a jury under oath can.

The actual arguments presented at trial, though, do not match the grandeur of the institution. The spectator is likely to feel sympathetic toward Orestes because Apollo pressured him to commit the crime, because he had to overthrow Aegisthus to return from exile (and his mother, when she realizes Aegisthus's death, calls for an axe with which to fight, 889–90), and because he shows none of the glee Clytemnestra took in killing Agamemnon and Clytemnestra. The Erinyes are eager to blame Apollo, but otherwise they have no concern for Orestes' situation. They say again that they did not pursue Clytemnestra because her husband was not a blood relative (605), but to the spectator this quibbling must seem manifestly unjust. (It is also perplexing, since Apollo warned Orestes that his father's Erinyes would pursue him if he did not take revenge, and he is mindful of this threat, *Libation Bearers* 283, 925.)

The Erinyes' distinction between killing blood relatives and others makes possible Apollo's argument, based on contemporary scientific speculation, that mothers are not really parents. Greeks were accustomed to seeing a parallel between human reproduction and agriculture, so the idea would have seemed less bizarre to them: the male plants a seed, and the woman is like the earth that nurtures it. Apollo cites Athena as an example of birth without a mother (663–6). Yet the Erinyes seem to be parthenogenetic daughters of the goddess, Night (321–2). Furthermore, Apollo's own argument makes the mother the nurturer of the child and puts them in the sacred relationship of hospitality. That relationship was also traditionally protected by the Erinyes, and Agamemnon and Menelaus were called Erinyes in the entry song of Agamemnon because they were avenging Paris's violation of hospitality. Even if Apollo were right, it would not settle the question – and it is by no means certain how the original audience would have responded. Apollo reminds the jury that, as the oracle, he told Orestes to kill his mother, and that the oracle cannot lie but always follows the orders of Zeus – and he advises the jurors that the will of Zeus is more powerful than an oath (614–21). We would expect

Apollo to speak with the authority of his oracle, but suggesting that the jurors could ignore their oath would not have made Athenians trust him, and the theory about reproduction that he presents was not common belief.

In the end, the decision is about gender hierarchy. Athena votes for Orestes because she belongs so closely to her father and prefers the male in every way, except for remaining forever a virgin (736–8). For that reason, she agrees with Apollo that Orestes' murder of his mother is less heinous than her murder of her husband (739–40). What is at issue is not the nature of reproduction, but patriarchy. The actual arguments are almost irrelevant. Athena votes as she does, not because her existence proves that mothers are not real parents, but because her nature makes her a supporter of the patriarchal order. The irrelevance of the clever argument of Apollo must be intentional, for the value of the court does not depend on the wisdom of everything that is said there, but on the mechanism it creates for preventing endless cycles of bloodshed.

E. *EUMENIDES*: THE POLITICAL CONTEXT

Eumenides is one of the few tragedies that unquestionably refer to recent events. Three times in the play, Orestes promises the Athenians that in return for their help, Argos will become their ally forever (289–91, 669–73, 762–74). Indeed, he pledges that after his death, if the Argives attack Athens, he will send bad omens and make them change their minds (767–71). His ghost will repay kindness, while the earlier angry ghosts of the trilogy sought revenge for themselves. The Athenians had entered into an alliance with Argos only three years before the production of the *Oresteia*, in 462–461 BCE. This was not a minor matter. The Athenians had previously been allied with Sparta, the traditional enemy of Argos, and this move was a significant realignment of Athenian foreign policy. By the time the play was produced, Athens was engaged in the long, intermittent conflict with Sparta and Sparta's allies known as the First Peloponnesian War. The play strongly supports this policy, for nothing suggests that the alliance promised by Orestes is anything but an unequivocal good for Athens.

The implications of Athena's founding of the Areopagus are trickier. Here, too, Aeschylus was probably innovating; another myth has the gods try Ares for murder on the Areopagus (the "Hill of Ares"). The Athenians may have had an earlier story that Orestes was tried in the ancient court, but probably not that it was founded for his trial. Historians disagree about the development of the Areopagus, and about exactly what powers it possessed before the reforms of Ephialtes. Clearly, however, before 462–461 BCE, it was not just a court for cases of intentional homicide, but a division of government with large though amorphous powers to "protect the laws" and the ability to respond to citizens' reports of serious crimes. Its members were former holders of the archonship, the annual magistracy that was restricted to the two highest of the four property classes in Athens. Under the leadership of Ephialtes, all its powers, except that of judging deliberate homicide and wounding, poisoning, and arson, were described as "additional" and moved elsewhere. Ephialtes himself died soon after the reforms were passed, and the Athenians believed he had been murdered, and some of them believed he had been the victim of a conspiracy.

It was in this atmosphere of lingering suspicion that Aeschylus produced the *Oresteia*. While the play emphatically supports the Argive alliance, *Eumenides* avoids taking a straightforward position on the reform of the Areopagus. Athena founds it as a homicide court. Yet she also calls it a "council" and praises it in terms that seem grandiose for a court with restricted jurisdiction (700–6). The goddess emphatically warns the Athenians against changing their laws (693–5), which she describes as the equivalent of polluting clean water with filth. Scholars disagree about what she is opposing: the reforms of Ephialtes, the "additional" powers the council had before the reforms, or changes in the law on homicide itself (which had not been changed). Athena also urges the citizens to revere "neither anarchy nor despotism" (696), but she is not specific about what particular measures would tip the constitutional balance one way or the other.

Above all, however, in her pleas with the Erinyes, she begs them not only not to curse the fertility of the land, but not to rouse the passions of the citizens so that they fight each other (858–63). Athena has no objection to war with external enemies, but in pleading with the Erinyes, she implies that civil conflict is the product of the same angry powers who caused the miseries of the royal family of Argos. The Erinyes, persuaded by her promises that they will be revered in Athens, bless the city with fertility, healthy young men and marriages for its young women, and with the absence of conflict and revenge killing. Instead, they wish that the Athenians repay joy with joy as they share the same friends and enemies with a single mind (976–87). So it matters that the play has endorsed a particular foreign policy. As long as the citizens are united in their alliances outside, they will be protected against civic conflict internally.

Eumenides does not exactly resolve the problems of the earlier plays, but it glosses them over by representing a utopia of civic harmony. The joyous procession that accompanies the Erinyes, now incorporated into the religious life of the city, is a final gesture of unity. Whatever people's views of the reform of the Areopagus, nobody could object to the blessings showered by the Erinyes on the city, and the Erinyes of the play are recognizably the *Semnai* of familiar worship. So the play, by bringing its audience together in celebration of the city, briefly enacts the utopian fantasy with which it ends.

SOURCES AND SUGGESTIONS

For the stagecraft of the trilogy, I am heavily influenced by Taplin 1977 (not accessible for nonspecialists). Goldhill 1992 is a short introduction to the trilogy; Goldhill 1986 is a major work but difficult. The most influential study of imagery is Lebeck 1971. Herington 1986 is an introduction to Aeschylus that concentrates on the *Oresteia*; it is a stimulating essay, not a guide to critical opinion.

MacIntosh/Michelakis/Hall/Taplin is a collection of essays about performances of *Agamemnon* from antiquity to the recent past.

7

ANTIGONE

Although the larger story within which *Antigone* takes place was among the most familiar of Greek legends, the tragedy itself had a mostly invented plot. Everyone knew that Oedipus had killed his father and married his mother, although there were many variants on what happened after the truth was revealed, and in some accounts his children were born of another marriage. Then the two sons of Oedipus had quarreled over who would rule Thebes. Polynices, the exiled son, brought together six allies from other Greek cities, but in the attack of the Seven against Thebes, all but one of the Seven were killed. Polynices and his brother Eteocles killed each other. Aeschylus, in his *Eleusinians*, had dramatized the story that Thebes refused burial to the army of the Seven until Athens intervened. The army is, in fact, left unburied in the play, but the fact is not mentioned until Tiresias warns Creon that the dead men's cities of origin are becoming disturbed (1080–3). Mimnermus, a seventh-century poet, told how Ismene had a love affair with Eteoclus, one of the Seven (the source says with Theoclymenus, but that is almost certainly a mistake), and was killed by another of the Seven, Tydeus, at Athena's command. Haemon, the son of Creon, in the epic *Oedipodeia* was a victim of the Sphinx, while Creon had another son who died fighting the Seven. This son's death is briefly mentioned in the play as a further cause of grief and anger for Creon's wife, Eurydice (1302–3). She blames Creon for his death, but it is not clear why. Eurydice has no existence outside Sophocles. Of Antigone there is no trace before Sophocles. Although she appears at the end of Aeschylus's

Seven against Thebes, most scholars believe that this scene is a later addition to that play, after the great popularity of Sophocles' tragedy had made Antigone's story part of the standard version. So much has been lost that we cannot say that Sophocles invented her, but the audience had few assumptions about the characters and no real idea how the story would go.

Interpretations of *Antigone* split loosely into two groups. One side sees Antigone as wholly in the right, Creon as in the wrong. The other side is influenced by the famous treatment of the play in Hegel's *Phenomenology of Mind.* For Hegel, both Antigone and Creon are "right," for each stands for a significant good. Creon upholds the state and its laws; Antigone the instinctive rights of family and religion and the individual conscience these nurture. Each, however, in defending these goods, denies the value of the other. Any interpretation is limited, however, if it moves too quickly from the ambiguities and complexities of the drama itself to a general and abstract moral. For example, neither an interpretation along Hegelian lines nor a reading of Antigone-as-protector-of-individual-conscience will give much consideration to the chorus's speculation that Antigone is paying for a ancestral "ordeal" (856), a thought that Antigone herself takes very seriously (857–71).

Antigone, like *Agamemnon,* presents a female protagonist who transgresses against gender norms. She is not a likable heroine. Indeed, in her defense of family ties, she rejects her sister, the only surviving member of her family. However, she fails to fit one crucial measure of the woman who will not stay in her proper place – in her conflict with Creon, her uncle and guardian, and ruler of the city, she is right, for Tiresias, whose prophecies are always true, says that refusing Polynices' burial was offensive to the gods. Every culture has its own social and moral schemata or stereotypes, frameworks that allow people to make quick judgments. The moral schemata allow different kinds of action to be placed in the same category ("chasing the impossible" is a Greek moral schema), while stereotypes assign individuals to types that are linked to these categories ("bad woman," "tyrant," "young man in love"). *Antigone* evokes schemata and stereotypes, but they are not quite satisfactory, either for the audience or for Creon, who relies too readily on them (commentators have pointed out that his speech is full of generalizations).

So, for example, the chorus in its second stasimon (582–625) considers the possibility that the gods have sent a form of madness to Antigone, "a folly of speech and an Erinys of the mind" (603). This song applies to Antigone a kind of thinking familiar from the *Agamemnon* – when a family is cursed, each generation fails to avoid its own injustices, so that evil reproduces. Yet the moral of the song, that "bad seems at some time good to someone whose mind a god is leading towards destruction" (622–4), applies as much, if not more, to Creon. It is Creon who fails to see disaster coming until it is too late, although Antigone's family, with its history of incest and murder, seems evidently cursed, while there is no evident reason for a god to be pursuing Creon.

In classical Athens, the bodies of traitors and temple robbers were legally forbidden burial in Attica (Xenophon, *Hellenica* 1.7.22), but nothing prevented relatives from burying them elsewhere. Athenian attitudes do not seem to have been completely straightforward. Criminals could be thrown into a pit where they did not receive ritual burial but the corpses were not exposed. In Greek literature, refusing burial and mutilating a corpse were nearly always condemned. Creon's decree is thus unusual, for he does not just forbid Polynices' burial in Theban soil, but orders guards to make sure that it is left alone, so that the damage done by scavengers will be a spectacle, and he expressly forbids lamentation. The decree, though, is not so strange as to be incomprehensible.

From the start, the play gives the issue of burial completely different contexts for Antigone and Creon. Antigone in the prologue emphasizes that the decree is aimed at herself: "he has declared through a herald even to me – yes, to me" (32). Actually, Creon gives no indication that the sisters have even entered his mind. As the nearest male relative of Polynices, he abjures any familial obligation in favor of what he sees as his duty to the city. Creon believes that he has political enemies, and when he hears that someone has buried Polynices, he assumes that these opponents have bribed the guards (289–303).

The prologue offers several schemata for understanding the characters' behavior. Antigone, after she describes Creon's decree, challenges Ismene: she will soon show whether "you have a noble nature, or are bad from good parents" (38). It may seem astonishing that Antigone does not hesitate to call on the family's noble nature, despite its horrifying history, but they are the royal family of Thebes. Antigone speaks an aristocratic moral language (though one Athenian democracy could adapt by treating all Athenians as noble descendents of Erechtheus). When she says it would be "fine" to die after performing the burial (72), she speaks in the traditional voice of Greek heroism. Ismene calls on two main arguments. First, she tries to convince Antigone that she cannot act because she is a woman. She says: "But we have to remember that we were born women, not supposed to fight against men" (61–2). In the Greek, "have to" is a more clearly moral term than the future participle I have translated "not supposed to" – for women to fight men is unnatural and unexpected, and it is wrong to forget this. Ismene's other argument is closely linked to her point about gender. She does not believe that Antigone has any chance of actually accomplishing what she wants to do (90, 92), and Greek moralizing is often concerned with the dangers of trying to do the impossible. Ismene makes a meaningful argument that Antigone's proposal is morally wrong, but not because she thinks Creon's edict is justified or that it would not be right for someone in a better position to oppose it.

So the prologue sets two genuine Greek values against each other. The "nobility" that makes heroes willing to risk their lives is not exclusively male – in Euripides, this exultation of noble death is found in women who sacrifice themselves and is unequivocally admirable. Against it, however, is the good sense, a form of *sophrosyne*, that should restrain people from ignoring the limits on their power. Gender complicates the matter. Antigone has no man to act for her, and it is simply not clear to what extent Athenians would typically admire or blame a woman who went outside female boundaries in an extreme situation. The judgment would probably have varied not only from individual to individual, but also depending on exactly how the action was described. When Antigone exits, Ismene calls her "crazy, but rightly loving to your relatives" (but it could also mean "rightly loved by your relatives"). Since Ismene is "normal," her responses can guide those of a spectator, and they place the emphasis clearly not on her transgressiveness but on her unwillingness to accept that she will not be able to achieve her goal. Since she does, to a certain extent, achieve it – she cannot protect the body from scavengers, but she is able to perform basic funeral rites – this schema does not fully apply, but it is clear that Antigone's determination does not rest on any calculation that she has a real chance of success.

Evaluating Antigone's ferocity is difficult because Sophocles is interested in polarization, perhaps having seen how Homer depicts the process. Antigone's presentation of her proposal is aggressive from the beginning, but as the prologue continues, she speaks ever more passionately, sounding almost eager to die, and demanding that Ismene publicize what she is doing. Ismene comments that she has "a warm heart for cold business" (88). She tells Ismene that her advice not to chase the impossible will mean "you will be hated for my part, and you will be justly added to the dead's enemies" (93–4). This polarization effect complicates how the audience should hear her statements. She insists to Creon that, for her, death is actually a good thing, and that the prospect does not pain her at all (460–6). Yet later in the play, she laments her imminent death at length. Antigone is certainly not insincere, but she states her views strongly and pushes herself into ever more extreme statements.

Creon addresses his speech to the chorus, elders whom he has summoned to hear it (155–61, 162–9). These men have been consistently loyal to the Labdacids whose heir Creon is. Initially, the relation between Creon and chorus evokes a positive stereotype; the ruler properly summons his loyal advisors. It gradually becomes clear, however, that Creon does not want advice, and that the elders are not eager to give any.

Creon has inherited power because he is the closest male relative of Eteocles and Polynices, and the points he wants to make in his opening speech to the chorus are those that pertain to his understanding of the situation. Creon's principles are often close to those of the Athenian state. He begins by commenting that it is impossible really to know a man's character until it is revealed by political power (176–7). His theme – that in between personal loyalties and public interests, he will always choose the public interest – was resonant in the fifth century, and what he says is in itself right. Creon stresses that he will not be constrained by fear from doing what is best (178–86). He also insists that he despises someone who has a friend greater than his fatherland (183), and that he would never have as a friend someone who was hostile to the city, because it is the security of the city that makes friendship possible (187–90).

These are good and patriotic views; complexity arises when we consider why he enunciates these particular principles at this particular time. The city is no longer in danger, and Creon is not about to make friends with any of its enemies. These principles are cited in order to explain his decision to forbid the burial of his own nephew, and the decision is not so much explained by the principles as it is a further emphatic declaration of them; both the principles and the following proclamation flow from his statement that a man can only be known from how he handles power: he is showing what kind of man he is. Creon is dissociating himself from Polynices, and he evidently expects his decision to shock the Thebans and to be, at least in some quarters, unpopular – that is the only plausible reason for him to talk about how he will not yield to fear. He sets guards to make sure that the body is disfigured because he expects opposition to the decree, though not the kind of opposition that has already arisen. Creon is evidently taking this extreme action as a public demonstration of his own patriotic character and of his own decisiveness and fearlessness; if he did not think anyone would object to his treatment of the corpse, he would not need to abuse it or to present the principles that lead him to abuse it.

So Creon speaks of the *philoi* (friends or relatives) we make for ourselves (190), because he is implicitly claiming that people make decisions about friendship even about their relatives, so that he can remove Polynices from his *philoi*. Everything he says about his policy as a ruler is directed at this symbolic gesture by which he intends to define himself. This allows a spectrum of judgments about Creon. The spectator may respect his commitment to the city, or feel discomfort that his first act as a ruler is not an attempt to unite the city but to prove something about himself.

Beyond Creon's own intentions, the speech articulates how differently and how alike he and Antigone think. Antigone, although she has threatened to hate her sister, takes the demands of kinship as a given. She never says anything that implies that she is personally grieved for Polynices or for Eteocles. Nothing confirms that she ever knew her brother. For Antigone, family members seem to be fixed in their identities as if they were chess pieces. Yet Creon also views people primarily in defined roles, just in different roles – Polynices was a traitor, therefore no longer a member of the family. And Antigone and Creon are strikingly similar in a kind of self-centeredness. Both see disagreement as a challenge to themselves and take everything personally. This is characteristic of both Achilles and Agamemnon in their quarrel in the first book of the *Iliad,* but it is not a stereotype.

The scene with the guard introduces at least two more schemata. First, the chorus suggests that the burial the guard reports could be "divinely driven" (278–9). Creon reacts angrily (his warning "stop before you fill me with anger" at 280 means that he is already furious). Like Antigone, he speaks so energetically that he confirms his own positions. A character in tragedy who angrily rejects advice, especially from a chorus, is likely to be in trouble soon; this refusal to listen invokes both a narrative pattern and ethical assumptions – a ruler who rejects any advice he does not want to hear is on the path to tyranny, though he may have a long way to go. Creon's immediate suspicion that the guards have been bribed and his threats to the guard point in a similar direction. Creon is slipping into the stereotype of the paranoid tyrant. At the same time, he tells the chorus that the gods could not possibly have wanted to help Polynices, who sought to burn their temples, and asks indignantly whether the gods honor bad men (282–8). Here and elsewhere, Creon is a rationalist, and he assumes that the gods, too, are reasonable. This gives him contemporary, sophistic associations, and it also invokes a narrative pattern: anyone who is not a prophet and in a doubtful situation believes he knows how the gods think is likely to be wrong.

The great stasimon that follows this scene, the "Ode on Man" (332–75) introduces a further schema. The song celebrates human effort and the ingenuity that has enabled humanity to achieve all the skills of civilization. Yet all this intelligence can bring either good or evil; "cityless is the man with whom evil lives because of his daring" (370–1). Apparently having adapted Creon's view of the burial as an act of political rebellion, the elders – who have just survived the worst of all forms of such rebellion, an attack by an exile with external support – see it as an example of ingenuity (since whoever did it slipped by the guards) and as dangerous to civic order. Insofar as the song creates a profile of the criminal, it is entirely wrong, and Antigone's entrance as it ends has a powerful theatrical effect. The song, though, gives a more sympathetic presentation of Creon's views than he himself can, and it presents not just his view of this event, but an attractive view of the world.

When Antigone is captured and brought before Creon, she raises a new set of issues. When Antigone argued with Ismene, they did not talk about the gods but only about the dead. She could assume that Ismene would sympathize with her belief that Polynices should be buried, but she wanted to convince her that, as his sister, she should risk her life to see that done. In addressing Creon and the chorus, however, she wants to make it clear that there is a general justification for the burial. So she explains her daring by insisting that Zeus did not make the proclamation, "and the Justice who lives with the gods below did not define such customs among people" (451–2), and she introduces the "unwritten and secure ordinances of the gods" in contrast to Creon's "proclamations" (454–5). These apparently require that all the dead receive funeral rites. But when she says that if she had feared a man's thought, she would be punished by the gods (458–9), she has probably shifted to a slightly different point. In *Libation Bearers*, Apollo warned Orestes that his father's Erinyes would persecute him if he failed to take vengeance. The murder of Agamemnon was wrong, but only Orestes was required to avenge it. Any Greek who happened to find a corpse was expected to perform a minimal rite for it. That is why the guard describes the covering over Polynices' body as "light dust, as if from someone avoiding pollution" (256). But a stranger would not be expected to undergo the risk of his life for a stranger's corpse. So Antigone goes from what she puts forward as a general rule, that the gods want the dead buried, to the gods' requirement that she, as Polynices' sister, perform the burial, to her further, prudential reasons for not being afraid of death. Given the troubles that surround her, on a rational calculation, death would be her best outcome. She concludes with an insult to Creon: if he thinks that she is stupid, he is the stupid one (469–70).

Predictably, Creon responds not to her substantive argument, for he says nothing to defend his decree, but to the challenge itself. Antigone's behavior, both in defying his decree and in defending her action, is *hybris*, and if she goes unpunished, she will be the man, not Creon (484–5: the "bad woman" stereotype). Creon then infers, because he has seen Ismene in distress inside, that she, too, must be guilty. Antigone claims that she could not win better fame than by burying her brother (the heroic schema), and that the elders of the chorus would agree with her, if they were not afraid (504–5). The chorus made the tentative suggestion that the gods were involved in the burial, and the elders never speak in favor of Creon's decree, but on the whole they are the least sympathetic chorus any protagonist receives in Greek tragedy. They do not seem to be afraid of Creon, but they place more importance on maintaining legitimate authority than on anything else. Later, Haemon says that the people are praising Antigone (688–700), and although he is not a neutral reporter, nothing suggests that he is lying. Antigone is right that people are afraid to tell Creon what they think, but she does not understand why the chorus acts as it does.

In her last stichomythia with Creon, she rejects Creon's insistence that honoring Polynices dishonors Eteocles with her famous "I was born with a nature not for joining in hate, but in love" (523). The scene with Ismene complicates responses again. Ismene wants to claim a share in the burial and to die with Antigone, but Antigone not only rejects her but mocks her (536–60). Only in her last words to Ismene does she soften: "Cheer up: you are alive, but my soul has been dead for a long time, so that I could be helpful to the dead" (559–60). Throughout this sequence, the actor can choose whether Antigone is as hostile as her words, or whether, as her last line hints, she is trying to save her sister even as she expresses her resentment (the prologue makes it impossible to believe that her anger at Ismene is entirely feigned). This scene offers the kind of paradoxical situation in which tragedy delights, for to accept her sister's love is to accept her suicide. It is much easier to join in loving the dead than the living.

In her following exchange with Creon, Ismene introduces an entirely new topic: Antigone is betrothed to Creon's son, Haemon. Creon, of course, does not care because he views Antigone as like Polynices, a bad woman to be replaced by someone better, even though Ismene insists that these two have a special bond (570). At line 572, according to the manuscripts, Ismene exclaims "Dearest Haemon, how your father dishonors you!" Ancient copies of plays did not mark the names of speakers after they had their first lines but simply put a line in the margin when the speaker changed. So the attribution is a guess, and many editors have given the line to Antigone. She never mentions him elsewhere.

When Haemon enters, Creon presents all the reasons why Haemon should let Antigone die. The arguments all fit standard schemata: sons should obey their fathers; Antigone is a bad woman who would be a bad wife; allowing disobedience in the family encourages it in the city; men need to be superior to women (639–80). Everything he says is standard Athenian ideology, even when he says that one should obey the person appointed by the city even when his orders are unjust (667). Haemon attempts to respond first by claiming that the people support Antigone, and then by offering another available conventional schema: it is wise to take good advice, even from a younger person (701–23). The chorus comments that both have spoken well, without recommending any decision, but the following stichomythia leads to complete polarization. Creon is pushed much further into the tyrannical mode when he denies that the views of the citizens matter, and he defines Haemon entirely as a woman-dominated male, finally threatening to execute Antigone in his presence (760–1). The quarrel makes Haemon what Creon believed he was from the beginning – a supporter of Antigone against his father.

When Haemon exits, Creon announces that he will now execute both girls, and the chorus makes its first real intervention. The chorus leader asks whether he really means to kill both, and this objection, tentatively phrased as it is, makes Creon decide to spare Ismene (769–71). He then announces a mode of execution. Antigone spoke, in the prologue, of stoning (36) – not an official judicial sentence in classical Greece, but occasionally practiced by mobs as a form of lynching against alleged traitors. Creon, however, decides to entomb her in a remote place with a little food so that the city will avoid ritual pollution (773–6). A stoning would have required popular support. The entombment seems to be intended as poetic justice, since she cares so much about burial (and it means that Creon will not need to decide how to bury Antigone).

At this point, the entire tragic mechanism has been created; from this point, the catastrophe unfolds. Pathos mainly replaces argument. After a song about the power of Eros, there is an extended lament between Antigone and chorus. Many critics have been confused that Antigone, who was so eager to die, now laments especially that she must die unmarried. She changes in part because her earlier declarations were made in the heat of argument; because as her death approaches, she feels it more powerfully; perhaps because she hoped the gods would intervene to help her; and because the death Creon has chosen is peculiarly terrible, leaving her trapped between the dead and the living. The chorus's attitude is unchanging. In the *parodos*, they attributed the failure of the Seven to Zeus's hatred for arrogance, and allude to how he struck Capaneus with the lightning bolt as he scaled the wall (127–33). Antigone, similarly, they see as an offender against Justice (853–5), though perhaps one influenced by a family curse. Their attempts at consolation are strange: when Antigone laments that she will die like Niobe, who turned to a weeping stone on a mountain, the elders comment that is a great thing to have a fate like that of a demigod – it is not surprising that she complains that she is being mocked (823–39). The exchange of songs does not contribute much that is new to the audience's intellectual understanding of the events; most of the rest of the play is devoted to pathos.

Antigone's final speech was formerly controversial, because many readers found 904–15 tasteless and thought it must be interpolated. It certainly interrupts the pathetic mood. The passage is obviously based on the story of Intaphernes' wife from Herodotus (3.119). When all her male relatives have been arrested for a conspiracy against King Darius, the king tells her that she can save one. She chooses her brother above her husband and sons, because he cannot be replaced. Antigone explains that she would not have defied the edict for a husband or child because these could be replaced, but that she could not have another brother. The argument makes no sense, since her brother is dead and she would die herself after burying him. But although the speech is nominally addressed to Polynices, she directs it to Creon (914). If he cared about family ties, he would probably be attracted by an argument that put them in a stable hierarchy.

The choral ode that follows Antigone's exit is one of the most difficult in tragedy. Danaë, like Antigone, was imprisoned (by her father), although she was pregnant by Zeus. Lycurgus had mocked and abused Dionysus, and was also imprisoned. The last example is the most perplexing. The sons of Phineus were blinded by their stepmother, and wept for their "birth in a bad marriage" (980). Yet their mother was the child of the North Wind and the ancient royalty of Athens. The mother's suffering (Cleopatra, though the ode does not name her) seems to be the point. The chorus seems unable to find any truly meaningful way to connect Antigone with the past; they can only assert that whether Antigone was innocent, like Danaë, or fought with the gods, like Lycurgus, her fate is what it is.

When Tiresias the prophet enters to announce that the pollution of Polynices' corpse has cut Thebes off from communication with the divine, Creon again reflexively moves to resist his advice. He accuses the prophet, like the guard earlier, of being bribed, and insists, with his characteristic rationalism, that gods cannot be polluted (1033–47). When Tiresias angrily predicts disasters for both the city and Creon (in another case of polarization), the chorus tentatively intervenes again to say that Tiresias has never been wrong (1092–4). Creon agrees to follow their advice, and so sets out to bury Polynices and free Antigone.

He will of course be too late. The gods have, in a sense, acted, but not in time to help either Antigone or Creon.

The gods have not really intervened as Zeus did in the *parodos*. Instead, the gods have responded almost mechanically. Because Creon has improperly confused the realms of the dead and living, he has spread ritual pollution, and this pollution has closed the regular channels by which the gods send messages to humanity. The chorus follows Creon's exit with a beautiful but futile song to Dionysus, begging him to come to Thebes and purify the city (1115–54). Dionysus is not a god of purification, but he was born in Thebes and so might come when other gods would refuse.

The worst possible chain of events follows. The expected messenger enters and narrates to the chorus and to Creon's wife, Eurydice, how they first buried Polynices then went to free Antigone. But she had hanged herself, and Haemon, who was there lamenting, tried to run his father through, and when he failed, turned the sword on himself. (He is as excessive and driven by *erôs* as Creon thought, but his irrationality has been driven by Creon himself). Eurydice goes inside, and Creon has hardly entered in lamentation with the chorus when he is told that she, too, has killed herself. Pity for Antigone is transformed into pity for Creon. Antigone goes to her death still insisting, against the chorus, that she acted piously, and almost complaining about the gods' failure to intervene, and wishes that her enemies suffer no more than she (921–8). Creon is left with the realization that he has caused the deaths of his wife and son. *If* they had gotten to the tomb faster, *if* Antigone had not been so quick to commit suicide, *if* someone could have stopped Haemon, the disaster would have been averted.

Antigone can serve as an inspiration, despite her abrasiveness. Nobody has ever wanted to emulate Creon. But the tragedy is about their collision. It can be seen as a study in the dangers of schemata: the chorus thought Antigone was a typical example of the kind of arrogance that the gods destroy, but Creon turned out to be more typical. If there is a simple moral, it is the standard tragic advice to avoid overconfidence, listen to advisors, bear in mind that the gods are hard to know; but the effect is not that of any simple moral.

SOURCES AND SUGGESTIONS

I have treated this particular tragedy in terms of the complexity of schemata in part as a response to Sourvinou-Inwood 1989, an influential article which argues that Antigone violates norms of female behavior and would therefore have been viewed negatively by the Athenian audience, who would have been sympathetic to Creon's concerns for order and hierarchy). Foley 2001 (172–200) ("Antigone as moral agent") is also in part a response to that paper.

Hester 1971 gives a fine overview of "Hegelian," pro-Antigone, and anti-Antigone views (although it is a very scholarly discussion, it is unusually clear). Nussbaum 1986 (51–82). Segal's essay on the "Ode on Man," "Sophocles' Praise of Man and the Conflicts of the *Antigone*," Segal 1986 (137–61) (originally published in *Arion* 3 1964: 46–66) discusses patterns of imagery and thematic issues throughout the play. Zeitlin's paper "Thebes: Theater of Self and Society in Athenian Drama" in Winkler/Zeitlin 1990 (130–67), discussing *Antigone* and other plays set in Thebes, influentially argues that Thebes in tragedy is an anti-Athens.

8

MEDEA

Medea is a revenge tragedy. Euripides inherited a story in which Medea, the princess of Colchis (on the eastern shore of the Black Sea, in modern Georgia), fell in love with the hero, Jason, when he came to her country on his quest for the Golden Fleece. She used her knowledge of magic to help him with the ordeals set by her father, and when she fled with Jason and her father came in pursuit, she murdered her brother so that her father would be delayed picking up the mutilated pieces. When they returned to Iolchus, she took revenge on his enemy, Pelias, by convincing his daughters to cut him up as a way of renewing his youth. They fled to Corinth. There Jason abandoned Medea and her children to marry the princess, daughter of King Creon. Medea killed the princess and her father, and fled to Athens where she was received by King Aegeus. The Corinthians murdered the children of Jason and Medea, who later received a cult as heroes (see glossary) at the temple of Hera Akraia.

Scholars disagree about whether Euripides was the first tragedian to make Medea the killer of her own children. The hypothesis (see glossary) quotes Dicaearchus, a student of Aristotle, and Aristotle himself for the guess that Euripides took this element of the plot from Neophron, a very prolific (120 plays) but obscure tragedian. Three fragments survive from Neophron's *Medea*, and they would make Euripides heavily indebted: one has Aegeus asking Medea's advice about an oracle, in the second Medea speaks to her own heart as she hesitates to kill her children, and in the third she prophecies to Jason that he will eventually hang himself. It seems unlikely that Euripides would have imitated another tragedian so closely or that, if he had, the comic poets would not have mocked him so relentlessly that we would know about it. So some believe that another *Medea* imitating Euripides' famous play had been confused with the earlier *Medea* of Neophron. Opinions, however, are divided. Neophron's tragedy may have had weaknesses in Euripides' eyes that invited him to "fix" it.[1] Tragedians constantly competed with their contemporaries and predecessors.

Euripides may not have been the first tragedian to make Medea the killer of her own children, but this murder is the center of his play. The play sets out to achieve an almost impossible task: to lure the audience into feeling sympathy with Medea and to share her heroic view of herself, and so force the spectators to continue to identify with a woman who chooses to kill her children, even as her actions repel us. The play indirectly endorses one side of Athenian culture against another. Medea hates, above all, the thought that her enemies could laugh at her, and she is willing to suffer almost anything to ensure that nobody is in a position to triumph over her. This fear of humiliation as the ultimate evil is characteristic of Greek heroic ethics; it is one of the most important supports for the belief that it is better to die well than to live badly (a belief Antigone, for example, endorses). But there was also an opposite impulse in classical Athens, most visible in the speeches from the lawcourts, where speakers often insist that they have put up with considerable abuse from their opponents rather than commit violence or even bring legal action. Being forbearing in the interests of civic peace also had a positive value.

Medea presents the issues in a peculiar form, since Medea is such an unlikely representative of Greek heroic values. First, she is female; women, like men, were expected to fear humiliation, but it was not usually their task to defend their own honor. Men were supposed to do this for them. While sexual fidelity was not expected of married men, they were expected to show respect for their wives by keeping within limits – not spending too much money on other women, not establishing a concubine in the house, not pursuing other sexual opportunities

---

[1] Michelini 1989 argues for the priority of Neophron.

in a way that would create a public perception that the man had no sexual interest in his own wife. The male relatives of a woman were supposed to protect her against such bad behavior by a husband, and in extreme cases, divorce was a possibility. Elite Greek men gave substantial dowries when their daughters married, and in the case of divorce, these had to be returned, which provided a strong financial incentive for husbands not to antagonize their wives and their wives' families.

Tragedies frequently depict women who lack male protection. Hecuba in *Hecuba*, enslaved after her husband and sons have been killed in the Trojan War, takes vengeance for herself on the murderer of the son she had sent away for safety. Electra in Sophocles' play, believing that her brother has died, plans to kill Aegisthus herself. Medea, however, is an unusual case. She has no natal family because she betrayed them for Jason's sake. So Medea's dreadful situation is her own fault. By violating the rules of female behavior, she has put herself in this vulnerable position. At the same time, Jason is under an exceptional obligation to her. What makes it easy for Jason to abandon her also makes it an abominable thing to do. The play refers to his oaths (161–3). The oaths are especially important because the most solemn Greek oaths prayed for the obliteration of the oath-taker's line if he violated the oath – the deaths of his children are an appropriate punishment for Jason's perjury.

Medea is both an abnormal, transgressive woman and absolutely typical. Jason ends his extended reply to Medea's complaints in the *agon* (see glossary) by claiming that Medea would have understood his reasons for marrying the princess had she not been afflicted by sexual jealousy:

> You women are at such a point that if your sexual life is going well, you think you have everything, but if some misfortune happens to your bed, you make what is finest and most beneficial your worst enemy. There should be a way for mortals to produce their children from some other source, and the female race not exist. If that were so, people would have no trouble. (569–75)

Medea, near the end of the play, seems to agree that jealousy was her motivation:

Ja. Did you really think it was right to kill them over sex?
Me. Do you imagine that this is a small pain for a woman?
Ja. Yes – one who is sane and self-controlled [*sôphrôn*]. But
      to you it is all evils. (1367–9)

Medea does not object to his characterization of her anger as all about sex, even though it is obvious that it is not just jealousy that enrages her but the dishonor that is inextricable from sexual betrayal. She identifies herself consistently and powerfully with womanhood and even with Greek misogyny. She says herself:

A woman is full of fear and cowardly in battle and at looking
at steel. But when she has been wronged about her bed, no
other heart is more bloodthirsty. (263–6)

She reminds herself that she will be able to find a way to take revenge:

Besides, we are by nature women, who are most helpless
when it comes to good, but are the cleverest contrivers of all
evils. (407–9)

Since she is an adept manipulator, however, the audience should not assume that her generalizations are simply what she thinks. Medea may be saying what she really believes, but she also wants the chorus of Corinthian women to serve as reliable confidantes who will keep her plans secret (259–63). So she wants them to see her as one of them, and she overcomes differences from them both by inviting them to see them as like her by generalizing about women, and by persuading them to see her as more like them.

The latter is the tactic of her famous opening speech when she complains about the misfortunes of women in general. "We women," she says, of everything that is alive and conscious, "are the most miserable creature" (230–1). She goes on to enumerate the miseries of women's lives, starting with dowry: a woman must pay a great sum of money to get a master (in an implied contrast with the rest of the market, where masters pay for their slaves). Then the husband may be bad or good, and divorcing a bad one damages a woman's reputation. A woman has to be a prophet, entering a new household, and figure out what kind of man her husband is and how to deal with him. If, then, the wife is successful in all this and the husband is contented, the woman's life is enviable, but otherwise, it is better to die, since he has alternatives if he dislikes his wife, but she has none. Men think that they are entitled to privilege, since they must be warriors and women live a life without danger – but Medea would rather enter battle three times than give birth once. Only after this assimilation of herself to an ordinary Greek woman does she give an account of why her situation is even worse than theirs would be, removing any allusion to her own part in depriving her of family support. She even speaks of herself as "plundered" from her country (256).

The chorus accepts Medea's presentation of herself as an exemplary female victim. In their first stasimon (see glossary), the women sing about how, because men have made the songs, the traditions all describe women as false and untrustworthy, but the example of Jason will change this, and women will have more honor (410–45). This is evidently not the final outcome of the play. In *Medea*, as often in tragedy, extremes become hard to distinguish from each other.

Medea is also a foreigner from a very distant and exotic land. Today, it invites a postcolonial perspective. Jason is confident in his cultural superiority – he tells Medea that she should be grateful that he brought her to Greece where the rule of law has been established, instead of the might that has power in her barbarian home (536–8). The ironies are blatant. Jason believes that he mistakenly brought something dangerous and foreign to innocent Greece:

> Now I am sensible, but then I was not, when I brought you
> to a Greek home from your halls and barbarian land, a great
> evil, betrayer of your father and the land that reared you...
> (1329–32)

He claims that no Greek woman could have done what she has done (1339–40), although the chorus has been able to think of one, Ino

(1282–92), and Procne and Althaea, Meleager's mother, were other famous examples. The play opens, however, with the Nurse's wish from the opposite perspective that the colonial encounter had never taken place:

> I wish that the ship Argo had never sailed through the dark
> Clashing Rocks to the land of the Colchians, and that the pine
> cut in the glens of Mt. Pelion had never fallen...

Most Athenians certainly shared Jason's confidence that Greeks were superior to barbarians, who lived in either primitive savagery or under despotism. Jason, though, is not an appealing spokesman for Greek chauvinism. (Similarly, in other plays, Euripides' Trojans are often much nobler than his Greeks.) If Medea were a betrayer, he was happy to use her to his advantage, and now he has betrayed her.

In any case, Jason brought Medea to Greece, and from the perspective of the audience, she is part of the distant past of Greece. After Medea tricks Aegeus into promising her a refuge after she leaves Corinth (dictating an oath, which will be kept this time, 946–55) and announces that she will kill her children (792–3), the chorus sings in celebration of Athens. The Athens of the strophe and antistrophe of this ode is an aesthetic-erotic utopia. It is Athens where the Muses created Harmony (or possibly the opposite – the Greek is ambiguous), and Aphrodite blows moderate and sweet-smelling breezes. She sends "the Loves that are seated alongside Wisdom, co-workers of every kind of excellence" (843–5). So how, after murdering her children, can she go to that land of holy rivers? Of course, the audience knew that she did. If Medea's mere presence spread contamination, Athens cannot be quite as the song made it.

Finally, Medea is not only a woman and an exotic foreigner, she has arcane knowledge, including knowledge of drugs/poisons. She honors Hecate, the goddess of witchcraft, above all (395–7). The play blurs this esoteric knowledge, however, with Medea's ability to manipulate and fool others. Much of the play is a series of Medea's encounters with her victims: she wins the sympathy of the Corinthian woman, who promise their silence; she convinces Creon, against his better judgment, to allow her to stay for one day; she traps Aegeus into taking an oath to protect her; and she makes Jason believe that she has realized that he was right all along, and overcomes his reluctance to let her send her children to his bride with gifts. Her skill is uncanny, but there is nothing supernatural about it, at least not until she has the gifts brought out, for they are not only the most beautiful objects in the world (947–8) but came from Medea's grandfather the sun-god (954–5).

Medea's manipulations require that she be in absolute control of herself, and much of the energy of the drama comes from both the alternations between the false Medea and the "real" Medea, as well as from the tensions between the vehemence of her feelings and the surface of rational argument. Euripides' style is an ideal vehicle for conveying these contrasts. After her scene with Creon, the chorus cries out in a short burst of sung anapests, but Medea simply answers that the situation is certainly bad but it isn't over yet (364–5), and she expatiates on how stupid Creon was before considering the advantages and disadvantages of various ways she could kill her enemies. Typically, she calls poison the "straight" method (384). In the *agon* with Jason, however, the "real" Medea speaks without any purpose except to make herself feel better by abusing him and to cause him pain (473–4). However, even in her rage, she is a Euripidean debater who begins at the beginning: how she saved his life in the ordeals in Colchis, how she betrayed her home for him, how she destroyed his enemies in Iolcus. His repayment for this was to betray her, even though he had children – because had he been childless, his seeking another wife would be pardonable. She asks Zeus why he has not made it possible to tell from the body when a man is bad (516–19).

Jason's point-by-point answer relies on the paradoxes so beloved by fifth-century Athenians: Love actually forced Medea to help him – but he does not want to be too precise (another late-fifth-century buzzword) in assessing this. Instead, he argues that she received more than she gave, not only in being rescued from her barbarian country, but because she became famous. As for his marriage, he was both wise and *sôphrôn*, since he did not marry the princess for sex or for more children, but in order to give his children powerful brothers. His wish that women did not exist answers Medea's question of Zeus. The chorus leader comments that he is a good speaker, but he has not treated his wife justly. When Medea points out that if he had meant well, he could have persuaded her before his marriage, he replies that she would hardly have been acquiescent then, since she is so angry "even now" (585–90).

How would the original audience have reacted to Jason's self-presentation? This is not a trivial question for the texture of the tragedy as a whole, since Jason's clever rhetoric is set against Medea's manipulative skill. Jason does not convince Medea or the chorus, and although they are women, and so prejudiced against him, both Medea and chorus comment on his skill at speaking, which is a direct flag to the audience to look for sophistic rhetoric rather than truth. The argument that gives credit to Aphrodite and Eros for saving Jason rather than to Medea can be inverted to excuse women for sexual misconduct; it is, for example, how Helen defends herself in *Trojan Women* (946–50). It does not sound good there.

How Athenians would have heard his argument that he had married prudentially is hard to know. There are several different questions here. Would his reasons justify his treatment of Medea? Would his scheme be likely to work? Is he telling the truth about his motives? The answer to the first, in the usual terms of Greek ethics, would clearly be "no." Since she saved his life, and he took oaths to her, nothing can entirely justify him. However, if his motives were good, a spectator could be inclined to feel sympathetic. Whether it would have been a good plan, had Medea accepted it, is hard to say. We know of Athenian families in which relations among stepbrothers were hostile, and we know of Athenian men who neglected the children of a first marriage after they married again. Stepmothers did not have a good reputation. But it might indeed have given the children wealth and a secure social position, and these are not goods Greeks would have taken lightly – as an exile in Corinth, Jason's situation would be precarious, although he evidently has in abundance the bankable glamour that won Medea in the first place. In any case, Greeks would not have blamed him for marrying prudentially – that was the norm, not marriage for love. Finally, would he have seemed sincere? (This always depends, of course, largely on how he was played.) There is no reason to think that he is lying when he presents his motives, but Medea suggests that he thought the connection with Medea would be an embarrassment in his old age (591–2), and this sounds plausible. A spectator may well suspect that what he says is true but not the whole truth.

Jason's explanation that he did not try to persuade her because he knew he would not succeed is hard to evaluate. Jason and Medea were in a relationship of friendship, and not deceiving your friends is a basic rule of Greek ethics. (It lies at the center of Euripides' *Alcestis*, where Admetus deceives Heracles by not telling him that Admetus's wife has died, and Heracles, having won her back from death, deceives Admetus into taking her, veiled, into his house as if she were a slave woman.) However, this rule always had exceptions, and Jason's assumption that Medea was incapable of a rational assessment of the best interests of the family probably found more sympathy in the Theater of Dionysus than it generally would now. Ancient audiences, however, like modern audiences, would have realized that the deceit has made his offence that much worse, and that her anger now does not prove that she would not have been able to consider his scheme had he proposed it to her.

Jason fails to acknowledge that he has behaved badly in any way, and his moral smugness is repugnant. It is also his vulnerability. Believing, as he evidently does, that his policy has been so self-evidently best that only sexual jealousy keeps Medea from seeing its excellence, he is helplessly vulnerable to Medea's deceit when she pretends to have recognized his wisdom. Even though Medea's superior intelligence saved his life, and even though the speech in which she says that she now realizes how right he was is ludicrously excessive (in 885–8, she talks about how she should have attended his new wife), he hopelessly underestimates her. By accepting one tenet of Greek misogyny, that women are less rational than men, he fails to remember another (one Medea herself endorses) – that they are more devious. He does not understand Medea at all, while she knows everything about him that she needs to know.

Although the audience has access to Medea when she speaks honestly to herself, she is not a fully transparent character even to the audience. Why does Medea kill her children? Both the dramatic development of her plan and her reasoning are difficult. The Nurse is worried about the children from the beginning, but she seems finally to decide that the children must die to complete her revenge after the Aegeus episode, which demonstrates how important it is for a man to have an heir.

In her great monologue (1021–80), Medea repeatedly hesitates, but returns to her intention of killing the children. It is a confusing speech. Initially, she defines the problem as a calculus; by killing the children, she can hurt Jason more than she could in any other way, and the question is whether the pain she will cause herself will be great enough to outweigh the satisfaction of this revenge. In 1046–52, she describes the outcome arithmetically: she will suffer twice as much as Jason, so she decides, for a moment, that it is not worth it, before the possibility of being laughed at makes her change her mind again. She briefly refers to the possibility of taking the children with her when she flees, but never considers it closely. She says that the children must die, and so it is better that she kill them rather than someone else (1240–1). Because she has used them as tools in the murders of the princess and Creon, they are doomed unless she takes them with her, and at least some in the original audience would have known the version in which the Corinthians killed them. And taking them with her would seriously interfere with her future career. When she announces her exit at 1385, she says that she is going to "live with" Aegeus, with a clear hint that their relationship will be sexual.

However, at the end of the speech, she says:

> And I understand what kind of evils I am about to do. But anger is the ruler of my plans, which causes the greatest evils for mortals. (1078–80)

She is not performing a sort of cost–benefit analysis but being overwhelmed by her need for revenge. These are among the most famous lines in the play; they appear to be a response to the teaching of

Socrates that nobody really does wrong knowingly. However, they are very difficult. I have translated "passion is the rule of my plans" instead of the more obvious "anger is more powerful than my plans" because the word "plans" has meant the killing of the children earlier in the speech. Some scholars believe that this part of the speech is an actor's interpolation.[2] The lines are weirdly brilliant, whether Euripides composed them or not. Medea here acknowledges that all the calculation in which she has engaged is fundamentally irrelevant, because for all her appearance of rationality, she is acting out of pride and anger that are not under rational control. She announces her own irrationality, however, in highly controlled language, even generalizing about the human condition. Both Jason and Medea are studies in the limits of a purely instrumental rationality: they are skilled at thinking about how to achieve what they want, but they do not think about whether they want the right things.

She never considers whether it would be wrong to kill the children, or whether they have any right to their lives: she loves her children but does not think about them except as objects of her feeling and so of potential loss. Children are never realistically portrayed in tragedy; when they briefly speak or sing, they express the sentiments adults project onto them, and they serve only as a focus for pathos, never having individuality. Yet when Medea actually murders the children, they cry for help (1271–8) and the chorus considers trying to interfere – and they do not address her at all, but call to each other and to the chorus. Although a plea to Medea would be emotionally powerful, the spectator realizes that they know that begging their mother for mercy would be futile. So at the same moment, the children become, briefly, characters whose death is a loss in itself and not only as a loss to Medea or Jason, and figures through whom the audience can see how inhuman Medea has become.

The Medea of the end of the play, after she kills the children, although she says that she suffers for their deaths, is satisfied with her balance sheet (1362). She feels absolutely no guilt. While the play up to this

[2] Kovacs 1986; on the other side, Seidensticker 1990.

point avoids making her too much a witch or more than human, in her final appearance she drives a flying chariot given to her by her divine grandfather. Both vase paintings and literary sources make it clear that, at least in productions in the fourth century and later, Medea's chariot was drawn by flying serpents. Like a god, she flies, and she speaks as only gods ordinarily speak. She predicts Jason's miserable death, and she announces the future cult of her children: the ends of Euripidean plays often link past to present by describing a religious practice as a memorial to the events of the play, but this kind of proclamation is the task of a god or an incipient hero (1378–88). Because the play has avoided giving Medea supernatural powers before the murders, her transformation into something like a god after them is truly chilling. She describes the murder of his children as if it were a sacrifice (1054), and it seems actually to be an effective ritual, making her both less and more than human.

The Aegeus scene has already pointed toward the darkness of Medea's future in Athens. Aegeus comes to consult Medea about an oracle he has received at Delphi about his childlessness. This oracle has told him not to take the cap off his wineskin until he is home in Athens, and, in accordance with narrative conventions, he does not understand it, although its basic meaning is obvious to the audience. Medea does not interpret the oracle for him, but promises him help with childlessness when she comes to Athens (716–18). He leaves with the intention of consulting his friend, Pittheus, in Troezen, and the audience knows that Pittheus, who understands the oracle, will lure him into sexual relations with his daughter, Aethra, who will bear the great hero, Theseus. (The oracle's meaning is not that Aegeus will not have a child unless he avoids sex until he reaches home, but that the next time he has sexual relations, the woman will conceive.) The story of how Medea tried to murder Theseus when he came to Athens as a young man was well known. If she kills her own children for revenge on a man who has wronged her, she will try to kill Theseus when neither the young man himself nor his father has injured her. Against Theseus, however, Medea will fail, and flee without accomplishing serious harm.

Medea is thus both misogynist and feminist, invoking stereotypes on both sides. The first stasimon suggests that the play will begin a new tradition of poetry to redress male bias, but the tragedy does not quite do that. It is not just about gender, however. An Athenian man would have to see something of himself in Medea, even though she is as unlike what an Athenian man would have liked to be as can be imagined. Like other revenge tragedies, it pushes the audience to consider the values that lead to revenge: if you believe that being laughed at is the worst imaginable fate, you can make yourself a monster to avoid it. *Medea* can also be seen as a study in the limits of reason. Medea is extraordinarily skilled at understanding other people so that she can manipulate them, and she is exceptionally intelligent at scheming. At the end, she is alone on her magic chariot, and nobody would want her abilities at the cost of having to be like her.

SOURCES AND SUGGESTIONS

Allan 2002 is an excellent introduction to the play. Luschnig 2007 aims at a political interpretation. Hall/Macintosh/Taplin 2000 is a collection of essays about productions and adaptations of *Medea*.

The "heroic" Medea was identified by Knox in "The Medea of Euripides," *Yale Classical Studies* 25 (193–225), reprinted in Knox 1979 (250–74). Easterling 1977 is a sensitive treatment of the infanticide within the play. Gill 1996 (216–25) is a study of Medea's self-awareness within a broader study of Greek ideas of the self.

There is a feminist reading in Foley 2001 (243–71). Zeitlin famously argues in her essay "Playing the Other: Theater, Theatricality and the Feminine in Greek Drama" (in Winkler and Zeitlin 1990, 63–96, and Zeitlin 1996, 341–74) that women in drama are the Other that enabled male audiences to explore their own concerns, and are never an end in themselves as women. I see no reason why women in tragedy could not both represent real women and serve as instruments for men to explore themselves.

9

HIPPOLYTUS

Euripides produced two plays entitled *Hippolytus*. One, produced in 428 BCE, was in a victorious tetralogy (Sophocles' son Iophon was second, Ion of Chios third). Ancient scholars called one the *Hippolytus-Covered-Up*, because Hippolytus was so shocked by Phaedra's advances that he pulled his cloak over his head so as not to hear them, and the other, which survives, the *Hippolytus-with-a-Garland*, because he first enters carrying a garland of flowers for the statue of Artemis on one side of the central door (there was a statue of Aphrodite on the other side). The *Hippolytus-Covered-Up* was a shocking play. Phaedra was not only shameless in trying to seduce Hippolytus but also probably defended her behavior, as Euripidean characters so often did. She accused Hippolytus directly to Theseus, and killed herself only after the truth came out. The ancient scholar, Aristophanes of Byzantium, judged that the surviving *Hippolytus* was Euripides' second treatment of the material because it fixed what was "unsuitable and deserving of criticism" in the first. Most modern scholars agree that the surviving play was the second, though not for this reason, since Euripides never reacted to criticism of any other play by rewriting it. However, the surviving play does show signs of being designed to be different from other versions – the setting in Troezen instead of Athens, for example – which seems likelier in a second visit to the material. The story was familiar in any case. Hippolytus, the illegitimate son of King Theseus of Athens by the Amazon Hippolyta, hated women and lived a celibate life. Phaedra, Theseus's wife, fell wildly in love with him, and when he rejected her, told her husband that Hippolytus had tried to rape her.

Theseus prayed to his divine father, Poseidon, to destroy his son, and a great bull came from the sea and caused his chariot to be wrecked. When it was revealed that Phaedra had lied, she killed herself.

In the extant *Hippolytus*, Euripides set out to do something extraordinary: he composed a drama in which Phaedra is a sympathetic character. The resulting play is constructed with exceptional skill. It portrays two people who profoundly misunderstand each other, and who destroy each other without ever actually meeting, even though language, false, misleading, or simply careless, is the medium through which they bring ruin on each other and themselves.

Hippolytus initially presents itself as an example of a standard Greek story pattern. Hippolytus has been brought up by his grandfather in Troezen. Aphrodite, in an expository prologue, explains that Hippolytus refuses to worship her and avoids her sphere in human life completely, giving all his devotion to Artemis. To avenge herself for this insult, she has caused his stepmother, Phaedra, to fall desperately in love with him when he visited Athens to be initiated in the Eleusinian Mysteries. Now, Theseus is in exile for a year in Troezen, and Phaedra has told nobody of her passion. However, Aphrodite will see to it that Theseus finds out and kills his son with the power of a curse his father Poseidon gave him. Phaedra, though she will keep her good name, will perish, too, because Aphrodite cannot worry about collateral damage when she needs to take vengeance (48–50). This prologue is unclear – Theseus would not curse his son because he found out that his wife was afflicted with lust for him – and surprising, since Phaedra did not have a good reputation in Athenian tradition.

Hippolytus then enters from the *parodos* with a secondary chorus of his servants who have just come from the hunt. They sing a short hymn to Artemis, and Hippolytus gives a garland of flowers to her statue. His prayer is a compressed revelation of his character, and has also invited Freudian interpretation. He presents a garland from a beautiful, untouched meadow where "those who have nothing learned, but to be *sôphrôn* has been assigned in their nature – for them it is right to pick, but not for the bad" (79–80). It was common for Greek sanctuaries to have land attached where there were restrictions on use.

It was also standard belief that a person needed to be pure to enter a holy place, but this would mean not having bloodguilt or recent sex or contact with the dead. Hippolytus, though, sets an extraordinarily high standard, and calls everyone who is not completely self-controlled by nature "bad." To this elitist attitude, he adds an absolute distinction between learning and nature that marks his views as an exaggeration of the traditional Greek aristocratic belief that excellence in anything requires an inherited ability. There is also something odd about the association of the untouched meadow with a young man, because Greek poetry regularly associates such places with young unmarried women. Persephone, picking flowers when she is carried off by Hades, provides the type. Hippolytus says that he is so close to Artemis that he spends time in her company, although he never sees her but only hears her voice, but Artemis also is usually associated with girls approaching the age for marriage (in the *Odyssey*, Nausicaa is compared to Artemis at 6.102–9 and 150–2). Hippolytus, hyper-masculine in his misogyny and devotion to hunting and athletics, is potentially feminized by the image of the meadow. His refusal of sex has no place in Greek life, where it would be normal for a man to live chastely for a time in order to be ritually pure or as part of athletic training, but not permanently – a man was expected to marry and continue his family line.

A slave then attempts to persuade him to offer at least token reverence to the statue of Aphrodite, assimilating worship of the goddess with having good manners and not being *semnos*, a word whose range extends from "entitled to reverence" to its sense here, "stuck-up" (93–4). Aphrodite, as a goddess, is *semnê* (99, 105). Hippolytus refuses. After Hippolytus enters the house, the servant prays to Aphrodite to forgive him – he is young and foolish, but gods should be wiser than mortals (114–20). This scene enacts what Aphrodite described in the prologue. At this point, the play seems to be a standard cautionary tale about the folly of refusing respect to any god.

But when the chorus enters, the focus shifts completely. The chorus consists of women who have heard, while doing their laundry at a spring, that Phaedra is sick and has been refusing to eat, and they have come to find out what is wrong and to offer their support. As in *Medea*, the tragedian brings his primarily male audience into the hidden world of women. Phaedra is brought outdoors on a sofa, fantasizing about how she would like to be hunting in the wild or driving horses (that is, doing what Hippolytus does).

For Phaedra, Euripides creates a subtler dilemma than those faced by most tragic heroes. Phaedra is a married woman who is sexually obsessed with her stepson. In a sexually segregated society like classical Greece, such a man is not a surprising object of desire, since he would be one of the few men with whom she would have regular contact. However, she wants to be a good woman, and he is dedicated to chastity anyway, so he is nearby but unavailable. Phaedra hoped that if she kept silent and resisted her feelings, they would go away, but they have not (since Aphrodite herself has inspired them). So she has decided to starve herself to death. This decision creates a further tension. She is already torn between her unbearable desire and her moral code, and she desperately wants to confide in someone about her suffering. To die rather than do wrong is noble. For a Greek, it would be paradoxical to want to behave well without being praised for it. So dying in silence is the best way for Phaedra to protect her reputation – and she is trying to die in a way that could be taken for an illness – but if she really dies without telling anyone the reason, she loses credit for her nobility.

So when the Nurse supplicates her, she yields and tells the Nurse that she is in love, and manipulates the conversation so that it is the Nurse who names Hippolytus (352). She then explains her reasoning to the chorus at length (373–430). Like other Euripidean characters, she discusses her own situation in terms of fifth-century philosophical debates: she has often pondered why people's lives are ruined, and she has decided that it is not because they do not know what is good but because they do not carry out their good intentions. She takes issue here with the intellectualism argued by Socrates. Her catalogue of the reasons people fail to do what they know is right is odd. First she mentions laziness, then pleasures – but the pleasures she lists are "long gossips and idleness, and *aidôs*" (384–5). The first two are, in effect, forms of laziness. *Aidôs* is inhibitory shame, the feeling that stops people from performing actions that are "inappropriate" for them. It is usually a

virtue – Homeric heroes, for example, rely on *aidôs* to make them fight
rather than let their friends down – except when it keeps someone from
an action that is embarrassing but necessary. Phaedra complains that
it is not right that there is only one name for good and bad *aidôs*. So
these general reflections also characterize Phaedra, whose life has been
so quiet that she has never felt a real temptation to pleasure. She does
not even mention sex. Her desire for Hippolytus is not, for her, a desire
for pleasure – it is simply a powerful force with which she contends.

However, the Nurse, initially shocked to silence by Phaedra's revelation, recovers and tries to persuade her that her plan of suicide is
not only unnecessary but wrong. She adapts the conventional ideas
of Greek morality to defend the extremely unconventional position
that it is better to commit adultery than to die. Her first argument is
that desire is a universal force, and even gods are subject to Aphrodite,
so that it is actually *hybris* to want to die to escape desire. Her second main argument is just as perverse. It was a commonplace of Greek
moralizing that no human life could be perfect. No mortal could ever
be praised if only perfection were worthy of praise. When the Nurse
says "as a human being, you would be doing well if you have more
goods than evils" (471–2), she is speaking entirely in accordance with
Greek conventional thinking. She is completely outrageous from the
Greek perspective, however, in treating adultery as if it were a relatively minor offense. The responses of both Phaedra and the chorus to
the Nurse's speech clearly mark it as sophistic speech, as fine-sounding
talk that does harm. The Nurse then becomes blunt: she needs not fine
(but false) talk but the man (490–1). When Phaedra weakly begs the
Nurse to stop, the Nurse changes direction and promises charms that
will "stop your sickness without shame or damage to the mind" (511),
and Phaedra agrees, although the spectator knows that she should know
better than to trust the Nurse.

After a choral song about the terrible power of Eros comes the
scene that determines everything. Phaedra, listening at the door, hears
Hippolytus shouting at the Nurse, and realizes that her secret has been
betrayed. Hippolytus then bursts through the door onto the stage,
followed by the Nurse. Phaedra remains on stage, but the Nurse and

Hippolytus either do not see or pretend that they do not. This is a significant difference that a director must consider. If Hippolytus does not know that Phaedra hears everything he says, he assumes that the Nurse will convey what needs to be conveyed to Phaedra, and he says the rest because he feels the need to say it, as he concludes by answering an imaginary interlocutor who complains that he abuses women all the time (664–9). If he does see her, everything he says is actually directed at her.

The actual approach is already over; what the audience hears is Hippolytus's cries of indignation, and the Nurse's pleas to him to be quiet. She tells him not to dishonor the oath he swore (the audience learns that she swore him to silence before telling him what she wanted), and he replies "The tongue has sworn but not the mind" (611–12). He must mean that he does not believe the oath is truly binding because he took it without knowing what a horrible secret he would be asked to keep, so that although he said the words, he did not really consent. This became one of the most parodied of all Euripidean lines. For Greeks, the exact wording of oaths was binding, whether the oath was understood or not, and whether a choice of words made the promise broader or narrower than the participants intended. Hippolytus actually keeps his oath, even though the oath makes it impossible for him to defend himself to his father. Phaedra, though, hears him threaten to ignore it, and then hears his protracted misogynist tirade, an utterly immoderate rant (616–68). It evidently never occurs to Hippolytus that the Nurse has not faithfully represented Phaedra. Although he does say in the course of his tirade that he will keep his oath (656–8), he also threatens to watch how both the Nurse and Phaedra look at Theseus. Phaedra has already shown how sensitive she is to scrutiny.

So Phaedra believes that Hippolytus will tell Theseus (689–92). The Nurse suggests that there is still a way for Phaedra to be saved (705). Although she forcefully rejects any more advice from the Nurse, in dying she does exactly what the Nurse would surely have suggested – in order to save her reputation and the good name of her children – and because she resents Hippolytus's arrogance, she devises a way to die that brings credit to herself and ruins him. She says, indeed, "by sharing in this illness together with me he will learn to be *sôphrôn*" (731), turning his favorite word against him. For him, *sôphrosynê* means, above all, sexual self-control, but she uses it in the broader sense of "moderation." Phaedra does not explain *how* she will involve Hippolytus in her ruin. The letter is a surprise.

Phaedra's suicide takes place during one of the finest examples of a Euripidean specialty, the escape ode. The chorus daydreams about being somewhere else. They wish to be a bird and fly across the Adriatic to where the sisters of Phaethon weep amber, or to the garden of the Hesperides at the western edge of the world. Then, however, they sing about how unspecified bad omens accompanied Phaedra's departure from her native Crete and her arrival at Athens, and to the present: the omens were fulfilled in her unlawful desire, so that she will hang herself, thereby saving her reputation and freeing herself from her painful desire. It is a very pretty ode but not very intelligent.

This play replaces her accusation against Hippolytus with a suicide note. This is a brilliant variant on Euripides' favorite theme of deceptive speech. First, the Nurse comes out to tell the chorus that Phaedra has hanged herself. The chorus briefly divides, as one considers entering the house to cut her down, while another says that it is not their job. Then Theseus enters. He has been visiting an oracle and wears a garland, but when he hears what has happened, he tears the garland from his head and orders the slave to open the doors. Phaedra's body is brought out on the *ekkyklêma*. Only after singing a lament for her does Theseus see the writing tablet fastened to her dead hand, and he speculates that the note asks him not to remarry. As the chorus sings, he reads the tablet. This is the first surviving example of silent reading in the classical world; usually, people read aloud, and this is a powerful stage effect. Theseus reports that Hippolytus raped her (885–6). In the "standard" version, she may have said only that he had attacked her, not that he had succeeded, but the rape motivates the suicide and the suicide thereby makes the charge of rape credible. It is also, as revenge, perfect: Hippolytus unfairly believed the worst of her, so she will see to it that Theseus, even more unfairly, thinks the worst of him. Theseus believes Phaedra's dying words without hesitation or thought, and he immediately curses Hippolytus.

Here, Euripides faced a problem in dramatic construction. The plot depends on two indirect communications: the Nurse's proposal and the letter. One is misleading, the other an outright lie. The play also features an *agon*, in which Hippolytus tries to defend himself to his father but cannot do so effectively because of his oath, so that language misused is more powerful than truth. The *agon*, however, requires some fudging because Theseus has already cursed his son and it is not clear that he could retract it. So Euripides makes Theseus uncertain that the curse will be effective, and he also orders that his son be exiled. So when Hippolytus enters, Theseus calls him a hypocrite and imagines what he could say to refute the charges – for example, that Phaedra hated him because she feared him as a rival to her own sons, or that women are sexually uncontrolled, while men are able to control themselves (960–70). Phaedra has made her body into a more powerful witness than any argument, so he orders Hippolytus into exile.

Hippolytus, having heard Theseus's shouting, rushes in with his servants, and initially, Theseus refuses to speak to him. In fact, he speaks only in the third person from 915 to 946, when he finally decides that Hippolytus's presence has polluted him in any case and he may as well address him. Hippolytus, in the first part of this scene, is in the situation of Phaedra during Hippolytus's scene with the Nurse; he is accused as if he were not present. The spectator may have the impression that Theseus has never understood or trusted Hippolytus; although Theseus does not say that he has always been suspicious of Hippolytus's claims of intimacy with Artemis, the scorn he efficiently heaps on Hippolytus sounds as if Theseus was ready to believe accusations against him.

Hippolytus is in an impossible situation. Only the truth would provide Phaedra with a credible motive for the suicide and the false accusation, and he cannot speak the truth because of his oath. He tries to insist on his purity (some readers/spectators find his insistence on his own virtue unsympathetic). When his *sôphrosynê* does not convince, he resorts to arguments from probability: Phaedra was not so beautiful that he would have done this for her alone (the audience would think of Helen of Troy). Getting sexual possession of the queen could be the beginning of a conspiracy to overthrow Theseus, but Hippolytus has no interest in the throne. His argument is similar to that of Creon in *Oedipus the King*: Hippolytus has power without responsibility, and he most wants athletic victories in Panhellenic contests and to enjoy life among aristocratic friends. Finally, he swears an oath. At the end of his speech, he does something very rare in tragedy: he shows that he has genuinely learned something. He says of Phaedra:

> She acted with *sôphrosynê* when she was not able to be *sôphrôn*, and we, who were able, did not use the ability well.
> (1034–5)

This line uses the Greek distinction between the aorist mood, used for a single action ("she acted with *sôphrosynê*"), and the imperfective participle ("because/when/although she was unable to be *sôphrôn*) to show Hippolytus's enriched understanding of the human moral world, for the prayer to Artemis would not allow such a division. Hippolytus has realized that people are complex. Although he does not know that Aphrodite caused Phaedra's passion in order to avenge herself on him, or that the Nurse acted without Phaedra's full consent, he understands Phaedra's suicide as the only way she could subdue her desire, and he also realizes that his response to the Nurse's proposition was wrong. The one line cannot tell the audience exactly how Hippolytus understands his mistake. He may be saying only that it was tactically unwise for him to make Phaedra think that he would violate his oath, but he may be saying more – that in assuming that the Nurse's proposal meant that Phaedra was a typically bad woman and no more, he oversimplified a complex reality and misjudged her.

By this point, audience sympathy must be entirely with Hippolytus. Theseus's refusal to believe a solemn oath, or to consult prophets, leaves him with no chance of being believed. It is striking that Theseus, the Athenian national hero, in this play acts like a fool. The *agon* raises a contemporary issue in passing, when Hippolytus complains that Theseus will not wait for "informing time," but is banishing him immediately (1051–2). Athenian trials did not allow for any deliberation by juries or any reflection – as soon as the speeches of prosecution and defense were done, the juries voted. Thucydides presents a debate from the year immediately following the production of the play in which Cleon, the most important politician after Pericles' death, criticizes the Athenians for reconsidering the decision they had taken the day before to massacre the people of Mytilene, whose revolt had just been suppressed (3.38).

When Hippolytus finally exits, the chorus of women and the secondary chorus of his servants sing in responsion about his fall (1102–50): the servants find the changeable nature of human life perplexing, and do not comprehend the ways of the gods; the women pray for a fortunate life, and plan to live only a day at a time. The men express their deep confusion at the fate of "the brightest star of Athena, goddess of Greeks;" the women sorrowfully consider that he will no longer drive horses around the Lagoon (a famous feature of the landscape of Troezen), play the lyre in the house, give Artemis garlands, make young girls rivals for marriage with him. It is not clear who sings the final epode, in which the singers say that they "rage at the gods" and ask the Graces why they have driven an innocent man from his home. Hippolytus himself has complained that he is being destroyed by the very gods whom he reveres (1060–1).

After the messenger narrates the attack of the bull on Hippolytus's chariot, Theseus orders that the dying Hippolytus be brought back because Theseus believes that the fulfillment of his curse proves Hippolytus's guilt (1265–7) and Theseus wants to prove it to him. At this point, Artemis appears and tells him the truth, and Hippolytus is carried on in his death agony. Artemis explains Aphrodite's role in the events to Hippolytus, and promises him hero-cult in Troezen, as well as revenge. The gods, she has told Theseus, do not interfere with each other (1329–30); but she will kill with her arrows the mortal most loved by Aphrodite (1420–2). Artemis departs, because the gods avoid being polluted by death, and Hippolytus forgives his father, echoing a provision of Athenian law that a murder victim could, before dying, absolve the killer.

Artemis must appear because only a goddess can reveal the truth of Aphrodite's involvement. Her supernatural intervention, however, is needed only so that she can explain the initial supernatural intervention of Aphrodite. The other facts Theseus needs to understand could have been revealed by the Nurse. In this play, there is a divine level of action that the characters discover only at the end and that seems, in some ways, unnecessary. The play invites treatment as almost two different plays whose main action is exactly the same. If the spectator takes Aphrodite literally, this is a story about *theomachy*, fighting with a god. Hippolytus's rejection of Aphrodite is *hybris*, and she takes revenge, even though her revenge kills Phaedra and ruins Theseus's life. This play is a critique of the traditional gods. While the first part of the play emphasizes Hippolytus's offense against Aphrodite and his excessive rejection of sexuality, the second half shows him as giving his life rather than violate his oath. She is cruel. Even Poseidon, Theseus's father, promptly fulfills his curse instead of intervening to save him from killing his son.

But it is also possible to treat the goddesses as allegories. Phaedra herself reflects on the strange erotic history of her family: her mother, Pasiphaë, fell in love with a bull and gave birth to the Minotaur; her sister, Ariadne, was the beloved of Dionysus who ran away with Theseus and was killed on the island of Dia (337–40). (Crete, her native island, was associated with sexually transgressive women.) By bringing up this history, the play invites its audience to rationalize the story. Phaedra comes from a family subject to perverse desires, and Hippolytus's dedication to chastity could itself give him a strange allure (the chorus thinks that all the maidens want to marry him, 1140–1). The gods, in this perspective, are not cruel or unforgiving, for they are not personalities subject to moral evaluations. They represent the way human life is. This double view of the gods is one of the sources of the play's fascination.

Hippolytus is open to a rich variety of approaches and questions. It is obviously much concerned with problems of language and communication. Much of the play is about decisions to speak or to be silent, first Phaedra's, then Hippolytus's. There are many instances of the slipperiness of words themselves, marked by Phaedra's comments about how good and bad *aidôs* should be indicated by different words: the "medicine" promised by the Nurse and the *sôphrosynê* that Hippolytus claims are both tricky ideas. Beyond the ambiguities of words themselves are the difficulties people have in understanding each other when they speak from different premises and toward different goals. The characters are regularly aware of the differences among speaking situations. The Nurse, for example, tries to find out whether Phaedra's illness is one that women can talk about only among themselves, or one that could be communicated to a male doctor (293–6). Hippolytus says that he lacks skill for explaining himself to a crowd but is cleverer among small groups of his friends (986–9). It is not a coincidence that this play includes two scenes in which the real message goes to somebody who is not overtly addressed. Using the third person for someone present can be insulting in Greek as in English, but it is prominent in this play because this form of indirection denies the real addressee the possibility of participating in dialogue. It blurs the distinction between talking to and talking about.

"Talking about" is also central to the play. Phaedra is constantly concerned about her reputation, about what will be said about her. She is afraid that if her repute is bad, her sons will not be able to speak freely as citizens of Athens (421–5). The chorus initially enters because they have heard a rumor about Phaedra's illness (129–40). Artemis promises Hippolytus that Phaedra's love for him will not be left in silence (1428–30). This concern for reputation is two edged, for while it is the basis of Phaedra's attempt to die nobly rather than yield to her desire (405–7), it is also one of the reasons she writes the false accusation against Hippolytus. Phaedra believes that to compete in life, a person needs "a justice and good mind," and that time reveals the bad (426–30), but in her anger at Hippolytus, she gives no consideration at all to whether his action is just. Concern for reputation is a reliable guide for action only for someone who believes that what people say will be the truth.

Although the play's issues of language and reputation had political significance, this is not an overtly political play. Hippolytus is in some ways outside the city, consistently associated with wild places. This goes with his rejection of marriage, since the wild was associated with young men on the boundary of adulthood – Hippolytus, in some ways, has failed to make the transition to adulthood.[1] Yet Hippolytus is a bastard, who would not be obliged to marry as a citizen would be, since it is not his task to continue the household, although the young women of Troezen all want to marry him. He is not his father's heir, and his insistence that he has no interest in political power rings true. Some members of the original audience might have considered that he had found a way of life appropriate to his situation. At the same time, he evokes an Athenian type: the "quiet Athenian," the aristocrat who preferred to avoid public life as much as possible.[2] Tragedy's blurring of the distant past and the present makes Hippolytus's position ambiguous – while Phaedra's children are Theseus's legitimate heirs, it is not clear that Hippolytus's illegitimacy puts him under the same disadvantages it would in fifth-century Athens, and this blurring allows for a variety of reactions to the character.

Hippolytus is the most balanced of surviving diptych plays. Its two main characters are antagonists, yet it does not require its audience to choose between them. Its final moments, in which father and son finally understand each other and Hippolytus forgives Theseus, are particularly appealing to modern tastes. It manages to be accessible without being simple.

SOURCES AND SUGGESTIONS

Gibert 1997 argues that we have no real evidence that our *Hippolytus* was the second; he is convincing that we do not know, but most scholars believe that internal evidence suggests that it was. My discussion is influenced by Kovacs 1987 (untranslated Greek).

[1] Mitchell-Boysak 1999.
[2] Carter 1986, 52–6.

Mills 2002, in the Duckworth Companions series, is a very useful guide for students. A famous study of the play is B. M. W. Knox, "The Hippolytus of Euripides" (205–30) in Knox 1979 (originally published in 1952). An accessible feminist study of speech in the play is McClure 1999 (12–57). There is a fine treatment of *aidôs* and *sôphrosynê* in Gregory 1991 (51–84). Goff 1990 examines language in the play.

10

OEDIPUS THE KING

My teacher, Cedric Whitman, once said that reading *Oedipus Rex* made him feel as if he were being driven on a mountain road in Italy with a very skilled but utterly fearless driver: at every moment, it looks as if the car will lose the road and the play will fall into the abyss. He was talking about the dramaturgical and narratological risks the play takes, that the audience will stop believing in the drama, whose story depends on unlikely coincidences and the believability of whose action requires that the spectator remain completely absorbed at every moment. The effect of the play's flirting with being completely past belief, though, is easy to appreciate. Somehow, difficult though it is, we need to overcome the accumulated weight of expectation about this tragedy of all tragedies. The critical tradition pushes audiences to want a profound yet immediate message about the gods or fate or a valuable moral about life.

We do not know the date of production of *Oedipus the King*. Stylistically, it appears to be later than *Antigone*, and it is almost certainly earlier than *Electra*. The only other criteria for dating are the general similarity between Oedipus's intellectual self-confidence and the atmosphere of Periclean Athens, and the plague that initiates the action. Athens suffered a terrible epidemic in 430 BCE, with recurrences in 429 BCE and the winter of 427–426 BCE. (Analysis of a mass burial excavated in 1994–5 has suggested typhoid, but the issue is still under scientific debate.) The plague of the play, which includes crops, herds, and miscarriage (25–7), combines an affliction caused by pollution, and does not closely resemble the plague Thucydides describes, but other details, such as the emphasis on the hostility of Ares the war god (who is normally a protector of Thebes), do seem to evoke the combined war and plague that attacked Athens. Most scholars believe that the plague recalls the plague at Athens, though it is not certain.[1]

Critics continue to debate whether the play makes Oedipus guilty and the gods just. This may not be the right question, at least not the question with which to start. After all, the play follows Oedipus's investigation, and the work of the tragedy really happens on that thrill ride. The play functions on two levels simultaneously. The ancient audience, like modern audiences, knew that Oedipus had killed his father and was married to his mother, but not how, in this particular version, this had come about. As we see Oedipus look for the answers to his questions, we follow his experience and also, from our situation of greater knowledge, establish the back-story. The tragedy conveys its meaning through the audience's emotional and intellectual responses, as prior knowledge of the story keeps meeting the difficulties Oedipus encounters in finding it out in the play's famous dramatic ironies.

This parallel process of Oedipus's investigation and the audience's gradual understanding of how the oracle has been fulfilled has a very particular effect. Most people have at some time had the experience of having misunderstood what was happening around them, most often because others deceived them, whether benignly (a surprise party) or cruelly (a spouse's affair). Human beings universally tend to make their lives into stories, and Oedipus is about someone who finds out that the story of his life has been completely other than he thought it was. Several tragedies culminate in such revelations that change the significance of entire lives, but *Oedipus the King* is the grimmest and perhaps the most powerful of them, because Oedipus is defined as somebody who is supremely competent at understanding and managing his circumstances, and his entire life turns out to have been organized and patterned to make him the most polluted human being imaginable.

This tragedy therefore, perhaps more than any another, invites examination of how the drama interacts with the story. The drama

---

[1] Knox 1956; Mitchell-Boysak 2008, 56–66.

follows a series of questions, each of which gives way to a new question. The original audience could not know exactly how the investigation would proceed, so that even though everyone knew the essentials about Oedipus, the plot of the actual play was entirely new. The final revelation will be aesthetically satisfying, since it will bring together the audience's knowledge and the character's, but also very painful to watch.

In the prologue, the question is what has caused the plague and how to end it. This question is almost immediately answered when Creon returns from the Delphic Oracle: pollution from the murderer(s) of Laius has caused the plague, and removing the killer(s) will cleanse the city. So, at the end of the prologue, Oedipus promises to do all he can (145–6), and the play has introduced the second question – who killed Laius. Yet immediately, this question is unhelpfully framed. Creon very explicitly says that the one survivor of Laius's murder said that he was attacked by a gang of bandits (122–3). Oedipus immediately assumes that the killers must have been hired and the murder political (124–5) because bandits by themselves would not dare attack a king on a sacred embassy.

The prologue places heavy emphasis on one aspect of the backstory: that Oedipus came to Thebes and saved the city from the Sphinx. The priest who addresses him on behalf of the people urges him to repeat that success. The priest and Oedipus both speak within the norms of Greek piety, so that Oedipus is "best of men" (33) but must have saved Thebes with the help of a god (38). This is characteristic Greek religious thought, especially familiar from the poet, Pindar, in the first half of the fifth century: any exceptional human achievement must have had divine support. That does not make it any less worthy of praise. In fact, human greatness lies precisely in having the qualities that attract the gods' help. Oedipus must be a person whom the gods love. Oedipus is also immensely sympathetic within the scene. He initially comes outside because he does not regard it as right to hear his people's problems from messengers (6–8). To a modern ear, perhaps, his analysis of how he suffers more than anyone else, because everyone else grieves individually, while he feels for the entire city, may sound pretentious or self-serving (60–4), but this is appropriate for a tragic king (and it is characteristic of Oedipus to describe his feelings through arithmetic). He has wept for his city but also thought about how to act, and he has sent Creon to the Delphic oracle already.

After the chorus enters, singing of the horror of the plague and praying for its end, Oedipus first pronounces an extended proclamation and curse that seeks to enlist the entire population in the search, making it as difficult as possible for anyone to protect the guilty. Then the investigation quickly goes astray. Creon has advised asking the prophet Tiresias for help. Tiresias has special knowledge from the gods, but he is a human being. He is reluctant to say what he knows, and Oedipus infers from his reluctance that he must have guilty knowledge. Since Creon suggested asking Tiresias for help, when Tiresias finally says that Oedipus himself is the killer, Oedipus further infers that Creon must be involved in a conspiracy with Tiresias to overthrow him. He probably does not even hear Tiresias's final angry prophecies (449–62) – a director has a significant decision to make in timing Tiresias's exit as he is guided down the *parodos*, and Oedipus's exit into the house. Even the chorus hesitates to believe Tiresias. Oedipus is stopped from having Creon executed only by the intervention of Jocasta, his wife and Creon's sister.

The Tiresias scene is a hairpin curve, where only Oedipus's rage makes it believable that he does not connect Tiresias's statement with the man he killed. Oedipus's anger can arouse a complex response because the spectator knows that Oedipus is wrong and unjust but can also sympathize with his frustration – it is incomprehensible to him that Tiresias is unwilling to save the city (322–3). His accusation that Tiresias was no help against the Sphinx (390–6) is telling for the spectator who knows the truth because it points to the apparent arbitrariness of the gods.

The speech in which Jocasta tries to calm Oedipus is another tricky passage (707–25). She wants to prove to Oedipus that human beings have no prophetic ability, and therefore that Tiresias need not be lying because Creon has bribed him: he is simply wrong. So she tells the story of how an oracle told her and Laius that his son would kill him.

He, however, was killed at a meeting of three roads by "foreign bandits," while the baby was exposed (715–19). Here, Oedipus is so intent
on the detail of the three roads that he pays no attention to the rest
of the story. His recognition of this detail means that the question of
Laius's killer has almost been answered, except that the discrepancy
between many bandits and one person remains.

This recognition prompts Oedipus's narrative of his life. (The for-
mality of the narrative does not imply that he has never told Jocasta
or the Thebans who his parents are; he tells the story properly, from
the beginning.) This is perhaps the trickiest twist. Oedipus tells how
someone insulted him by saying that he was not really the son of his
parents. They denied that he was adopted, but the rumor was persis-
tent enough to make him consult the Delphic Oracle. And the oracle,
he says:

> sent me away dishonored as to what I had come about, but
> spoke and revealed other, terrible, unfortunate things to me,
> so that I was miserable – that I would have sexual relations
> with my mother and bring to light offspring unendurable for
> people to see, and become the murderer of the father who
> begat me. (788–93)

Oedipus does not fail to notice that Apollo did not answer his question.
Here is the hardest part of the story: why does he assume that this
response means that Polybus and Merope are his parents, as he obviously does, since he decides not to return to Corinth in order to avoid
fulfilling the oracle? The word "dishonored" seems to be crucial. He
thinks Apollo did not answer the question because it was a stupid question that did not deserve an answer. Oedipus is naïve about the gods,
and assumes that if the identity of his parents were important, Apollo
would have responded to his question.

At this point, the audience understands the entire story except how
the baby Oedipus came to Corinth. Oedipus, Jocasta, and the elders
of the chorus all realize that only the arithmetical discrepancy stands
against the conclusion that Oedipus killed Laius. Jocasta repeats her
argument that prophecy has no value (848–58), although it has become

irrelevant, since the evidence now points to Oedipus as the killer quite apart from Tiresias's accusation. This disturbs the chorus, who sing a prayer for purity and a demand that the oracles be proven true (863–910). Yet their assumption that disbelief in oracles means disbelief in the gods is immediately disproved when Jocasta enters with offerings for Apollo.

The messenger from Corinth arrives to announce the death of Polybus and Oedipus's selection as king there. For Oedipus, this represents a possible solution: if he has killed Laius and must leave Thebes, he could simply go back to Corinth. However, despite his skepticism about oracles, he is still nervous about his mother, so that the messenger, seeking to relieve him of anxiety, explains that he was not the son of Polybus and Merope. The messenger himself gave the baby that he had received from a slave of Laius when they were both pasturing summer flocks on Cithaeron. So Oedipus pursues yet another question – who his parents are. The audience knows the entire story. When the chorus says that the slave who was a herdsman in the mountains is the same man who survived the killing of Laius (1051–2), the audience also knows that this question will be answered as soon as this man speaks. Jocasta, desperately trying to stop further investigation, also obviously now knows.

As Oedipus follows one question, the last is abandoned. Nobody ever really talks about the plague once the search for the killer begins, and once Oedipus is seeking his parentage, he never confirms that he was, in fact, the killer of Laius. It is not necessary, since the oracles link his origin and the murder. The back-story seems strongly determined, since the oracles make the outcome seem inevitable. It depends on coincidences and on lies. The coincidences belong to the expectation created by the oracles; if the gods have determined that these events will happen, the coincidences necessary for them to happen will take place. The coincidences have more meaning because they also depend on the nature of the characters. Oedipus is the son of Laius and shares Laius's pride and hot temper, so that when they meet, it is not surprising that Laius pushes Oedipus out of the road and that Oedipus reacts by killing Laius and his attendants. That is the kind of people that they are. The lies are also necessary though: if Polybus and Merope had told the truth about his origins, or if the survivor of Laius's murder had identified the victor over the Sphinx as the killer, there would be no disaster. Finally, Apollo brings about the fulfillment of his own oracle by choosing to deliver the prediction instead of answering the question that Oedipus had asked. It is not the case in this story that Apollo knows the future but does not cause it; when he refuses to tell Oedipus what Oedipus has asked, he intervenes actively to bring these events about.

The aftermath of the revelation is a typically tragic sequence of events in its contingency, and here, too, different causes interact. The household slave who serves as messenger describes how Jocasta locked herself in her room and lamented. The slaves were then distracted by the entry of Oedipus, who demanded a sword while looking for Jocasta. When they refuse him, he manages to break into the bedroom, finds Jocasta hanging, and puts out his eyes with her brooches. Had he found a sword, he would presumably have killed her and himself. Had he not arrived when he did, she might not have killed herself or might have been prevented. The messenger believes that a god directs Oedipus to Jocasta's room (1258). It is impossible to know whether a god is involved.

The chorus asks how Oedipus brought himself to blind himself, and then what god drove him, on the assumption that he could only have acted under an impulse sent by a god. Oedipus responds that it was Apollo, but also gives a reason for his action – that there was nothing sweet for him to see (1329–35). Later, when the chorus asks why he did not kill himself, Oedipus delivers a speech justifying his action (1367–90), as if he had deliberated. He then begins to demand that he be killed or removed from the city (1436–7, 1440–1). He evidently still believes that he can properly interpret his fate. Oedipus is both a rationalist and a rationalizer, who will not accept either that he cannot make sense of his situation, or that his own actions were not a proper response to it.

If the play has a simple moral, it would seem to be one that has interested very few of its admirers, beginning with Aristotle – the validity of oracles. It is a general rule of tragedy that oracles and prophecies are fulfilled, so that they serve as announcements for the audience. Insofar as the truth of oracles is a tragic convention, it says nothing about what the poets believed or were trying to convey. In this play, however, belief in oracles is explicitly at issue, and whether mortals could receive communication from the gods was a real controversy in the fifth century. Herodotus insists that he will not try to discredit oracles or accept the arguments of others who do, because he knows, and cites, an oracle of the legendary prophet, Bacis – clearly, in the view of modern historians, composed after the fact – that predicts the battle of Salamis (8.77). Herodotus himself, however, reports stories in which the Delphic Oracle was bribed, and relates with some relish how the Lydian King Croesus experimentally tested various oracles and found most of them useless (46.3–49). The historian Thucydides, in contrast, evidently puts no faith in oracles, and sophists were critical (Herodotus's reference to those who "discredit" oracles seems to refer to the title of a book by Protagoras). For Herodotus, the truth of some oracles was important, even if it might not be very useful in practice (since he had no good way of knowing which oracles would prove true).

Like Herodotus, the chorus is willing to doubt an individual prophet. They do not initially believe Tiresias, though they are shaken by what he says, because they apply general criteria of plausibility to what he says. There would have been no motive for him to kill Laius, and they know Oedipus as wise and a civic benefactor (483–511). Jocasta, however, argues that humans have no share at all in a prophetic craft (708–9). This troubles the elders deeply. Perturbed by both her story of the unfulfilled oracle and by the possibility that Thebes is endangered by political conspiracy, and that human life is governed by chance, in the second stasimon (863–910), they pray for purity in relation to eternal, divine laws (akin to those invoked in *Antigone*). It is not at all clear exactly what they mean, for the preceding scene does not demand the invocation of such laws. Greeks would not ordinarily have thought that either disbelief in oracles or political murder violated these most sacred rules (although incest and parricide did, and the song is full of double meanings).

The song then warns against *hybris*. *Hybris*, they say, brings forth the "tyrant." So far in the play, "tyrant" has been a word simply for "ruler," but here it seems to have the negative associations of everyday rather than tragic language. *Hybris* climbs high but then falls. However, the chorus wants "the wrestling that is good for the city" to continue, and the song continues by singing about the kind of man who recognizes no limits and does not fear justice. Evidently, up to this point, it is political turmoil they fear most. "If such practices are honored," they sing, "why should I dance?" It is one of those rare moments at which a chorus seems to be inside the play and in contemporary Athens at the same time. In the second antistrophe, they turn to the oracles and ask Zeus to see that the oracles are fulfilled because faith in the gods is waning; they themselves will no longer visit oracular shrines unless these oracles are shown to be true.

The elders, then, connect a loss of faith in oracles with a loss of belief in the gods, and they also believe that the kind of man who would have had Laius killed, or who might have bribed a prophet, would do anything, including breaking the holiest laws. They imagine and fear a breakdown of social order, and this order can only be preserved if the truth of the oracles is established, the murderer of Laius is found and removed, and political stability ensured. Ironically, Oedipus's discovery of the truth accomplishes everything they demand. J. P. Vernant, in a famous article, connects Oedipus with the Greek ritual of the *pharmakos*.[2] A *pharmakos* was a scapegoat, a criminal who was feasted and then driven out of the city, carrying evil with him. Oedipus, however, is not someone chosen as a scapegoat because the city can easily spare him; he is the true source of the pollution and the legitimate king of Thebes.

While the choral song puts faith in oracles at the center of religious belief and so of the city, and the plot triumphantly vindicates the oracles, the play does not tell its audience how to use oracular knowledge in their lives. Jocasta argues there is no good way to predict anything, so that "it is best to live at random, as one can" (977–9), that is, without

---

[2] Vernant 1981; Foley 1993.

directing excessive attention toward the future. Oedipus, after Jocasta had already realized the truth, describes Chance as his mother (1080–5). Chance is what appears random to the individual, what cannot be predicted: nobody could have known that the baby given to Polybus would become ruler of Thebes. Part of the mystery of the play is how hard it would be to differentiate belief in chance from belief in oracles in actually living one's life. If Laius and Jocasta on one side, and Oedipus on the other, had not received the oracles or had ignored them, the outcome would presumably have been the same because the reliability of the oracles is absolute. Jocasta's imagined life without any attempt to control the future and a life of complete dependence on oracles would end the same way. Oracles are useful only if they offer choices (as many literary oracles do).

Oedipus has obviously acted freely throughout; Apollo has never forced him to do anything. Equally obviously, it is not his fault that his story has taken the shape that it has. To be sure, Oedipus is a far from perfect hero. Although Laius began the fight at the crossroads, Oedipus did not need to kill several people because he had been rudely pushed out of the way. Within the play, he jumps to conclusions and loses his temper too easily. He is too confident in his own abilities. It is debatable whether he should be considered impious because he follows Jocasta in rejecting oracles (but not the gods). The flaws that can be attributed to him are mainly irrelevant, however, since the oracle dooms him before he is born. In Aristophanes' *Frogs* (1182), Euripides quotes the first line of his *Antigone*, "Oedipus was at first a fortunate man," only to have Aeschylus point out that Apollo had predicted that he would kill his father before his birth, so that he was miserable from the beginning.

Sophocles could easily have alluded to some cause for the gods to be angry with Oedipus's family. Aeschylus's *Seven against Thebes* was the third play in a tetralogy about Laius and his descendants. The chorus sings allusively about past events, and evidently Laius was warned by the oracle not to have children and disobeyed (*Seven against Thebes* 742–9). In Jocasta's account, the oracle says he will be killed by his child, whoever was born of Jocasta and Laius (713–14), but there is no hint of disobedience. Nothing in Sophocles' version hints at any reason at all for the gods to doom Oedipus. So it is not clear that the play has very much of value to say about human freedom and responsibility. It rests on the assumption that Oedipus acts with complete freedom – the gods do not interfere with his mental processes, as gods sometimes do – but that whatever he does, he will kill his father and marry his mother.

The play does have an obvious moral as a warning not to believe that a human being can control his life or that the world is fundamentally available for rational understanding. Oedipus is slow to realize that he must be the murderer because he has faith in arithmetic: "one could not be equal to many" (845). The answer to the problem is not at all profound – the eyewitness lied because it was so incredible that one man had killed all the others that he feared telling the truth, or because when he arrived with his report, Oedipus was already installed as king. The chronology is not entirely clear but the slave's motives are not hard to infer, especially since Jocasta explains that he asked to be sent away to the countryside when he saw Oedipus in power (758–64). One can be equal to many if the many were a fiction. The issue of number also has eerier resonances; Oedipus is one man who is equal to many (as son and husband, father and brother). In the end, though, it does not matter whether the collapse of arithmetic in the play has a trivial cause like a lie, or a deep cause like the confusion of categories caused by incest. In the world as this play shows it, the most basic form of logic is unreliable.

The play critiques the optimism characteristic of sophistic thought. Oedipus is initially confronted with what appears to be a difficult but straightforward problem. He sends Creon to the oracle to learn the cause of the plague, and then tries to enlist Tiresias to help him find the killer, while he delivers a curse that seeks to ensure that nobody in Thebes will conceal information and that may even produce a confession. Although he relies on supernatural mechanisms, the mood is practical, energetic, and reasonable: Oedipus is the capable and efficient administrator. The play shows the complete downfall of a person regarded by both the priest at the beginning of the play and by the chorus as supremely competent.

Oedipus is not impious; he evidently respects the gods. At the moment he realizes that he may be the murderer, he cries out to Zeus (738). He is not even initially overconfident, although in his anger with Tiresias, he boasts of solving the riddle of the Sphinx "which was not for anybody who came by to solve, but it required prophecy" (393–4). When he summons the chorus as representative of the Theban people and promises to do everything possible, he declares "either we will turn out to be fortunate, with divine help, or fallen" (145–6). Greeks would typically be euphemistic in even mentioning the possibility of failure (direct speech is ill-omened), and the lines carry ironic weight for the external audience. But they are also a compressed demonstration that the speaker is pious, recognizing that if he is successful, it will be because the gods have helped him, and that nothing he does on his own can guarantee success. The beginning of the play defines Oedipus as a man especially good at solving terrible problems; he combines contemporary thought, with its belief in the power of human reason, with the traditional idea that some men are able to achieve beyond others because the gods love and help them. The revelation, however, proves that he is, on the contrary, most detested by the gods.

After the revelation, Oedipus does not complain that the gods have been unjust, although he would have had good grounds for such a complaint. The gods' justice simply does not seem to be the issue. He is not interested in assessing whether he is guilty either. In *Oedipus at Colonus*, Oedipus argues that the men of Colonus in the chorus who want to drive him away are afraid only of his name because he really was not to blame for actions he suffered more than he did (*Oedipus at Colonus* 265–74), but there is no trace of such self-defense here. Oedipus repeatedly laments what he *is*: impure, accursed, hateful to the gods. Oedipus enjoyed what would seem to a Greek supreme good fortune: he saved Thebes from the Sphinx, and so was praised and admired; he was king, happily married, and had children. The very things that made him lucky are catastrophes. As the play goes on, Oedipus's desire for the truth becomes more intense and relentless, and the spectator feels at once a longing for the revelation and dread of it: this is a man putting all his energy into learning what will utterly ruin his life. This irony is the moral of the play: that human good fortune is always supremely fragile. As a moral, it is banal because it has no real force once it is framed outside the drama that brings it to life. Because the play forces the audience to feel very close to the protagonist and yet to be distanced from him by a greater knowledge that makes his blunders obvious, watching it (or reading it) conveys that fragility so that the message transcends its familiarity.

The end of *Oedipus the King* is strangely inconclusive. Tiresias predicts that the blind Oedipus will wander as a beggar in a foreign land, using a staff to find his way (455–6). Yet in the final scene, Creon first insists on consulting the oracle again about what should be done with Oedipus (1438–9, 1442–3). This is especially striking because there were versions of the story in which Oedipus died at Thebes (the *Iliad* refers in passing to his funeral games, 23.679–80). In Euripides' late play, *Phoenician Women*, Oedipus is driven into exile after his sons kill each other. The conclusion does not indicate exactly what is going to happen.

The plague is forgotten, as Creon, after explaining that he has not come to reproach Oedipus for Oedipus's earlier injustice toward him, insists that such pollution should not be exposed to the light (1424–31). He brings Oedipus's daughters to him, and Oedipus speaks sadly of their likely future as social outcasts (1486–502). Oedipus is not concerned for his sons, who are grown men (1459–61), but he begs Creon to care for his daughters and not allow them, his relatives, to be wandering husbandless beggars (1506). Finally, after Creon promises that if the gods approve, Oedipus will be sent away, Creon takes the girls from him over his protests and they enter the house. The reference to Oedipus's sons avoids any allusion to either their quarrel with each other or Oedipus's curse on them. This curse was found already in the epic and central to Aeschylus's *Seven against Thebes*. At the same time, Oedipus's request to Creon to take care of his daughters points unmistakably back to *Antigone*. The Creon who will not act without another consultation of the oracle is not the same character as the Creon of *Antigone*, but his last act in the play is to separate Oedipus from his daughters, which does not bode well.

The tone of the final scene is hard to judge. Oedipus is still trying to get his way – he has not learned not to be confident about what he believes – but perhaps rightly so. Creon behaves generously, but there is something odd about his worry over polluting the sun when he is not worried about the pollution of Laius's killing. The oracle warning the city to expel Laius's killer seems clear enough. Oedipus first says that he wants to be cast out on Mt. Cithaeron, to die as his parents originally intended, but then considers that he will not die there of illness or by any other predictable cause because he has been kept alive for some terrible evil (1453–7). We might think that what has already happened is enough, but Oedipus is sure that this story is not over.

Insofar as the play teaches its audience about the fragility of mortals, it perhaps allows the ordinary members of the audience some complacency. Because we are not as great as Oedipus, we are unlikely to be targets of the gods. This may be one reason why the play quietly hints at future calamities. Seeing Oedipus reenter the house is a reminder that many more terrible events will take place and that even the careful Creon will be destroyed. Nobody can afford to be smug.

SOURCES AND SUGGESTIONS

Oedipus, for much of the second half of the twentieth century, was the center of a debate between those who admired Sophocles' heroes and thought the tragedies criticized the traditional gods (nicknamed the "hero worshippers"), and those who thought that, on the contrary, the tragedies affirmed traditional religion ("pietists"). The most eloquent version of the hero-worshipping position is Whitman 1951; the best book on the pietist side, especially good on the play's implicit critique of fifth-century rationalism, is Knox 1957. The most famous essay on this play is Dodds 1966; it attacks oversimplifications. While most interpretation in the English-speaking world moved on to other questions starting in the 1970s, R. Griffith 1996 is a pietist interpretation. Winnington-Ingram 1980 is an exceptionally lively study of the Sophoclean hero.

Vernant/Vidal-Nacquet 1981 includes two important essays by Vernant: "Ambiguity and reversal: On the enigmatic structure of *Oedipus Rex*" (87–119) and "Oedipus without the complex" (63–86). The difficulty of the end of the play was brought to the notice of scholars by Taplin 1978, 45–6.

11

HELEN

Helen is one of the tragedies that does not at all conform to expectations of "the tragic." It is, indeed, much closer to a modern idea of comedy (though not to fifth-century Greek comedy). Through the nineteenth century and most of the twentieth, the play was typically dismissed as frivolous and escapist. It is an unusually clear instance of how modern history influences the reading of ancient texts: *Helen* came back into favor in North America very suddenly. In 1967, a commentary by A.M. Dale was published and a German commentary in 1969 by Richard Kannicht, which stressed the antiwar aspect of the play. Then, in the early 1970s, there were three significant articles in three years. Evidently, *Helen*'s treatment of the Trojan War resonated with American disillusionment in Vietnam.[1] There was no corresponding revival in the theater, for *Helen* was not familiar enough, and *Trojan Women* has always been the obvious choice for a director who wants an antiwar tragedy.

Euripides did not invent the variant of the Trojan War story in which Helen never went to Troy but spent the war in Egypt in the care of King Proteus, while an *eidolon*, a fake Helen fashioned by the gods, went to Troy: it went back to the "Palinode" of the lyric poet, Stesichorus. According to legend, he had begun to perform a poem that followed the standard version when Helen – who had the status of a goddess in Sparta – struck him blind. After he wrote the "Palinode," he regained his sight. Euripides referred to the story briefly in his *Electra* (1280–3),

---

[1] Podlecki 1970, Segal 1971 (reprinted in Segal 1986, 222–67), and Wolff 1973.

where the Heavenly Twins explain that Zeus created it in order to cause the Trojan War. *Helen*, though, was probably the first work of Greek literature to consider the implications of this tale in several directions. The play rests on the questions that the story of the phantom prompts. First, whether Helen was a sufficient cause for war was already an issue in Greek literature (in Aeschylus's *Agamemnon*, for example): what would it mean for the Trojan War to have been fought over a phantom? Second, what would it be like for Helen in this situation to know that she had a double that was (deservedly) loathed? Finally, the doubling of real person and *eidolon* offered obvious possibilities for exploration of the favorite fifth-century theme of the contrast between word (*logos*) and reality (*ergon*). Greek intellectuals of this period were fascinated by the philosophical problems created by the inadequacies of perception – if we cannot believe our senses, what basis for knowledge can we have? – and by their recognition that language does not always fit external reality.

These, then, were the issues. Since Menelaus, already in the *Odyssey*, wandered to Egypt after the Trojan War, and Stesichorus probably included a reunion of Helen and Menelaus in his poem, the play could be about the reunion of Helen and Menelaus. But a tragedy required obstacles. The first of these would be Menelaus's belief that Helen was already on board his ship, so that the recognition would be complicated. But a lively plot needed more than that. So Euripides had Proteus die before Menelaus arrives, and invented Theoclymenus, a son of Proteus, who has sexual designs on Helen, and who hates Greeks. Helen thus becomes not only the innocent victim of the gods' decision to start the Trojan War, but a damsel in distress to be rescued by her husband (although, as it turns out, she rescues him as much as he rescues her). Finally, Egypt was a land with which the Greeks were fascinated, and which they saw as peculiarly religious. So Euripides complicated the rescue plot by giving Theoclymenus a sister, Theonoë, with prophetic powers.

This combination creates three difficulties for Menelaus and Helen. First, they must recognize each other. Then, they must get Helen away from Theoclymenus, and that will require deceit. Third, they must prevent Theonoë from betraying their plans. By combining the intrigue plot with the themes of language and reality prompted by the *eidolon*, Euripides concocted an extraordinary mélange – a romantic adventure with philosophical implications. He also decided to exploit the humorous potential in the confusion between Helen and the *eidolon*.

The funniest sequence is the first encounter of Helen and Menelaus. She has heard from Teucer that Menelaus is believed to have perished on the way home from Troy, and while Theoclymenus is away hunting, she has left her usual refuge, the tomb of Proteus (where Theoclymenus does not dare molest her), to ask Theonoë whether Menelaus is alive. Meanwhile, Menelaus, who has been shipwrecked and is wearing not just rags but pieces of torn sail, has come to the palace to seek help and been driven away by an old woman. She has told him that the king hates Greeks, because in his household is Helen, daughter of Zeus, the child of Tyndareus (Helen has both a divine and a mortal father), from Sparta who came from Lacedaemon. Menelaus tries to understand how there could be two women, both named "Helen," both children of someone called "Zeus," from different places called "Sparta" and "Lacedaemon." He finally concludes that there are so many people and places in the world with the same names that the coincidence is not astonishing (483–500). Even though ancient Greeks did not have a modern theory of probability, Menelaus's reasoning is patently ridiculous. Then, as Helen returns to the tomb, she is accosted by Menelaus, a wild-looking man, whom she thinks is trying to catch her for Theoclymenus. (There is a similar sequence in Euripides' *Electra*, when Electra takes Orestes and Pylades for potential rapists.) After reaching the tomb, she gets a better look at her stalker and recognizes Menelaus (560). He, however, sees only a strange woman with an uncanny resemblance to Helen, and refuses to believe that she is Helen even when she explains the truth. The recognition succeeds only when a messenger arrives to announce that Helen has mysteriously disappeared – and turns to Helen to complain that he did not know she could fly, and to tell her that she should not make fun of them this way after all the trouble she caused at Troy (605–21). The comic potential of the two Helens is fully exploited.

Still, although this part of the play is very funny, the jokes have an edge. For one thing, an audience that knows it is watching a tragedy could not simply relax and enjoy how ludicrous it all is, because the tragic style is a constant reminder that there is no guarantee that it will all come out well. To be sure, the style itself contributes to the humor. Menelaus's loss of dignity is ridiculous: he is not an Odysseus, who can be shipwrecked and naked but still know how to maneuver. Menelaus in *Helen* enters in his tattered sails and speaks in tragic clichés, wishing that his ancestor, Pelops, had died before Atreus was born and enumerating his troubles (386–434). Menelaus is clearly an ordinary person who is acutely embarrassed at his situation, and the gap between the pretensions of tragedy and his mediocrity is almost a parody of tragedy itself. (This is a characteristically Euripidean effect.) Still, he is pathetic too. He has overcome his embarrassment to try to beg some help for his men. If he is no great hero, he is clearly a decent leader doing his best. Most importantly, the play never lets the audience forget the Trojan War. Teucer and Helen quickly summarize the misery: Helen, hearing that the city has fallen, says "Wretched Helen, because of you the Trojans perish," and Teucer answers, "And Greeks, too" (109–10). Menelaus refers to the great army he led, all volunteers (393–6). So when Menelaus is confused because there are two Helens, it is absurd but it is also appalling, for the phantom Helen was created by the goddess, Hera, and has been used by Zeus to cause massive and terrible suffering. The *eidolon* is a figure of pure supernatural malice.

The tone of the play fluctuates so that its effects are varied and disconcerting: sad, funny, exciting, and full invitations to philosophical reflection. For example, in the prologue, Helen says that "there is a story" that Zeus came to her mother, Leda, in the form of a swan – "if this account is true" (18–21). Later she says, again with doubt, that Leda gave birth to an egg from which she was born (257–9). There were various stories about Helen's birth, but Euripides selected, and may have invented, this particular variant to make the story as grotesque as possible. Helen's doubts about this story echo contemporary debates about mythological stories: contemporary intellectuals often assumed that they were exaggerated accounts of events that had really happened and so rationalized or allegorized the supernatural parts. This play, though, presents a Helen who is doubtful about the weird story of her birth but whose present situation is the result of divine intervention: Hermes took her invisibly through the sky to Egypt and promised her that, as long as she remained faithful to Menelaus, she would eventually live with him again in Sparta and he would know that she had never gone to Troy. Helen can explain that, in her anger at losing the Judgment of Paris, Hera created the *eidolon*, and that Hera's action coincided with Zeus's decision to cause a great war in order to reduce the burden of human population on the Earth and to give Achilles his opportunity for glory (presumably Hermes told her all this). Helen's skepticism is confined to this particular story, since she has so much direct knowledge of equally peculiar actions by the mythological gods. Helen's doubts about the story of her birth evoke contemporary intellectual speculations that would deny the entire basis of the play. The effect can be similar to that of postmodernist fictions that acknowledge their own fictionality.

The story that Zeus caused the Trojan War to reduce overpopulation was already found in the post-Homeric epic *Cypria*, and Euripides refers to it again in *Orestes* (1639–42). In the *Cypria*, he begat Helen (on the goddess Nemesis, not Leda) for this purpose, and he invited the goddess Strife to throw the golden apple that led to the Judgment of Paris. He did not need to manipulate human beings any further, for the war followed through human folly. Zeus's plan to reduce human population, cruel as it is, is not the result of Zeus's personal concerns but serves the cosmic order. However, Zeus's need to reduce human population could easily be moralized. In the *Orestes*, for example, the number of people is called a *hybrisma*: mortals have become so numerous that they have exceeded their proper limits, and the word may also suggest that they are morally deserving of destruction (especially to an audience that has just seen the play). In *Helen*, however, there is no hint that mortals deserve to be destroyed, and by adding the motive of glorifying Achilles, Euripides threatens to trivialize Zeus's plan. The phantom, furthermore, is created by Hera for purely personal motives.

Paris thinks he has Helen, but he has an "empty fantasy" (35–6; Helen at this point does not know that the war is over and that Paris is dead). Helen's narrative, and the rest of the play, places little blame on the human beings who caused the war but lays much stress on the suffering of the innocent, both Greeks and Trojans. Even when Menelaus says that Paris utterly destroyed his house, Helen agrees and extends the destruction to tens of thousands of Greeks – but the subject of her response is not Paris but "this" (691–2), so that the individual dissolves in the complex web of causes. Whether Helen would have been an adequate cause of war is no longer the real question, since in this version, the war was fought for nothing at all. The issue of human responsibility is muted by the emphasis on the phantom, a very nasty joke played by the gods on humanity.

This intrusion of divine quarrels into human life does not end when the phantom disappears. When Theonoë speaks prophetically to Helen and Menelaus at 878–93, she says that the gods are in disagreement and holding a council: Hera, who was formerly hostile to Helen, wants Helen and Menelaus to reach home, so that everyone will know that Paris's marriage was a fraud. Aphrodite wants them to perish, so that people will not know that she paid for her victory in the Judgment with a spurious marriage. The myth of the Judgment of Paris is bad enough – the goddesses bribe the judge in a beauty contest with no concern for the consequences. The phantom makes it worse – Hera creates it entirely so that Aphrodite will not be able to fulfill her promise. Hera was not really hostile to Helen before or "well disposed" (881) to her now – Helen is only an instrument. This is probably the harshest view of the gods in tragedy, since they do not care about mortals at all.

Yet Theonoë ends her speech with a remarkable pronouncement. The decision is up to her, not, as the audience would expect, to Zeus (887–91). If she tells her brother who Menelaus is, Menelaus will be killed and Aphrodite will win. If she sides will Hera and keeps the secret, Helen and Menelaus will escape. The relationship between Theonoë's decision and that of the gods' council is not clear, but in the rest of the scene, Helen and Menelaus plead with Theonoë, and she decides to save them. The dispute among the goddesses is not mentioned again except in Helen's prayer to both Hera and Aphrodite as she goes to prepare herself for the deception of Theoclymenus (1093–106; her prayer to Aphrodite is more a reproach than a request). The Twins declare in the final epiphany that Helen "must remain in her marriage" and go home with her husband (1654–5). Nothing explains whether that *must* indicates that this outcome was always fated, or was the will of Zeus, or is the morally right end. Theonoë's decision matters, and the rest is obscure. So it may be significant that there is one passage that explicitly criticizes the choice to fight the Trojan War, in the second antistrophe of the first stasimon (1151–64), after Theonoë has made her decision and after Helen and Menelaus have planned their deceit. In this song, the chorus directly criticizes war as a way of ending disputes and says that the Trojan conflict should have been resolved diplomatically. It is as if human responsibility has been restored. However, the traditional criticism of the Trojan War was not that a peaceful settlement was not attempted (it was, but Paris prevented it) but that the Greeks should have realized that Helen was not worth it.

The stasimon, though (which also expresses great perplexity about the gods), makes a significant point: "you are foolish who acquire glory for achievements through war and the points of the strong spear, stupidly bringing your efforts to their end by death" (1151–4).[2] Whether a particular war is justified or necessary, the chorus finds the pursuit of military glory stupid. Both glory and the necessity of violence run uneasily through the play. Zeus evidently endorses the ideal of glory in war, since he caused the Trojan War in part in order to give Achilles the chance to win it. When Helen and Menelaus discuss what they will do if Theonoë does not help them, they join in a suicide pact, and Menelaus slips into pointless bluster, offering to fight any challenger and refusing to shame his Trojan fame (843–51). The passage is bitterly funny, since Menelaus lists some of those who died – Achilles, Ajax, Nestor's son Antilochus – and asks rhetorically whether he will not think it right to die for his wife. It is as if he has forgotten that these

---

[2] The text of 1154 is uncertain.

heroes died for his wife – except that they actually died for an illusion in the form of his wife.

The plan to escape has Helen trick Theoclymenus into thinking that Menelaus is a survivor of Menelaus's ship who has seen him drown. Before marrying Theoclymenus, she wants to conduct a funeral ritual at sea. Menelaus's men are invited to assist, and when the ship is at sea, Menelaus and his followers attack. Helen urges them to show the glory they won at Troy against the barbarians (1603–4). They kill the Egyptians and steal the ship. After all the emphasis on the sadness of military violence, while some spectators could doubtless see the Egyptians as cardboard enemies who can be killed without scruple, like the enemy troopers in *Star Wars*, some might wonder whether this is such a wonderful success for the Greeks. No resolution without violence would be possible, however. Theoclymenus would not be persuaded to let Helen go home. So the chorus may be naïve in imagining that words would have made the Trojan War unnecessary. At the end of the play, when the Heavenly Twins appear to stop Theoclymenus from killing Theonoë (and the women of the chorus, who are trying to stop him), Castor explains that they would saved their sister sooner but had to yield to fate and the gods who decided "that these things would be so" (1658–61) – but he does not say when they made this decision.

In this play, then, human beings are both terribly deluded by the gods and easy victims of deceit and their own posturing. The messenger comments at the end of his report, "Nothing is more useful for mortals than a *sôphrôn* mistrust" (1617–18). Only a prophet like Theonoë has the ability to distinguish appearance from reality, word from deed. When Teucer, who has come seeking Theonoë's advice on how to find his way to Cyprus, sees Helen, he says that although she looks like Helen, she has proved to have a very different mind, and he wishes that Helen die miserably but the woman to whom he is speaking have good fortune (160–3). Helen herself cannot entirely sustain the distinction between herself and her reputation; at 52, she speaks of those who died "because of me"; at 198–9, she sings about the fall of Troy "because of me, the killer of many, because of my name, cause of many miseries." Teucer tells her that Leda has committed suicide in her shame, and

Helen feels guilt even though it is in no way her fault – at 280, she calls herself her mother's "murderer," and at 687, she sings that her mother hanged herself "because of the shame of my bad marriage." It is just too difficult to keep them clearly separate, partly because the evil done by the phantom depends on the beauty of Helen. Helen's body exposes her to this confusion. Helen brings together her strange birth (if true) and the miseries that her beauty has caused to call herself a *teras*, a freak of nature and a supernatural sign, and to wish that she could wipe her beauty away as if it were paint (256–66). Reasonable action would seem impossible in such confusion.

Yet once Menelaus recognizes the real Helen, they conduct a successful intrigue. After the profound deceptions of the phantom, an ordinary deceit of one person by another is reassuring because only somebody who knows what is true can actually lie. Theoclymenus is a perfect victim. The play takes different Greeks ideas about Egypt specifically and non-Greeks generally and simply divides them between Proteus and Theonoë, who are mysteriously close to the gods, pure and wise, and Theoclymenus, who is a bully. Helen sees herself as enslaved because in a monarchy only the ruler is free (273–6), and the monarch's attempt to force an unwilling woman to marry him fits the Greek stereotype of the tyrant. So it was eminently satisfying for him to be outwitted by more intelligent Greeks.

The intrigue is Helen's work. In another comic sequence, Menelaus proposes two possible ways of escape, but Helen shows that each is impractical: Theonoë will not permit them to kill Theoclymenus, and, while they could obtain a chariot, they would not know where to go (1033–48). Menelaus's suggestions are straightforward; Helen proposes a deception that will win them a ship. It creates yet another division between word and reality, as Menelaus will "be said to have died, in word, without having died" (the phrase is significant enough to appear twice, at 1050 and 1052). It is as if Helen, who has known for so long that her suffering was caused by such a confusion, is primed to see how she can use a similar falsehood, and as if the two will be a more fully matched couple when Menelaus, too, has been doubled. During the intrigue, the real Menelaus shadows the false, dead Menelaus. The resourceful, clever Helen is a benign version of Medea, a woman who uses her seductive powers to save her marriage.

The other savior in the play is Theonoë. She is a remarkable Euripidean synthesis. Her extraordinary piety and concern for purity exploit Greeks ideas about Egypt as the most religious place in the world, and probably Herodotus's belief that the mysteries connected with Dionysus and Orpheus were of Egyptian origin (2.81). However, the gods to whom she refers are Greek. Indeed, the play's Egypt is a peculiarly undefined place. The opening lines refer to Anaxagoras's theory about the cause of the Nile flood – one of the great popular scientific debates of the day – but otherwise Theonoë is the only Egyptian feature of the play. There are no Egyptian customs or landmarks. Even the actual location of the drama is vague: somewhere near the sea at one of the mouths of the Nile. In Euripides' time, Egypt had been part of the Persian Empire since 525 BCE and there was no pharaoh, but Herodotus had written at length about the geography, history, and customs of Egypt, information the play does not use. Instead, Theonoë combines a loosely Egyptian need for purity – she even has the space in front of the palace purified with fire and sulphur before she goes outside (865–70) – with contemporary Greek philosophical thought. She needs the air purified so that she can receive pure breath, which probably alludes to the theories of Diogenes of Apollonia, who thought that Air – which, after all, people breathe – was the substance of the mind. Diogenes was the philosopher implicated in the scene in Aristophanes' *Clouds* in which Socrates is suspended in a basket so that he can think better in purer air (223–35).

Theonoë's explanation of why she has decided to keep the secret brings together a variety of ideas. She does not want to "pollute" the fame of her father or to lose her own good reputation (999–1002). She also upholds the Greek aristocratic belief that virtue is inherited, and sounds almost like Hippolytus:

> There is a great sanctuary of Justice within me – in my nature. And having this from Nereus, Menelaus, I shall try to preserve it. (1002–4)

Although she is far more careful than Hippolytus, scrupulously apologizing to Aphrodite, she also adduces her desire to remain a virgin and her lack of affinity for that goddess to explain her decision (1005–8). But finally, she mentions the danger of punishment in an afterlife for wrongdoing:

> For there is requital for these things both for those below and for all human beings above. The mind of the dead does not live, but it has immortal awareness falling into immortal aether. (1013–16)

This is an extremely confusing passage: what exactly are "above" and "below" here, if the dead become part of the immortal upper air? However, it sounds very much as if Theonoë is, in a very abbreviated way, engaging in a recognizable intellectual practice of the late fifth century, combining the doctrines of mystery religion about the afterlife with philosophical speculations about air. This is what the treatise known as the Derveni Papyrus, whose text is close in date to *Helen*, does.[3] It is hard to see how her rarified beliefs can cohere with goddesses who quarrel or with a decision of Zeus to reduce the population by causing the Trojan War.

While Egypt is vague in the play, Sparta is a real place. This is significant, since in 412 BCE when it was produced, Athens was again openly at war with Sparta. Although extant tragedy can present Menelaus as stereotypically bullying, nasty Spartan (Menelaus in both Sophocles' *Ajax* and Euripides' *Andromache*), he is not one in this play. Helen is homesick for Sparta, and references to Sparta are designed to allow the audience to sympathize with her longing to go home. Helen laments that her brothers have left the gymnasia by the "reedy Eurotas" (209–10): the Heavenly Twins, Castor and Polydeuces, were revered across the Greek world, especially as helpers in peril at sea, while the river, Eurotas, was always closely associated with the city. The chorus laments that Helen will not make blessed "the goddess of the Bronze House" (228) – Athena, whose famous temple at Sparta was known as

---

3 Betegh 2004.

the Bronze House. When the chorus imagines Helen's return, they see her as joining the daughters of Leucippus (the wives of her brothers) by the Eurotas or before Athena's temple, or as participating in the revels of the Hyacinthia. These are among the most famous landmarks and holy spaces of Sparta, and they are part of the audience's sense of the sacred landscape of Greece. Sparta in the play is not Athens' enemy, but one of the ancient centers of a shared culture. Helen at the conclusion is promised a share in the cult of her brothers, with a specific allusion to the ritual called *Xenia* (1667–9). Stesichorus first created the Helen-in-Egypt version to appease the divine Helen; by referring to her divine status at Sparta, the play locates itself within Spartan tradition.

Also at the end of the play, the Heavenly Twins announce that an island off the coast of Attica will henceforth be called "Helen" (1670–5). Such naming, like the proclamation of future cult, is one of Euripides' regular ways of linking the past of his plays to the world of his audience, but this one is odd – while the island might be a plausible stop on the way from Sparta to Troy, it is a very eccentric choice for rest when Hermes is flying with Helen to Egypt. The poet seems to have been determined to connect his play not only to Sparta but to Attica. The play seems to be attempting to remind its audience that these stories formed a shared past for all Greeks.

It is hard to know, however, exactly what to do with these hints. When Greeks argued that Greeks should not fight each other, they typically said not that they should avoid war but that they should unite against their foreign enemies. The Trojan War was the great mythical example of Hellenic unity against barbarians. In *Helen*, though, the Trojan War is fought for a phantom, while Greek unity is no more than an inference from shared reverence for holy places and a shared mythic past. The play is a puzzle with no easy answer.

SOURCES AND SUGGESTIONS

Besides the three articles that initiated the revival of interest in the play, see Wright 2005 and Holmberg 1995.

12

ORESTES

Orestes, produced in 408 BCE, was one of the most popular of all trage-dies in antiquity, often reperformed in the Hellenistic period. It is, how-ever, not an edifying play. The characters are not heroic or virtuous, and they move through a world in which people do not act out of a sense of honor or justice but in pursuit of ordinary self-interest or political partisanship. Furthermore, too much happens. It may seem a surpris-ing complaint about a plot that is so meticulously constructed, but the play lacks conventional unity – its main character is not consistent, and its tone varies wildly from scene to scene. *Orestes* is about people who are desperate, and in their desperation, they grab at one possible solution to their situation after another. At its end, Apollo appears from the machine. Usually, the final appearance of a god clarifies what has happened already and predicts the future of the characters, but in this play (as in Sophocles' *Philoctetes*), the god must move the characters in a new direction. *Orestes* was neglected or treated with hostility in the nineteenth century. It was easily put into what I have called "The Story," an instance of Euripidean decadence. The play began to receive more sympathetic attention in the second half of the twentieth cen-tury, when the moral confusion of late Euripides seemed to parallel the difficulties of modernity, and the play's reworkings of earlier versions attracted readers interested in intertextuality.

The play is set during a gap that Euripides has created in the tradi-tional story. Orestes has killed his mother and is being pursued by the Erinyes, who are strongly psychologized and hard to distinguish from his own feelings of guilt. In earlier versions, including Euripides' own

Electra, Orestes went to Delphi immediately after the murders. Here, however, he is still in Argos five days later, suffering attacks of madness and, between them sick and weak, cared for by his sister, Electra. Meanwhile, the people of Argos are treating Orestes and Electra as murderers: they have been banned from contact with the people, and the city is about to vote on whether they should be stoned. Electra herself calls Apollo "unjust" for telling Orestes to kill his mother, a deed "that does not bring glory in everyone's eyes" (30). The only hope Electra and Orestes have lies in their uncle, Menelaus, who has just returned from his wanderings at Troy and has sent Helen ahead by night for fear that she would be stoned by the people if she came. So Helen is in the palace, mourning her sister, but happy at being reunited with her daughter, Hermione. While Helen in her play doubts the fabulous story of her birth, Electra hesitates to call her father, Agamemnon, "glorious" (17) and her opening narrative stresses how much of the story is inappropriate for her to talk about (14, 16, 25–6).

So from the very start, we are in a more "realist" and clearly a more "political" world than in most tragedies. Popular anger about the Trojan War expresses itself not just in murmured resentment, as in *Agamemnon*, but is an immediate threat. The city apparently has functioning democratic institutions. Elsewhere the play refers to "Agamemnon's scepter," but it appears to be in the gift of the Argive assembly (437). The constitution of Argos is extremely unclear. We are also immediately placed in a story that unpleasantly doubles the one we know. Orestes is supposed to be tried at Athens, but here he is apparently to be tried at Argos. Menelaus seems to have replaced Apollo as a possible savior.

This impression that actions familiar to the audience from other tragedies are being repeated is immediately confirmed when Helen enters. Helen, after inquiring about Orestes' and Electra's well-being, asks Electra to carry offerings to her sister's tomb on her behalf, since she is embarrassed and afraid to go out herself. This strongly recalls Clytemnestra's sending of Electra with offerings for Agamemnon in Aeschylus's *Libation Bearers*, where Electra turns the ritual against Clytemnestra. The scene is a display of social and ritual ineptitude.

Helen first addresses Electra as "girl long unmarried" (72) but is at first reluctant to send Hermione because unmarried girls should not go out in public (108), showing that she regards Electra as no longer capable of being married (so that her reputation does not matter) and that she is completely insensitive to how inappropriate such an errand would be. Meanwhile, Electra makes a dig at Helen, who only now feels normal social shame, and Helen answers, "You are right, but what you are saying is not friendly to me" (99–100). Helen tells Hermione to ask Clytemnestra's sprit to be kind to Helen, Hermione herself, Menelaus, and Electra and Orestes "whom a god destroyed" (119–21), but she does not win Electra over. Electra comments that Helen has in mourning cut only the tips of her hair, so as not to spoil her beauty (128–9), and then worries that the chorus of women, about to enter, will awaken Orestes. Many such passages in late Euripides come close to satire or comedy of manners (in *Electra* and *Ion*, for example). When Electra calls her "the woman she was long ago" (129), she also recalls by contrast the Helen of *Helen* from 412 BCE, who does cut her hair as part of the escape plot (and whom Aristophanes called "the new Helen" at *Women at the Thesmophoria*, 850). At the same time, the sending of Hermione in Electra's presence prepares for Electra's later suggestion that Hermione be used as a hostage. The little incident is what specialists in narrative call a "seed," a detail that becomes more significant than it at first appears to be.

The following scene with Orestes (211–315), however, is utterly different in tone. Orestes awakes, weak and sick, and Electra cares for him and tells him the news that Menelaus is coming. He suffers an attack of the Erinyes and thinks Electra is one of them. In Stesichorus's *Oresteia*, Apollo promised Orestes a bow that would ward off the Furies; here, he demands the bow (probably as invisible as the Erinyes) and fights them off. Recovering, he blames Apollo who told him to commit the deed and has not helped him, and expresses much concern for Electra, who in turn insists on her dependence on Orestes. The scene is serious and moving.

The chorus prays for Orestes and sings in sympathy for him (316–55). Menelaus, when he enters, is shocked at Orestes' appearance (385).

In a long stichomythia, he learns about his condition and about the danger that threatens him. In the city, the hatred against him is being fanned by Oeax, the brother of Palamedes (432), who was unjustly condemned to death at Troy, and by friends of Aegisthus (435). Orestes is pleading for Menelaus's help when Tyndareus, the father of Helen and Clytemnestra, enters (470). Tyndareus is in some ways the very embodiment of a rational restraint. He argues that Orestes should have prosecuted his mother not killed her; he praises Greek traditions of exiling murderers rather than pursuing blood feuds, and he condemns Clytemnestra. Yet he says all this in a style that is completely inflexible and self-righteous, criticizing Menelaus for even speaking to Orestes, claiming that he has "turned barbarian" by being among barbarians (485). Orestes, who has seemed thus far overwhelmed by guilt, suddenly defends himself (544–604). It is not perhaps so psychologically implausible that he should try to defend himself because everyone else has seen him as pitiable, while Tyndareus shows not the slightest sympathy. Strangely, however, he does not address Tyndareus's crucial point, that he should have prosecuted his mother and driven her out of his house. Instead, he argues in terms familiar from the *Oresteia*: he would have been pursued by his father's Furies if he had not taken revenge; he prevented the dangerous precedent of allowing a woman to escape after killing her husband; he did what Apollo told him to do. Orestes could have argued that he could not practically have done what Tyndareus wanted – that, for example, his mother would have killed him had he given her any opportunity – but he does not.

This debate seems to function completely separately on two different levels. At the emotional and dramatic level, the only argument that makes any difference is that Orestes actually blames Tyndareus for begetting Clytemnestra (585–7). Tydareus is furious that he dares defend himself at all (607–9). He announces that he will attend the assembly and do his best to secure the condemnation of Orestes and Electra, whom he hates even more than Orestes. At this emotional level, it hardly matters what the characters say but only that Tyndareus attacks Orestes and that he responds. Tyndareus overtly addresses most of his speech to Menelaus (he briefly speaks to Orestes, forgetting his pollution in his anger at 526–35). At this level, the debate is a realistic depiction of speakers who move to more extreme positions as they react to each other and to their own rhetoric.

Intellectually, though, Orestes' speech does not even try to persuade Tyndareus, and it is not clear that it is really aimed at Menelaus either. The play's vagueness about the constitution of Argos is crucial here. Tyndareus speaks as if Argos is very much like Athens, while Orestes speaks as if it is the Mycenae of Aeschylus. Later, in the Argive assembly, Orestes repeats his argument that the murder of Clytemnestra was a beneficial deterrent, but nobody says that Orestes should have found a way to punish his mother without killing her; it does not seem to be a meaningful argument at Argos. The effect is very odd (the nearest parallel is in Sophocles' *Electra*). The speeches allow the audience to recognize that Orestes' dilemma arises from the absence of the institutions Tyndareus says he could have used.

But when Tyndareus exits, warning Menelaus not to help Orestes, it is as if the debate begins again, because now Orestes pleads with Menelaus to help him, and his arguments are utterly different from those he used with Tyndareus. Now he admits that he is in the wrong but argues that Agamemnon committed injustice for his brother, going to war for an inadequate cause and sacrificed his daughter, so that Menelaus should repay him by supporting Orestes and Electra (640–79). Menelaus, in reply, says that he would like to help but has no troops, so he will try to persuade Tyndareus and the city but can do no more – and he turns to exit (680–716). Menelaus betrays Orestes not so much by what he says as by this action. Menelaus apparently leaves down one of the parodoi, following Tyndareus, and as Orestes expresses his despair, Pylades comes down the other (717–28). The meter changes to trochaic tetrameters, which indicate greater excitement and speed, as Orestes greets his friend and explains the situation. Pylades, who has been exiled by his father, acts as a loyal friend and helps Orestes make his way to address the assembly. We seem to have returned to a world of heroic values where a man is loyal to a friend in need.

At this point, the chorus sings its second stasimon. The strophe considers that the prosperity and proud valor of the family are now shifting away from good fortune under the influence of the old calamities of the house (807–18). In the antistrophe, the chorus recalls Clytemnestra's plea to her son; matricide, the women believe, is madness (819–30). The epode begins:

> What disease or what tears and what pity is greater in the world than to put blood shed in matricide on one's hand? (831–3)

The messenger speech narrating the assembly includes an unusual number of judgments, and because the messenger is deeply loyal to Agamemnon, it is hard to know whether the audience ought to resist accepting them (866–956). But there can be no question that the assembly does not represent a wise community in which each speaker seeks the best solution for the common good. The first speaker is Talthybius, the herald, a familiar character from epic and from other tragedies, and he speaks against Orestes, though he wildly praises Agamemnon, always with an eye on the friends of Aegisthus (887–97). Then Diomedes, an important hero though not one we would expect to find in the assembly of Argos (traditionally he comes from the same area but has his own independent realm), and urges that Orestes and Electra be exiled (898–900). Then a dema-gogue calls for the stoning of Electra and Orestes, actually speak-ing for Tyndareus (914–15). Then a small farmer praises Orestes, and warns that Clytemnestra's actions threatened the security of the city by making men unwilling to leave home on campaign (917–30). So up to this point there are four speakers (884–930), and both of those who call for Orestes' and Electra's death are really speaking not for themselves but in someone else's interests. Orestes then argues that he served the community as a whole by showing that women cannot murder men with impunity (931–42), but he does not persuade the assembly, except that he wins permission for them to kill themselves. Orestes and Pylades leave the assembly accompanied by weeping "friends" (950–1). These would seem to be political "friends," mem-bers of a pro-Orestes faction, since the play gives no hint that Orestes has real friends other than Pylades.

After a choral song, Electra sings an astonishing lament in which she wishes she could go into the sky to tell Tantalus all the sufferings of the family (982–1012). The monody includes a quick, impressionistic history of the disastrous history of the descendents of Tantalus (the song would be incomprehensible to anyone who did not know these stories, but they were very familiar). However, it combines this mythology with science: the rock that Tantalus fears seems to be the sun in the cosmology of Anaxagoras. In the traditional story, Zeus reversed the sun's course to honor Atreus's claim to the kingship, or in horror at Atreus's or Thyestes' crimes, as a one-time miracle. Here, Strife (a cosmic force in the philosophy of Empedocles) apparently causes the sun permanently to move eastward along the ecliptic (the Sun's path through the Zodiac) although the sun goes westward during the day, a topic studied by Euripides' contemporary, the mathematician Oenopides of Chios. While scholars disagree about exactly what this passage means (the text is also problematic), it is clearly steeped in contemporary science.[1] Two very different ways of thinking about the world are recklessly combined, so that in the same song, the Sun has a chariot and so must be a god, and is also a rock carried in the celestial vortex. Both mythology and science, however, operate through inexorable processes. Electra does not see her misfortune as contingent or as dependant on her choices and those of others but as inevitable.

The ensuing discussion among Pylades, Orestes, and Electra is the turning point of the play. First, as they discuss how they should die, Orestes notes that they have little chance of a shared tomb, since they lack friends to bury them, and this prompts Electra to ask about Menelaus's failure to help and Orestes to speculate that he deliberately did not help them so that he could take power in Argos. This leads to his request to Pylades to care for their funeral (1051–68). Pylades first insists on dying with his friends, and then suggests that they could take revenge on Menelaus before they die by murdering Helen. He presents a plan for the murder and an argument in its favor: everyone hates Helen, so that by killing her, they can cancel the public obloquy

[1] The ecliptic: Morrison 1970; doubtful: Egli 2003, 58–69.

of the matricide. If they cannot kill Helen, he proposes, they can burn down the palace (1098–152). This is the first stage of their descent into wild destructiveness – they hope that another murder will excuse the first. Then, Orestes, happy at the thought of making Menelaus miserable, comments that if only they could be saved, they would be positively fortunate (1172–6). This prompts Electra to suggest that they take Hermione – who is completely innocent – as a hostage, to force Menelaus to save them.

None of these three would create such an appalling scheme alone. The assembly's verdict left them helpless, but by creating this scheme, they enable themselves to escape passivity and recover control. It is a complete reversal from the mood of Electra's song. They visibly cheer up as they plan. Apollo's oracle was the impulse for their first killing, while here it is the isolation; once they begin to see a way that they can overcome their sense of utter defeat, each eggs on the others, and none of them considers anything but the plan itself. If killing Helen is supposed somehow to compensate for killing Clytemnestra, they do not consider whether they will be admired if they kill Hermione also.

The revenge plot resumes the repetition–compulsion of the beginning but with a new twist. The *Oresteia* suggested that judicial processes would end the cycle of revenge. In *Orestes*, this mechanism fails. The assembly's verdict does not end violence but starts it again. However, what continues is not the standard cycle of retaliation. Instead, the murder of Clytemnestra is repeated in the attack on Helen, because Orestes, Electra, and Pylades see Menelaus's failure to help them as an offense deserving vengeance just as an overt act of violence would be, and because they grant the assembly no special legitimacy. Euripides often creates characters whose suffering and victimization makes them resentful and potentially cruel, ready to avenge themselves on the innocent (Hermione in *Andromache*, for example, who blames the failure of her marriage on her husband's slave concubine). Those who seem helpless are the most ferocious in revenge if an opportunity presents itself (as in *Medea* and *Hecuba*).

So the friends have become conspirators and terrorists. Scholars disagree about the relevance to the play of Thucydides' discussion of the civil war at Corcyra (3.82–3), in which the faction became more important than all other loyalties or values. The similarity should not be pushed too far, but there is a real similarity in atmosphere.[2] It was already clear in the first part of the play that when Orestes was in the company only of Electra and the women of the chorus, who sympathize with him, he was paralyzed by guilt, but when others asserted his guilt, he defended himself. Now this pattern is extended to Electra and Pylades. The assembly works to polarize the two groups, so that Orestes and his friends no longer feel guilty for the matricide.

Precisely because the play has made the heroic world so politically similar to his own, and his characters have been sympathetic without being heroic, the progress of the episode suggests that this could happen to anyone. While Orestes initially will not assist Electra in dying, because his mother's blood is enough to have on his head (1039–40), by the end of the scene, the prospect of more murder seems to make him gleeful. Each step leads to the next. Discussion of the funeral leads Electra to ask about Menelaus, and Orestes' view of his treachery prompts Pylades' idea of revenge. This lightens Orestes' spirits enough that he fantasizes that there might be a possibility of survival after all, and that in turn causes Electra to suggest the kidnapping of Hermione. Once they start on this path, they simply continue. The Orestes who needed physical support from Pylades to go to the assembly (799–800) is now able to fight energetically, and he has no further visits from the Erinyes. Action is medicinal.

The plan is no sooner formulated than it is carried out; Orestes and Pylades go inside while Electra has the chorus stand guard. Helen cries out for help inside, while Hermione returns from the tomb. Electra asks her to plead with her mother to persuade Menelaus to help her and Orestes, and Hermione readily agrees, entering the house to be captured. The plan seems to be going "well."

Instead of a messenger to report what happened during the attack on Helen, one of her Phrygian slaves (i.e. from Troy, possibly a eunuch – this

---

[2] Longo 1975; Rawson 1972, 160–2. West 1987, 36–7, denies the connection. Porter 1994, 327–32, is balanced.

is not quite clear) comes out and sings about the event. This is the song most strongly influenced by the "New Music" in Euripides. The song advertises that it is Asian, foreign (for example, 1396–8). It mixes apostrophes to Troy and Troy's gods with a subjective account of how the slaves were fanning Helen when Orestes and Pylades entered to supplicate her. Orestes lured her to the hearth while Pylades locked most of the attendants in other parts of the house, and then they attacked. The slaves managed to break out and try to defend Helen, but they were weak compared to Orestes and Pylades. Helen disappeared, and the Phrygian has fled. Orestes follows in pursuit, fearing that the slave will raise a hue and cry – but after sparing the slave, whom it would be beneath him to kill, he declares that he is not afraid of Menelaus before he goes back into the house. The episode is disconcerting in various ways. The slave is such a crude caricature of a cowardly Asian that his pleas for his life are almost funny, even as the chauvinism makes a modern reader cringe – but they are at least straightforward pleas. Orestes' contempt for the slave does not go well with his own willingness to threaten Hermione with death to save his own life, while an armed Orestes' threats to kill an unarmed man who is lying on the ground before him are unheroic.

When Menelaus appears, he has heard the Phrygian's song but does not believe that Helen vanished; he wants revenge for her and for Hermione (1561–6), and is astonished when the conspirators appear on the roof with his daughter. Orestes now demands not only that his life be saved but also that he become the ruler of Argos (1600–6). The extremes have become ever more extreme, so that the Orestes who was tormented by guilt at the beginning of the play now feels no remorse whatever and no concern about his ritual pollution. Their exchange is pointed, even darkly funny in its wit. When Menelaus finally cries "you've got me" (1617), Orestes orders the burning of the palace – whether as a bluff or because Menelaus's surrender does not mean that he will help but that he sees Hermione as doomed. Menelaus calls for help from the citizens – and Apollo, accompanied by Helen, appears on the machine. It is a very crowded and complex scene: the chorus in the *orchestra*; then Menelaus with his attendants and probably armed

Argives who respond to his call; then the conspirators on the roof, probably with attendants holding torches; then Apollo and Helen above.

Apollo quickly restores mythological order. Helen will be deified and protect sailors; Menelaus will rule Sparta; Orestes will go into exile for a year, then be tried at Athens, and he will marry Hermione (Apollo summarily dismisses the plot of Euripides' own *Andromache* at 1654–7) and rule in Argos; Pylades will marry Electra and live happily ever after. Everyone immediately acquiesces (as tragic characters do when a god appears) as though the play has been a nightmare and Apollo has allowed them all to wake up.

Orestes is crammed with surprises partly because it constantly invokes other versions, especially Aeschylus's, but refuses to follow the familiar story. Furthermore, even in the prologue, Electra is uncertain about or does not want to talk about much of the story she tells. The play thereby invites the audience to see it as a construct and to be continually aware that it is a fiction. At the same time, the excitement of the plot does not allow the spectator to be detached.

The thrill ride of a plot should be central to interpreting the play. As long as the audience believes that the prospect of revenge and possible survival could revive the pathetic Orestes of the first part of the play, everything, except the supernatural rescue of Helen, proceeds according to Aristotle's requirement of "probability or necessity" – even, given the conventions of Greek tragedy, Apollo's final epiphany. Since Apollo initiated this entire series of events by telling Orestes to kill his mother, he has a responsibility to end the havoc this command has caused. Given these characters in this setting, Menelaus would not help Orestes, being intimidated by Tyndareus and perhaps driven by his own ambitions; Orestes, Electra, and Pylades would react to the assembly's condemnation by seeking vengeance on Menelaus. At the same time, the play's surprises would seem to be the point. Like most tragedies, it works not by conveying a message easy to paraphrase, but by presenting a series of events at once unlikely and inevitable, both obviously invented out of other tragedies and completely absorbing.

The anachronisms, which push the world of the play closer to that of the audience, force a real question. Sophocles' *Philoctetes*, produced the year before *Orestes*, showed a young man, Neoptolemus, torn between a "modern" political operator, Odysseus, and the old-fashioned heroic values of valor and straightforwardness represented by Neoptolemus's dead father, Achilles, and by Philoctetes. In the end, he chooses Philoctetes, and Heracles, as *deus ex machina*, affirms their friendship. In *Orestes*, nobody successfully follows heroic models, both because these are not heroic characters and because their milieu is not heroic. If *Philoctetes* insisted that the old aristocratic ideals still had meaning, *Orestes* seems to question whether there is any useful way to adapt them to contemporary conditions. Such questioning might seem to undermine the very basis of tragedy, which assumed that the old stories shown in a grand style were meaningful – but the question did not mean that Euripides, or his audience, believed that there was no answer.

SOURCES AND SUGGESTIONS

Porter 1994 is a careful study of the play, which includes a full discussion of earlier work, but it is for scholars, with untranslated quotations from both ancient and modern languages. West 1987 has an introduction and extensive notes. Burnett 1971 has two chapters on *Orestes* (183–222), in which she argues that the main characters are impious in not trusting Apollo. There are two important papers on *Orestes* in Mossman 2003; Karl Reinhardt's "The Intellectual Crisis in Euripides" (16–47; originally published in German in 1957), and Froma Zeitlin's "The Closet of Masks: Role-Playing and Myth-making in the *Orestes* of Euripides" (309–41; originally published in *Ramus* 9 [1980] 51–77). Reinhardt's sees Euripides as a spokesman for the sophistic generation and compares him to Kafka; Zeitlin's explores the play's intertextualities. Also relevant for Orestes in that volume is Winnington-Ingram's "Euripides: *Poiêtês Sophos*" (47–63; originally *Arethusa* 2 [1969], 127–42).

13

TRAGIC MOMENTS

A. COMPARING THE TRAGEDIANS

How can we usefully compare the tragedians without slipping into The Story? There are significant differences in their individual styles – in the language of their dialogue, in their songs, and in their dramatic practice – and Greek tragedy did have a history, even though we do not have enough knowledge to reconstruct it in any detail. Neither Sophocles nor Euripides (as far as we know) composed very long songs like the *parodos* of *Agamemnon*, for example. Aeschylus seems to have preferred "simple" plots, in which there is a single source of dramatic action and the focus does not change. All three tragedians composed tragedies of this kind, such as Sophocles' *Oedipus Rex* and *Philoctetes*, or Euripides' *Medea* and *Bacchae*, but Sophocles also wrote tragedies like *Antigone*, where the center moves from Antigone to Creon, while Euripides wrote plays like *Andromache* and *Orestes*, which radically change direction.

There are also similarities. Euripides' *Hippolytus* and Sophocles' *Women of Trachis* have similar structures, in which a woman who is the initial focus of audience sympathy causes the suffering and death of a man who becomes the center of the last part of the play, but the two characters have no direct contact. One may have influenced the other, but such structures may have been common. The tragedians' interactions with each other were complex. Euripides used the *deus ex machina* frequently. In the surviving plays of Sophocles, the device is used only once, in *Philoctetes*. As in Euripides' *Orestes*, in *Philoctetes*, the characters are taking the story in a direction opposite to the one the myth demands, and the divine intervention restores mythological order; yet the effect is not the same as it is in Euripides, since most spectators and readers feel that the ending is "right" instead of imposed. Neither is per se better, but the emotion and intellectual responses they provoke are very different.

Since both Sophocles and Euripides composed Electra tragedies during the same period, probably in response to a reproduction of Aeschylus's *Libation Bearers* in the late 420s, comparing these three plays is an obvious and traditional way to look at the three poets. Each play, for example, handles recognition distinctively, and these differences are typical of the author.

The focal character of Aeschylus's play is Orestes. He appears first, and he watches as the chorus performs its entry song, accompanied by Electra. Clytemnestra, worried by a bad dream, has sent her with offerings to the ghost of Agamemnon. Electra asks the women's advice about what to do with her mother's offerings, and follows it in praying for revenge. Then she sees the lock of hair Orestes has left on Agamemnon's tomb, and matches both the hair and Orestes' footprint to her own. Orestes reveals himself and overcomes Electra's doubts by showing her a piece of her own weaving.

These proofs are not "realistic," especially the matching footprints. Yet they work dramatically and symbolically. The matching hair and footprints emphasize the biological tie between brother and sister, while the weaving implies that Electra is a "normal" Greek woman (since producing cloth was one of the most important women's tasks) and gives Orestes an ongoing connection to his family even though his mother is his enemy. The spectator is unlikely to ask why Orestes waits so long to reveal himself. For much of the scene, Electra is conducting a ritual, and rituals should not be interrupted, while once she sees Orestes' lock of hair on the tomb, the spectator knows that the recognition is about to happen.

Aeschylus's handling of the recognition is not complicated, but there is nothing primitive about it. It is typical of the ruthlessness of his dramaturgy that, once Orestes explains his plan for killing Aegisthus (he says nothing about his mother, and his silence generates suspense and unease), he sends her back to the house with very general instructions to make sure all runs smoothly (579–80). She then disappears from the play, where she is not needed; she might have served to cast doubt on whether Clytemnestra had ever been a "real" mother to Orestes, but the Nurse does that more effectively. The concerns of *Libation Bearers* are the terror of matricide, the recurrent cycle of revenge, the divine forces that drive Orestes, and the oppression from which he frees his household and city, all woven into its suspenseful action. Electra is minor.

Because Aeschylus had done this sequence so effectively, Sophocles and Euripides evidently both felt a challenge to handle it very differently. First, both made Electra the central character, very much as authors in recent times have often reworked familiar stories by changing the focus. Each, however, then made very different decisions about what their versions would be about.

Euripides imagined a series of events that would give his tragedy a different location and starting point. His prologue explains that Electra had noble suitors from around the Greek world, but Aegisthus feared that her children would want to avenge Agamemnon. He even feared leaving her unmarried, since even an illegitimate but noble child would be dangerous. Clytemnestra, however, was nervous about the odium that murdering her daughter would cause. So they married Electra to a very poor man of noble ancestry, a farmer in the countryside, where the play takes place, and put a bounty on Orestes' head. Typical of Euripides are the change in setting and the political calculations.

Also typical is the ensuing dramatic structure. Again, Orestes listens to Electra as she laments, although she is fetching water, not making offerings to Agamemnon's ghost. When Orestes and Pylades emerge, Electra starts to flee into the house: she thinks she is being assaulted. (The humor of the scene resembles that of Helen's meeting with Menelaus in *Helen*, or Xuthus's embrace of an embarrassed Ion in *Ion*.) Orestes identifies himself as a messenger from Orestes. When her husband returns, he is first shocked at seeing her with strange men, and then invites them to dinner, making her embarrassed that she has nothing good to serve. So she has him go to fetch her father's old peda-gogue, who can provide material for a meal. (This juxtaposition of the mundane problems of a housewife with the tragic action that will fol-low is a distinctly Euripidean technique.) Through all this, Orestes does not reveal himself.

When the Pedagogue arrives, he has seen a lock of hair on Agamemnon's tomb and the signs of offerings, but Electra does not think it possible that Orestes has returned (she does not think that he would come secretly). The old man thinks that this lock might match Electra's or that there might be a footprint that would fit hers, and he asks whether Orestes has anything she wove that would serve as a recognition token. She points out that men's and women's hair dif-fers, that men have larger feet and the ground is too dry for footprints anyway, and that she was a little girl when Orestes left, while a grown man would hardly be carrying around a cloak made for him when he was a child (509–44).

It is hard to know whether this discussion is making fun of Aeschylus or of the character or of both. Electra's critique of the Aeschylean signs is very reasonable, but she is entirely wrong, and her view of her brother as a hero who would not sneak around for fear of Aegisthus is com-pletely misguided. The exchange leaves the spectator wondering how the recognition will ever happen, when the old man simply recognizes Orestes and proves his identity by pointing to the scar left by an injury from a fall when the children chased a fawn. (The scar is reminiscent of Odysseus's scar in the *Odyssey*, but Euripides typically makes it the result of a childhood accident, not a hero's first exploit). The play never explains why Orestes was so reluctant to announce himself, but the play leaves no doubt that Electra is the active, moving party.

Sophocles again makes changes that are typical of his dramatic style. If Euripides offers a weak Orestes who is driven by Electra, Sophocles presents an Electra who is immensely strong but is accidentally a vic-tim instead of a participant in Orestes' plan for most of the drama. His Orestes does not listen to Electra's opening lament – the Pedagogue does not allow him to waste his time. Sophocles thus isolates his protagonist, as he so often does. He reuses Aeschylus's theme of

Clytemnestra's bad dream and her offerings, but his Clytemnestra does not send Electra but a usually more obedient daughter, Chrysothemis (whom Electra persuades to pray against her mother instead of on her behalf). It would not be likely that Clytemnestra would entrust this delicate job to a daughter she knew was her enemy, and Sophocles, like Euripides, is self-conscious about plausibility. This other daughter also allowed him to create sharp contrasts between the determined Electra and a more practical and self-interested sister, not unlike the contrast between Antigone and Ismene.

Sophocles' Electra is deceived by the false account of Orestes' death even as Clytemnestra is. This twist of plot allows Sophocles some effects that are peculiarly his own. His Electra, like Euripides', hears about the offerings he has left at Agamemnon's tomb, but dismisses them – not because she has romantic illusions that her brother would never act by stealth but because she has been convinced that he is dead. Then she rises to her most heroic, proposing to her sister that they kill Aegisthus themselves, a suggestion Chrysothemis regards as impossible. When Orestes arrives with the urn that supposedly contains his ashes, Electra takes the urn and speaks a lament over it (1126–70). Although her brother is beside her, her anguish is utterly real and excruciating, and perhaps the more powerful because she speaks rather than sings. Since she explains that she cared for Orestes when he was a child, we realize that she believes she has lost not only her hope of revenge and of escaping her intolerable life but a person she genuinely and deeply loved. Yet she does not know him, and he only recognizes her when he hears her speech; Sophocles first disappoints the spectator who, at the opening of the play, expects the Aeschylean model to be repeated, and then uses it with new power.

So in Aeschylus's play, the recognition comes early because the main action lies in the intrigue and its implications. It is about one-fifth of the way through the play – about where the first major plot point appears in a Hollywood film. In Euripides', the recognition is delayed until the middle. While the delayed recognition provides most of the dramatic tension for the first part of the play, Euripides, again typically, moves quickly to the plotting of the murders, their accomplishment, and the bleak conclusion in which brother and sister realize what they have done. Electra is the main planner of Clytemnestra's killing, and she must encourage Orestes to kill his mother (964–87). In Sophocles' *Electra*, Orestes declares his identity at 1221, in the most powerful scene of the play. While Euripides leaves no doubt that the killing of Clytemnestra is terribly wrong, Sophocles concludes in moral ambiguity, leaving at least the possibility that Electra, despite her share in the violent deaths (she replies to her mother's first cry from inside by shouting "strike again, if you have the strength," 1415) may truly have been saved.

A variety of other aspects of the three plays invite reading against each other: their treatment of the gods, their political implications, their choice of chorus, their handling of non-elite characters, their characterization of Aegisthus and Clytemnestra. This sketch, however, should give some sense of what we can see more clearly about each if we set their works side by side.

B. THE INHERITANCE OF GREEK TRAGEDY

Greek tragedy can be performed, translated, adapted, and imitated, and its indirect influence can be significant in works that do not directly borrow from any individual text. Much of it has been indirect. Greek tragedy was not available in the Latin West from the end of antiquity until the Renaissance. Even after tragedy was printed – Sophocles, for example, by Aldus Manutius in 1502 – it was not widely accessible. On the other hand, in the twentieth century, it was performed all over the world, and has been especially significant in Japan. So the reception of Greek tragedy is not a single story but many. Tragedy has been transformed by authors and in the theater. Its reception includes instances of indirect influence, of fruitful misunderstanding, and of conscious adaptation. Throughout, however, its cultural prestige and symbolic value as the origin of Western dramatic tradition have made it a significant object for imitation, reinvention, and appropriation. This brief discussion will point to a few examples that illustrate the complexity of tragedy's history.

Romans created a rich tradition of tragedy that imitated the Greeks in both structure and subject matter. Only the tragedies of Seneca (who died in 65 CE) survived antiquity intact, however. Seneca's tragedies are adaptations of Greek originals (although a historical play, *Octavia*, was also transmitted as his), and they follow the formal structure of Greek tragedy, alternating scenes with choral songs. Still, they are not by any means translations. Seneca's *Troades*, for example, combines elements from Euripides' *Trojan Women* and *Hecuba*, and the Senecan tragedies are shorter than the Greek. Most important, their overall mood and effect is very much their own. They are both more violent and more rhetorical than their Greek models, and their characters have a peculiar self-consciousness that is entirely their own.

Senecan tragedy is powerfully influential in the early modern period. Shakespeare, for example, is unlikely to have direct knowledge of any Greek tragedy, but his earliest plays show familiarity with Seneca, who is a profound influence on English tragedy in the early modern period. However, he does not borrow Seneca's plots or his formal structures. English tragedy allows a far more diverse register than classical models, with a far less rigorous decorum, and it is less unified in time and space. *Othello*'s movement from Venice to Cyprus, and *Julius Caesar*'s from Rome to Philippi, show a very different and more open vision of the task of theater. Yet Shakespeare's tragedy is not imaginable without the classical background.

The story is even more complicated than this, however. Shakespeare read Ovid's *Metamorphoses* in both Arthur Golding's translation and in Latin, and Ovid borrowed several tragic plots (he wrote a *Medea* that does not survive). Similarly, he relied on Plutarch for the plays based on Roman history, and Plutarch knew tragedy very well. Plutarch's biographies are an excellent basis for tragedy because they often present the life as a tragedian would see it. Yet the Greek historians contemporary with the great fifth-century tragedians, Herodotus and Thucydides, already see historical events in the shape of tragic plots, and we do not know whether they were influenced by the tragedies they saw in the theater or whether historians and tragedians shared a common way of seeing a series of events as a meaningful story. So it is impossible to decide to what extent the tragic element in Plutarch comes from his knowledge of tragedy itself and to what extent it reflects the affiliations between tragedy and ancient historiography.

Opera was invented as a deliberate attempt to revive Greek tragedy. Here, misunderstanding proved a powerful stimulus to creativity, for in the late sixteenth century it was falsely believed that in the original performances, tragedies had been sung throughout. Greek tragedy was an important and direct inspiration for the invention and early development of tragedy in the circle of Count Giovanni de' Bardi in Florence, but what it contributed was initially neither plots (relatively few operas have plots taken from ancient tragedies), for the most part, nor the sensibility that is so visible in Elizabethan tragedy, but formal possibilities, the idea of an emotionally powerful performance that would use music, language, dance, and spectacle as a unity. Opera would come to use tragic plots, but the first and most important contribution that tragedy made to opera was the idea. Wagnerian opera represents a return and a revitalization of that idea.

Seventeenth-century French tragedy arose in a milieu in which neoclassical criticism followed and narrowed Aristotelian precepts, requiring that tragedies observe the unities of time (one day), place, and action (no subplots) more rigidly than Greek tragedies themselves do. The greatest tragedian of the period, Jean Racine, was a careful reader of Seneca and of Sophocles and Euripides (in his prefaces, he avoids admitting his debts to Seneca, but they are powerful).[1] Some of his tragedies are direct adaptations of classical texts (*La Thébaïde, Andromache, Phédre, Iphigénie*), others are based on events of ancient history (*Alexandre le Grand, Britannicus, Bérénice*), while his last plays were adaptations of Biblical stories (*Esther, Athalie*). Only the last, Biblical plays, have a chorus. In French neoclassical tragedy, erotic passion is far more important than in Greek tragedy. In Racine's version of Euripides' *Phoenician Women, La Thébaïde* (not one of his

---

[1] Levitan 1989.

masterpieces, but a striking example), Creon desires Antigone and the throne equally, while she loves his son, Haemon. (They all die.)

Racine's works are formally tidier than Greek tragedies, with a five-act structure and rhymed verse. Euripides' *Andromache* is a strange play with sharp shifts of focus; Racine's Andromache is a tightly wound infernal machine. In Racine, significant characters have a *confidant(e)*, an intimate to whom the characters reveal their true feelings and intentions, so that the audience sees with exquisite clarity how the choices of each interact and cause the catastrophic outcome. The confidant can fulfill some of the functions of the chorus in resisting the character's extremes, but the convention can seem stiff, since the character is not interesting for itself.

In the twentieth century, it was easier to become familiar with tragedy than it had ever been. Translations were widely available and inexpensive, and film provided a new medium for seeing it. At the same time, it retained its special cultural prestige. Adaptations and productions often directly exploited the canonical place of tragedy in a variety of ways. Eugene O'Neill's use of tragic plots in New England settings is Freudian and universalizing – if the tragedies reflect basic patterns of human nature, they could happen anywhere. Yukio Ninagawa's 1978 *Medea*, on the other hand, deliberately brought together Kabuki and the Western tradition that Greek tragedy represented. Tragedy became a vehicle for anticolonial theater, as in Wole Soyinka's *Bacchae*.

In some ways, we moderns are well prepared for Greek tragedy, whether for producing it, seeing it in the theater, rewriting it, or reading it. We can find significance both in what is familiar and what is remote; we can treat it respectfully as cultural heritage, or radically transform it because it is cultural heritage. The genre often already played on the distance between the ancient, heroic, and mythological world in which it was set and the "modern" world of its audience. Our distance adds yet another layer. We can bridge the gap with imagination and openness to the emotional power of the tragedies, and we can use it for reinvention and even play.

SOURCES AND SUGGESTIONS

The reception of Greek tragedy has become a flourishing area of scholarship. There are excellent surveys of adaptations by P. Burian and of productions by F. MacIntosh in Easterling/Goldhill 1997, 228–83 and 282–323. Shakespeare's use of Seneca is controversial; Miola 1992 argues in favor of strong Senecan influence. Martindale 2004 is a collection of essays on Shakespeare's classical background. For Racine, Knight 1950 (in French) is still very valuable. On Eugene O'Neill, a recent study is Black 2004. On Greek tragedy in modern Ireland, MacDonald and Walton 2002. For twentieth-century production, an excellent start are Foley 1998b and, on Euripides, Foley 1998a. Hall and MacIntosh 2005 is a treatment of how adaptations in Britain have made Greek tragedies meaningful in their own time; Hall, MacIntosh, and Wrigley 2005 is a collection of essays about productions and adaptations since 1969.

GLOSSARY

Archon: One of nine Athenian public officials, originally elected but in the classical period chosen by lot.

Agon: A scene of formal debate, most often in the form: speech, short choral comment, answering speech, short choral comment, Stichomythia.

Aidôs: Inhibition, the shame that makes people avoid behavior that would diminish them in the eyes of others; respect for social norms and for people entitled to deference.

Chorêgos: The citizen who paid most of the costs of a production.

Ekkyklêma: A wheeled platform that was rolled out to make interior scenes visible.

Harmartia: A mistake (not "flaw of character").

Hero/heroine: A dead person believed to have powers to help or hurt the living. Offerings were made to heroes at their tombs.

Hybris: Behavior that shows disregard for the honor of others and an excessive valuation of oneself.

Hypothesis: A prefatory note, containing (depending on the type) a plot summary, production information, and comments on the mythological background and value of the play by ancient scholars.

Orchestra: The part of the performance space where the chorus dances.

Parodos: The side passages for entrances and exits from places other than the stage building; the song of the chorus when it first enters.

Polis: A city-state. A Greek *polis* consisted of a central town and surrounding countryside. Whatever the form of government of a *polis*, its citizens were distinct from noncitizens and were felt to "have a share" in it.

Prologue: The spoken part of the play before the first choral song.

Satyr play: The usual fourth play in the tragic tetralogy, presenting an episode from mythology with a chorus of satyrs, horse men who follow Dionysus and concern themselves with wine and sex.

Sôphrosynê (Adj. *sôphrôn*): Moderation, self-control, and awareness of one's proper place in the world; the opposite of *hybris*. For women (and Euripides' Hippolytus), chastity in particular.

Stasimon: A song performed by the chorus, without participation by actors in the *orchestra* between scenes, usually with the stage empty.

Stichomythia: Exchanges of single lines.

Telos: Literally, "end." In Aristotle's thought, goal, purpose, or perfect state.

DATES

The following chart includes most of the secure dates for the productions of the Three (all BCE). Sometimes we know the titles of the other plays in a tetralogy, sometimes not.

484	Aeschylus	First victory
472	Aeschylus	*Persians*
468	Sophocles	First production: *Triptolemus* (1st)
467	Aeschylus	*Seven against Thebes* (1st)
458	Aeschylus	*Oresteia* (1st)
455	Euripides	First production: *Daughters of Pelias*
441	Euripides	First victory
438	Euripides	*Alcestis* (2nd)
431	Euripides	*Medea* (3rd)
428	Euripides	*Hippolytus* (1st)
415	Euripides	*Trojan Women* (2nd)
412	Euripides	*Helen*
409	Sophocles	*Philoctetes*
408	Euripides	*Orestes*
405–440	Euripides	*Iphigenia at Aulis, Bacchae*
401	Sophocles	*Oedipus at Colonus*

Euripides' metrical practice in his spoken verse changes fairly steadily from his earliest surviving play to his last. So the other surviving plays can be approximately dated on metrical grounds. These are the *approximate* dates:

430	Children of Heracles
425	Andromache
425	Hecuba
423	Suppliant Women
420	Electra
416	Heracles
414	Iphigenia among the Taurians
414	Ion
411–409	Phoenician Women

Of the seven plays in the selection of Aeschylus, one is by someone else, three come from the same production, and the others are all at least roughly dated. *Suppliants* was part of a tetralogy with which Aeschylus was first while Sophocles was second, and the likeliest date is 463. (Until 1952, when *P.Oxy.* 2256 fr.3, a papyrus fragment from Oxyrhynchus in Egypt, provided this information, everyone assumed that *Suppliants* was the oldest surviving tragedy.) Sophocles is the most difficult. We have reliable dates for the last two plays. The hypothesis (see glossary) of *Antigone* says that Sophocles was elected general for 441–440 because of the success of *Antigone*. Since the dates of plays were in the public record, the story probably means that *Antigone* was produced in the years before 441–440, although some scholars have questioned this. Otherwise, stylistic grounds make most scholars agree that *Ajax* and *Women of Trachis* are relatively early, while *Electra* is relatively late, and *Oedipus the King* belongs between the early and the late plays. It is important to remember that although *Oedipus the King*, *Oedipus at Colonus*, and *Antigone* are often published together as if they belonged to a connected trilogy, they were composed and presented separately over a period of almost forty years.

WORKS CITED

Allan, William. 2002. *Euripides, Medea*. London: Duckworth.

Anderson, Greg. 2003. *The Athenian Experiment: Building an Imagined Political Community in Ancient Attica, 508–490 BC*. Ann Arbor: University of Michigan Press.

Barrett, James. 2002. *Staged Narrative: Poetics and the Messenger in Greek Tragedy*. Berkeley: University of California Press.

Betegh, Gabor. 2004. *The Derveni Papyrus: Cosmology, Theology, and Interpretation*. Cambridge, England: Cambridge University Press.

Black, Stephen. 2004. "*Mourning Becomes Electra* as a Greek Tragedy." *The Eugene O'Neill Review* 26: 168–88.

Blundell, Mary W. 1989. *Helping Friends and Harming Enemies: A Study in Sophocles and Greek Ethics*. Cambridge, England: Cambridge University Press.

Buck, Robert. 1979. *A History of Boeotia*. Edmonton, Canada: University of Alberta.

Burnett, Anne Pippin. 1971. *Catastrophe Survived*. Oxford, England: Oxford University Press.

Bushnell, Rebecca. 2005. *A Companion to Tragedy*. Oxford, England: Blackwell.

Buxton, R. G. A. 1982. *Persuasion in Greek Tragedy*. Cambridge, England: Cambridge University Press.

Carter, L. B. 1986. *The Quiet Athenian*. Oxford, England: Oxford University Press.

Clauss, James J., and Johnston, Sarah Iles, eds. 1997. *Medea: Essays on Medea in Myth, Literature, Philosophy and Art*. Princeton, NJ: Princeton University Press.

Collard, Christopher, and Cropp, Martin. 2008/2009. *Euripides VII and VIII: Fragmentary Plays*. Cambridge, MA: Harvard University Press.

Collard, Christopher, Cropp, Martin, and Gibert, John. 2004. *Euripides: Selected Fragmentary Plays*. Vol. 2. Warminster, England: Aris & Phillips.

Collard, Christopher, Cropp, Martin, and Lee, Kevin H. 1995. *Euripides: Selected Fragmentary Plays*. Vol. 1. Warminster, England: Aris & Phillips.

Conacher, Desmond. 1998. *Euripides and the Sophists*. London: Duckworth.

Connor, W. R. 1989. "City Dionysia and Athenian Democracy." *Classica et Medievalia* 40: 7–32.

Csapo, Eric, and Miller, Margaret. 2007. *The Origins of Theatre in Ancient Greece and Beyond: From Ritual to Drama*. Cambridge, England: Cambridge University Press.

Csapo, Eric, and Slater, William T. 1995. *The Context of Ancient Drama*. Ann Arbor: University of Michigan Press.

Dale, A. M. 1967. *Euripides: Helen*. Oxford, England: Clarendon Press.

De Jong, Irene. F. 1997. *Narrative in Drama: The Art of the Euripidean Messenger-Speech*. Mnemosyne Supplement. Leiden, The Netherlands: Brill.

Diggle, James. 1994. *Euripides Fabulae III*. Oxford, England: Oxford University Press.

Dodds. E. R. 1966. "On Misunderstanding the *Oedipus Rex*." *Greece and Rome* 13: 37–49. Reprinted in *The Ancient Concept of Progress*, Oxford 1973, *Oxford Readings in Greek Tragedy*, ed. E. Segal, 1983, and in M. O'Brien, *Twentieth Century Interpretations of Oedipus Rex*, 1968.

Dunn, Francis. 1996. *Tragedy's End. Closure and Innovation in Euripidean Drama*. New York: Oxford University Press.

Easterling, P. E. 1973. "Presentation of Character in Aeschylus." *Greece and Rome* 20: 3–19.

1977. "The Infanticide in Euripides' *Medea*." *Yale Classical Studies* 25: 177–91.

1985. "Anachronism in Greek Tragedy." *Journal of Hellenic Studies* 105: 1–10.

1997. *The Cambridge Companion to Greek Tragedy*. Cambridge, England: Cambridge University Press.

Egli, Frankziska. 2003. *Euripides im Kontext zeitgenössicher intellektueller Strömunger. Analyse der Funktion philosophischer Themen in den Tragödien and Fragmenten*. Beiträge zur Altertumskunde 189. Munich, Germany: Saur.

Foley, Helene. 1985. *Ritual Irony: Poetry and Sacrifice in Euripides*. Ithaca, NY: Cornell University Press.

1993. "Oedipus as Pharmakos." In *Nomodeiktes: Essays in Honor of Martin Ostwald*, ed. Ralph Rosen and Joseph Farrell. Ann Arbor: University of Michigan Press: 525–38.

1998a. "Twentieth-Century Performance and Adaptation of Euripides." *Illinois Classical Studies* 24–5: 1–13.

1998b. "Modern Performance and Adaptation of Greek Tragedy." *Transactions of the American Philological Association* 129: 1–12 (http://www.apaclassics.org/Publications/PresTalks/FOLEY98.html).

2001. *Female Acts in Greek Tragedy*. Princeton, NJ: Princeton University Press.

Fowler, Robert. 1999. "Three Places of the *Trachiniae*." In *Sophocles Revisited*, ed. J. Griffin. Oxford, England: Oxford University Press: 161–75.

Garvie, A. F. 2005. *The Plays of Sophocles*. London: Bristol Classical Press.

Gibert, John. 1995. *Change of Mind in Greek Tragedy. Hypomnemata* 105. Göttingen, Germany: Vandenhoeck & Ruprecht.

1997. "Euripides' Hippolytus Plays: Which Came First?" *The Classical Quarterly* 47: 85–97.

Gill, Christopher. 1996. *Personality in Greek Epic, Tragedy, and Philosophy*. Oxford, England: Oxford University Press.

Girard, René. 1977. *Violence and the Sacred*. Trans. P. Gregory. Baltimore: Johns Hopkins University Press. (First published in French 1972.)

Goff, Barbara. 1990. *The Noose of Words: Readings of Desire, Violence & Language in Euripides' Hippolytus*. Cambridge, England: Cambridge University Press.

1995. *History, Tragedy, Theory*. Austin: University of Texas Press.

Goldhill, Simon. 1986. *Reading Greek Tragedy*. Cambridge, England: Cambridge University Press.

1992. *The Oresteia*. Cambridge, England: Cambridge University Press.

2007. *How to Stage Greek Tragedy Today*. Chicago: University of Chicago Press.

Gould, John. 1978. "Dramatic Character and 'Human Intelligibility' in Greek Tragedy." *Proceedings of the Cambridge Philological Society* 24: 43–67.

Goward, Barbara. 1999. *Telling Tragedy: Narrative Technique in Aeschylus, Sophocles, and Euripides*. London: Duckworth.

Green, Richard. 1994. *Theatre in Ancient Greek Society*. London: Routledge.

Green, Richard, and Handley, Eric. 1995. *Images of the Greek Theatre*. Austin: University of Texas Press.

Gregory, Justina. 1991. *Euripides and the Instruction of the Athenians*. Ann Arbor: University of Michigan Press.

ed. 2005. *A Companion to Greek Tragedy*. Oxford, England: Blackwell.

Griffin, Jasper. 1998. "The Social Function of Attic Tragedy." *Classical Quarterly* 48: 3–61.

ed. 1999. *Sophocles Revisited: Essays Presented to Sir Hugh Lloyd-Jones*. Oxford, England: Oxford University Press.

Griffith, Mark. 1977. *The Authenticity of Prometheus Bound*. Cambridge, England: Cambridge University Press.

1995. "Brilliant Dynasts: Power and Politics in the *Oresteia*." *Classical Antiquity* 14: 62–129.

2005. "The Subject of Desire in Sophocles' *Antigone*." In *The Soul of Tragedy. Essays on Athenian Drama*, ed. V. Pedrick and S. Oberhelman. Chicago: University of Chicago Press: 91–135.

Griffith, R. Drew. 1996. *The Theatre of Apollo: Divine Justice and Sophocles' Oedipus the King*. Montreal, Canada: McGill-Queen's University Press.

Guthrie, W. K. C. 1977. *The Sophists (A History of Greek Philosophy, Vol. 3, Part 1)*. Cambridge, England: Cambridge University Press.

Hall, Edith. 1989. *Inventing the Barbarian. Greek Self-Definition through Tragedy*. Oxford, England: Oxford University Press.

1996. *Aeschylus. Persians*. Warminster, England: Aris & Phillips.

Hall, Edith, and MacIntosh, Fiona. 2005. *Greek Tragedy and the British Theatre 1660–1914*. Oxford, England: Oxford University Press.

Hall, Edith, Macintosh, Fiona, and Taplin, Oliver, eds. 2000. *Medea in Performance 1500–2000*. Oxford, England: European Humanities Research Centre.

Hall, Edith, MacIntosh, Fiona, and Wrigley, Amanda. 2005. *Dionysus Since 69. Greek Tragedy at the Dawn of the Third Millennium*. Oxford, England: Oxford University Press.

Halliwell, Stephen. 1986. *Aristotle's Poetics*. London: Duckworth.

Harrison, Thomas. 2000. *The Emptiness of Asia. Aeschylus' Persians and the History of the Fifth Century*. London: Duckworth.

Heath, Malcolm. 1987. *The Poetics of Greek Tragedy*. London: Duckworth.

Henderson, Jeffrey. 1991. "Women and the Athenian Dramatic Festivals." *Transactions of the American Philological Association* 121: 133–47.

Henrichs, Albert. 1994–5. "Why Should I Dance? Choral Self-Referentiality in Greek Tragedy." *Arion* 3.1: 56–111.

Herington, John. 1985. *Poetry into Drama. Early Tragedy and the Greek Poetic Tradition*. Berkeley: University of California Press.

1986. *Aeschylus*. New Haven, CT: Yale University Press.

Hester, David. 1971. "Sophocles the Unphilosophical: A Study in the *Antigone*." *Mnemosyne* 24: 11–59.

Holladay, Carl. 1989. *Fragments from Hellenistic Jewish Authors. II, Poets*. Atlanta, GA: Scholars Press: 301–529.

Holmberg, Ingrid. 1995. "Helen: Most Noble and Most Chaste." *American Journal of Philology* 116: 19–42.

Jacobson, Howard. 1983. *The Exagoge of Ezekiel*. Cambridge, England: Cambridge University Press.

Johnson, P. J. 1997. "Woman's Third Face: A Psycho-Social Reconsideration of Sophocles' *Antigone*." *Arethusa* 30: 369–98.

Jones, John. 1962. *On Aristotle and Greek Tragedy*. London: Chatto and Windus.

Kannicht, Richard. 1969. *Euripides, Helena*. Heidelberg, Germany: Winter.

Kerferd, G. B. 1981. *The Sophistic Movement*. Cambridge, England: Cambridge University Press.

Knight, R. C. 1950. *Racine et la Grèce*. Paris: Boivin.

Knox, Bernard. 1956. "The Date of the 'Oedipus Tyrannus' of Sophocles." *American Journal of Philology* 77: 133–47.

1957. *Oedipus at Thebes*. New Haven: Yale University Press.

1979. *Word and Action: Essays on the Ancient Theater*. Baltimore: John Hopkins University Press.

Kovacs, David. 1986. "On Medea's Great Monologue (Eur. *Medea* 1021–80)." *Classical Quarterly* 36: 343–52.

1987. *The Heroic Muse: Studies in the Hippolytus and Hecuba of Euripides*. Baltimore: Johns Hopkins University Press.

2002. *Euripides: Bacchae, Iphigenia at Aulis, Rhesus*. Cambridge, MA: Harvard University Press.

Lebeck, Anne. 1971. *The Oresteia: A Study in Language and Structure*. Cambridge, MA: Harvard University Press (for The Center for Hellenic Studies).

Lesky, Albin. 1983. *Greek Tragic Poetry*. Trans. Matthew Dillon. New Haven, CT: Yale University Press. (Translation of the 3rd German edition of 1972.)

Levitan, William. 1989. "Seneca in Racine." *Yale French Studies* 76: 185–210.

Lloyd-Jones, Hugh. 1972. "Tycho Wilamowitz on the Dramatic Technique of Sophocles." *Classical Quarterly* 22: 214–28.

Longo, Oddone. 1975. "Proposte di lettura per l'Oreste di Euripide." *Maia* 27: 265–87.

Luschnig, C. A. E. 2007. *Granddaughter of the Sun: A Study of Euripides' Medea*. Leiden, The Netherlands: Brill.

Macintosh, Fiona, Michelakis, Pantelis, Hall, Edith, and Taplin, Oliver, eds. 2005. *Agamemnon in Performance*. Oxford, England: Oxford University Press.

March, Jennifer. 1987. *The Creative Poet: Studies on the Treatment of Myths in Greek Poetry*. London: University of London, Institute of Classical Studies.

Marshall, C. W., and van Willigenburg, Stephanie. 2004. "Judging the Athenian Dramatic Competitions." *The Journal of Hellenic Studies* 124: 90–107.

McClure, Laura. 1999. *Spoken Like a Woman: Speech and Gender in Athenian Drama*. Princeton, NJ: Princeton University Press.

McDonald, Marianne. 2003. *The Living Art of Greek Tragedy*. Bloomington: University of Indiana Press.

McDonald, Marianne, and Walton, J. Michael. 2002. *Amid Our Troubles. Irish Versions of Greek Tragedy*. London: Methuen.

2007. *The Cambridge Companion to Greek and Roman Theatre*. Cambridge, England: Cambridge University Press.

Martindale, Charles, and Taylor, A. B., eds. 2004. *Shakespeare and the Classics*. Cambridge, England: Cambridge University Press.

Meier, Christian. 1993. *The Political Art of Greek Tragedy*. Trans. A. Webber. Baltimore: Johns Hopkins University Press.

Michelini, Ann. 1989. "Neophron and Euripides' Medea 1056 80." *Transactions of the American Philological Association* 119: 115–35.

Mills, Sophie. 2002. *Euripides: Hippolytus*. London: Duckworth.

Miola, Robert. 1992. *Shakespeare and Classical Tragedy : The Influence of Seneca*. Oxford, England: Oxford University Press.

Mitchell-Boyask, Robin. 1999. "Euripides' *Hippolytus* and the Trials of Manhood." *Bucknell Review* issue on *Rites of Passage in Ancient Greece: Literature, Religion, Society* Spring 43: 43–67.

2008. *Plague and the Athenian Imagination*. Cambridge, England: Cambridge University Press.

Morrison, J. S. 1970. "Passages from Aristophanes and Euripides." *Proceedings of the Cambridge Philological Society* 16: 83–90.

Morwood, James. 2002. *The Plays of Euripides*. London: Bristol Classical Press.

Mossman, Judith. 2003. *Oxford Readings in Classical Studies: Euripides*. Oxford, England: Oxford University Press.

Nussbaum, Martha. 1986. *The Fragility of Goodness: Luck and Ethics in Greek Tragedy and Philosophy*. Cambridge, England: Cambridge University Press.

Ormand, Kirk. 1999. *Exchange and the Maiden: Marriage in Sophoclean Tragedy*. Austin: University of Texas Press.

Pedrick, Victoria. 2007. *Euripides, Freud, and the Romance of Belonging*. Baltimore: Johns Hopkins University Press.

Pelling, Christopher, ed. 1990. *Characterization and Individuality in Greek Literature*. Oxford, England: Oxford University Press.

  ed. 1997. *Greek Tragedy and the Historian*. Oxford, England: Oxford University Press.

  2000. *Literary Texts and the Greek Historian*. London: Routledge.

Pickard-Cambridge, A. W. 1988. *The Dramatic Festivals of Athens*. 2nd ed. Revised by John Gould and D. M. Lewis, Reissued with supplement and corrections. Oxford, England: Oxford University Press.

Pippin, Anne. 1960. "Euripides' *Helen*: A Comedy of Ideas." *Classical Philology* 55: 151–63.

Podlecki, Anthony. 1970. "The Basic Seriousness of Euripides' *Helen*." *Transactions and Proceedings of the American Philological Association* 101: 401–18.

Porter, John. 1994. *Studies in Euripides' Orestes*. Leiden, The Netherlands: Brill.

Powell, Anton. 1990. *Euripides, Women, and Sexuality*. London: Routledge.

Rabinowitz, Nancy S. 1993. *Anxiety Veiled: Euripides and the Traffic in Women*. Ithaca, NY: Cornell University Press.

  2008. *Greek Tragedy*. Oxford, England: Blackwell.

Rawson, Elizabeth. 1972. "Aspects of Euripides' Orestes." *Arethusa* 5: 155–67.

Rehm, Rush. 1994. *Greek Tragic Theatre*. London: Routledge.

Reinhardt, Karl. 1960. *Die Sinneskrise bei Euripides*. In *Tradition und Geist*. Göttingen, Germany: Vandenhoeck & Ruprecht: 227–56. English translation: *The Intellectual Crisis in Euripides*, ed. J. Mossman, 2003, 16–46.

Rose, Peter. 1976. "Sophocles' *Philoctetes* and the Teachings of the Sophists." *Harvard Studies in Classical Philology* 80: 44–105. Reprinted in *Sons of the Gods, Children of Earth: Ideology and Literary Form in Ancient Greece*. Ithaca, NY: Cornell University Press: 1992, 266–330.

Rosenbloom, David. 2006. *Aeschylus: Persians*. London: Duckworth.

Scullion, Scott. 2002. "Nothing to Do with Dionysus: Tragedy Misconceived as Ritual." *Classical Quarterly* 52: 102–37.

Seaford, Richard. 1994. *Reciprocity and Ritual: Homer and Tragedy in the Developing City-State*. Oxford, England: Oxford University Press.

Segal, Charles. 1972. "The Two Worlds of Euripides' *Helen*." *Transactions and Proceedings of the American Philological Association* 102: 553–614. Reprinted in Segal, 1986, 222–67.

    1981. *Tragedy and Civilization*. Cambridge, MA: Harvard University Press.

    1986. *Interpreting Greek Tragedy. Myth, Poetry, Text*. Ithaca, NY: Cornell University Press.

    1997. *Dionysiac Poetics and Euripides' Bacchae*. Princeton, NJ: Princeton University Press. (First published in 1982.)

Seidensticker, Bernd. 1990. "Euripides, Medea 1056–80: An Interpolation?" In *Cabinet of the Muses*, ed. M. Griffith and D. J. Mastronarde. Atlanta, GA: Scholars Press.

Slater, William, and Csapo, Eric. 1995. *The Context of Ancient Drama*. Ann Arbor: University of Michigan Press.

Smith, Wesley D. 1960. "The Ironic Structure in *Alcestis*." *Phoenix* 14: 127–45.

Snell, Bruno, ed. 1971–. *Tragicorum Graecorum fragmenta*. Göttingen, Germany: Vandenhoeck & Ruprecht.

Sommerstein, Alan. 2009. *Aeschylus III, Fragments*. Harvard: Harvard University Press (Loeb Classical Library).

Sommerstein, Alan, Fitzpatrick, D., and Talboy, T., eds. 2006. *Sophocles: Selected Fragmentary Plays. Volume I*. Oxford, England: Aris & Phillips.

Sommerstein, Alan, Halliwell, Stephen, Henderson, Jeffrey, and Zimmermann, Bernhard, eds. 1993. *Tragedy, Comedy, and the Polis.*

Papers from the Greek Drama Conference, Nottingham 18–20 July 1990. Bari, Italy: Levante.

Sourvinou-Inwood, Christiane. 1989. "Assumptions and the Creation of Meaning: Reading Sophocles' *Antigone.*" *Journal of Hellenic Studies* 109: 134–48.

——— 2003. *Tragedy and Athenian Religion.* Lanham, MD: Lexington Books.

Stinton, T. C. W. 1986. "The Scope and Limits of Allusion in Greek Tragedy." In *Greek Tragedy and its Legacy. Essays presented to D. J. Conacher,* ed. M. Cropp, E. Fantham, and S. E. Scully. Calgary, Canada: University of Calgary Press: 67–102.

Storey, Ian, and Allan, Arlene. 2005. *A Guide to Ancient Greek Drama.* Oxford, England: Blackwell.

Taplin, Oliver. 1977. *The Stagecraft of Aeschylus.* Oxford, England: Oxford University Press.

——— 1978. *Greek Tragedy in Action.* Berkeley: University of California Press.

——— 1986. "Fifth-Century Tragedy and Comedy: A Synkrisis." *Journal of Hellenic Studies* 106: 163–74.

Vernant, Jean-Pierre, and Vidal-Naquet, Pierre. 1981. *Tragedy and Myth in Ancient Greece.* Trans. Janet Lloyd. Brighton, England: Harvester.

Vickers, Michael. 2008. *Sophocles and Alcibiades. Athenian Politics in Ancient Greek Literature.* Ithaca, NY: Cornell University Press.

West, M. L. 1987. *Euripides. Orestes.* Edited with translation and commentary. Warminster, England: Aris & Phillips.

——— 1989. "The Early Chronology of Attic Tragedy." *The Classical Quarterly* 39.1: 251–4.

——— 1990. *Studies in Aeschylus.* Stuttgart, Germany: Teubner.

Whitman, Cedric. 1951. *Sophocles: A Study of Heroic Humanism.* Cambridge, MA: Harvard University Press.

Wiles, David. 1997. *Tragedy in Athens: Performance Space and Theatrical Meaning.* Cambridge, England: Cambridge University Press

Wilson, Peter. 2000. *The Athenian Institution of the Khoregia. The Chorus, the City, and the Stage.* Cambridge, England: Cambridge University Press.

Winkler, John J., and Zeitlin, Froma, eds. 1990. *Nothing To Do With Dionysus. Athenian Drama in its Social Context*. Princeton, NJ: Princeton University Press.

Winnington-Ingram, R. I. 1969. "Euripides: *Poiêtês Sophos*." *Arethusa* 2: 127–42 (reprinted in Mossman, 2003, 46–73).

1980. *Sophocles: An Interpretation*. Cambridge, England: Cambridge University Press.

Wohl, Victoria. 1998. *Intimate Commerce: Exchange, Gender, and Subjectivity in Greek Tragedy*. Austin: University of Texas Press.

Wolff, Christian. 1973. "On Euripides' *Helen*." *Harvard Studies in Classical Philology* 77: 61–84.

Wright, Matthew. 2005. *Euripides' Escape-Tragedies: A Study of Helen, Andromeda, and Iphigenia Among the Taurians*. Oxford, England: Oxford University Press.

Zeitlin, Froma. 1980. "The Closet of Masks: Role-Playing and Myth-Making in the *Orestes* of Euripides." *Ramus* 9: 51–77.

1985. "Playing the Other: Theater, Theatricality, and the Feminine in Greek Drama." *Representations* 11: 63–94. Reprinted in Winkler and Zeitlin, 1990.

1996. *Playing the Other: Gender and Society in Classical Greek Literature*. Chicago: University of Chicago Press.

Zimmermann, Bernhard. 1991. *Greek Tragedy: An Introduction*. Trans. Thomas Marier. Baltimore: Johns Hopkins University Press.

INDEX

Actors, 4, 37, 38, 45

Aeschylus, 49–50

  Agamemnon, 20, 47, 48, 49, 58, 69, 76,
    85–94, 95, 97, 100, 107, 163, 175

  Eleusinians, 60, 106

  Eumenides, 19, 20, 28, 48, 57, 62, 64, 85,
    87, 97, 99, 100–5

  Libation Bearers, 4, 11, 27, 43, 56, 85, 87, 91,
    96, 97, 99, 100, 102, 113, 175, 187–8

  Oresteia, 23, 44, 47, 50, 85–105, 177,
    181

  Persians, 28, 44, 47, 50, 57, 60, 72–84, 94

  Phoenician Women, 3, 6, 159

  Prometheus Bound, 6, 16, 65, 200

  Proteus, 50, 85, 92

  Seven against Thebes, 6, 50, 60, 107, 156, 159

  Suppliants, 38, 39, 50, 56, 60

  Women of Etna, 2

Agathon, 3, 28, 42, 49

agon, 122, 126, 140, 141

aidôs, 136, 137, 144

Anaxagoras, 62, 171, 180

Anaximander, 70

antistrophe, 4, 77, 88, 125, 155, 168, 179

Aphrodite, 26, 69, 101, 125, 127, 133, 134, 135,
    136, 137, 141, 142, 143, 167, 172

Apollo, 5, 19, 29, 48, 51, 62, 69, 85, 87,
    96, 97, 100, 101, 102, 103, 113,
    151, 152, 153, 156, 174, 175, 176,
    177, 181, 183, 184

Archelaus of Macedon, 2

Archilochus, 35

Ares, 104, 148

aretê, 62

Arion of Methymna, 34

Aristophanes

  Clouds, 171

  Frogs, 15, 17, 27, 53, 59, 156

  Wasps, 39

  Women at the Thesmophoria, 54, 176

Aristophanes of Byzantium, 133

Aristotle, 17, 120, 153

  Poetics, 7, 8, 9, 13, 28, 35

Artemis, 88, 90, 93, 133, 134, 140, 141,
    142, 143, 144

Astydamas, 17

Atê, 76

Athena, 19, 20, 26, 46, 50, 64, 69, 85, 87, 97,
    101, 102, 103, 104, 105, 106, 142, 172

aulos, 3, 4, 39

Bacchylides, 35

Castor and Polydeuces, 5, 68, 163, 168,
    169, 172, 173

catharsis, 8, 17

Choerilus, 34, 36, 39

  Alope, 39

choral ode, 77, 117, 125, 139, 155, 180

chorêgos, 42, 43, 44, 53, 72

chorus, 4, 45

City Dionysia, 2, 33, 35, 40, 41, 45, 50, 52, 53

Cleophon, 17

Cyclic epics, 3

Cypria, 166

Dale, A. M., 162

Darius, 73

de' Bardi, Giovanni, 193

deconstruction, 30

Derveni Papyrus, 172

deus ex machina, 48, 185, 186

Dicaearchus, 120

Diogenes of Apollonia, 62, 171

Dionysia. *See* City Dionysia

Dionysus, 2, 6, 15, 17, 21, 23, 24, 25, 26, 31,
 34, 35, 36, 37, 40, 42, 43, 46, 47, 59, 69, 117,
 118, 128, 143, 171, 198, 205, 209, 211

dithyramb, 34, 35, 36, 37, 42, 44, 47

ekkyklêma, 48, 97, 99, 139

Empedocles, 180

Epigenes of Sicyon, 34

Erinyes, 87, 88, 93, 94–7, 98, 99, 100, 101,
 102, 105, 113, 174, 176, 182

Euphorion, 6, 50

Euripides, 24, 51–52, 70

 Aeolus, 67

 Alcestis, 52, 128

 Alecestis, 128

 Alexandros, 50

 alphabetical plays, 6

 Andromache, 2, 11, 19, 59, 67, 172, 181, 186, 194

 Andromeda, 53

 Antigone, 67

 Antiope, 7

 Bacchae, 6, 12, 23, 25, 26, 69, 186, 209

 Children of Heracles, 60

 Cresphontes, 7, 9

 Electra, 5, 27, 29, 68, 162, 164, 175, 176, 188–9

 Hecuba, 12, 64, 122, 181, 192

 Helen, 9, 29, 62, 66, 162–73, 176, 188

 Heracles, 10, 26, 48, 63, 64, 65

 Hippolytus, 10, 19, 25, 26, 59, 63, 64,
  65, 69, 133–45, 171, 186

 Hypsipyle, 7

Ion, 5, 7, 51, 59, 176, 188

Iphigenia among the Taurians, 7, 9, 11, 66

Iphigenia at Aulis, 6, 60, 64

Medea, 10, 48, 49, 64, 120–32, 135, 181, 186

Orestes, 10, 18, 20, 29, 60, 62, 166, 174–85, 186

Palamedes, 50

Phoenician Women, 60, 68, 159, 193

Phoenix, 64

Rhesus, 2, 6

Sthenoboea, 64

Suppliant Women, 60

Suppliants, 65

Trojan Women, 12, 50, 69, 127, 162, 192

euthynai, 79

Exagogê, 2, 13, 14

feminism, 30

Freud, 25

Freudian interpretation. *See* psychoanalyic theory

Furies. *See* Erinyes

Girard, René, 30

gods, 5

Goldhill, Simon, 41

Golding, Arthur, 192

Graham, Martha, 22

Gyges-tragedy, 3

Hall, Peter, 23

Hamartia, 9, 16

Happy ending, 5, 9, 19

Harrison, Tony, 23

Heavenly Twins. *See* Castor and Polydeuces

Hecataeus of Miletus, 66

Hegel, 107

Hera, 10, 26, 65, 101, 120, 165, 166, 167

Hermes, 166, 173

Herodotus, 3, 34, 39, 66, 68, 81, 117, 154, 171, 192

Hesiod, 94

Hieron of Syracuse, 2, 49, 77

Homer

 Iliad, 3, 11, 37, 63, 82, 83, 95, 112, 159

 Odyssey, 3, 11, 72, 85, 90, 135, 163, 189

hybris, 75, 76, 82, 92, 93, 114, 137, 143, 155

Ion of Chios, 42, 49, 50, 133
Iophon, 51, 133

Jones, John, 24

Kabuki theater, 194
Kannicht, Richard, 162

Lacan, Jacques, 25
Lenaia, 42, 53

Manutius, Aldus, 191
mêchanê, 48
metatheatricality, 4, 23
Mimnermus, 106

narratology, 30
Neophron, 120
New Historicism, 30, 73
Nietzsche, 18
Ninagawa, Yukio, 194
nomos, 66, 67
nostos, 73

O'Neill, Eugene, 194
Oedipodeia, 106
Oenopides of Chios, 180
Old Oligarch, 59
On the Sacred Disease, 62
oracles, 5, 68, 100, 131, 148, 153–6
orchestra, 46, 47
Origins of tragedy, 33–9
Ovid
    Medea, 192
    Metamorphoses, 192

Panathenaea, 11, 16
parodos, 3, 48, 116, 118, 134, 150, 178, 186
Pericles, 44, 51, 53, 56, 58, 60, 62, 142
pharmakos, 155
Philocles, 50
Philoctetes-plays, 10, 11
Phrynichus, 34, 39, 51, 72
    Alcestis, 39

Antaeus, 39
Capture of Miletus, 3, 39
Danaids, 39
Egyptians, 39
Phoenician Women, 3, 39, 44
Tantalus, 39
Women of Pleuron, 39
physis, 62, 63, 66, 67
Pindar, 51, 149
Plato
    Gorgias, 67
    Laws, 21, 43, 54
    Republic, 43, 67
    Symposium, 42
Pleiad, 2
Plutarch, 192
polis, 56, 58
Porson's Bridge, 13
post-colonial theory, 73
Pratinus, 34, 36, 39, 42
    Dymaenae, 39
    Karyatides, 39
    Perseus, 39
    Tantalus, 39
Proagon, 40
prologue, 3, 5, 26, 74, 87, 108, 109, 110,
    115, 116, 134, 135, 149, 165, 184, 188
Prometheus Bound. See Aeschylus
Protagoras, 65, 66, 154
psychoanalytic theory, 25, 26, 134, 194
Ptolemy II Philadelphus, 2

Racine, Jean, 193, 194
    Alexandre le Grand, 193
    Andromache, 193, 194
    Athalie, 193
    Bérénice, 193
    Britannicus, 193
    Esther, 193
    Iphigénie, 193
    La Thébaïde, 193
    Phédre, 193
Rhapsodes, 11, 37
Rhesus, 6, 40

Saïd, Edward, 73
satyr-play, 6, 13, 21, 35, 39, 40, 50, 85, 92
Selection, 6, 7
Sellars, Peter, 73
Seneca, 7, 192, 193
   Octavia, 192
   Troades, 192
Serban, Andrei, 22
Shakespeare, 7, 192
   Julius Caesar, 192
   Othello, 192
Socrates, 67, 130, 136, 171
Solon, 76
sophists, 15, 62, 64, 65, 154
Sophocles, 24, 50–1
   Ajax, 20, 28, 48, 49, 57, 63, 69, 172
   Antigone, 9, 12, 19, 24, 28, 59, 64,
      65, 106–18, 147, 154, 186
   Electra, 10, 20, 27, 28, 59, 63, 64, 122,
      147, 178, 189–90
   Oedipus at Colonus, 5, 12, 20, 28, 58,
      61, 63, 66, 158
   Oedipus the King, 5, 9, 17, 19, 26, 48, 60,
      63, 69, 141, 147–60, 186
   Philoctetes, 11, 28, 29, 58, 60, 63, 64, 65,
      68, 174, 184, 186
   Women of Trachis, 11, 12, 19, 20, 45, 69, 186
Sophocles II, 51
sôphrôn. See sôphrosynê
sôphrosynê, 89, 109, 123, 126, 134, 139,
   140, 141, 144, 169
Soyinka, Wole, 194
Star Wars, 169
stasimon, 108, 113, 124, 132, 154, 168, 178

Stesichorus, 29, 37, 85, 162, 163, 173
   Oresteia, 176
stichomythia, 114, 115, 177
"Story, the", 17–18, 174, 186
strophe, 4, 77, 88, 125, 178
structuralism, 30
Suda, 34, 36

Telephus, 10
Themistocles, 44, 72, 81
Theodectes, 17
theologeion, 48
theomachy, 143
Theophrastus, 53
Thespis, 33, 34, 35, 37, 38, 39
Thucydides, 83, 181
Titles, 5
Tragic flaw, 9
Tragic, the, 7
tragoidos, 34, 36

Vernant, J. P., 155

Wagner, 193
Wittgenstein, 13
Women, in the audience, 54

Xenophon
   Hellenica, 108
   Memorabilia, 66–67

Zeus, 5, 68, 69, 70, 85, 87, 88, 89, 91, 94, 95, 98, 99,
   101, 102, 113, 116, 117, 118, 126, 127, 155, 158,
   163, 164, 165, 166, 167, 168, 172, 180